# 1100 Words You Need to Know

**MURRAY BROMBERG** PRINCIPAL

*Samuel H. Wang High School, Queens, New York*

**MELVIN GORDON** ENGLISH DEPARTMENT

*Thomas Jefferson High School, Brooklyn, New York*

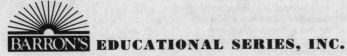

**BARRON'S** EDUCATIONAL SERIES, INC.

Woodbury, New York • London • Toronto • Sydney

*. . . Invest twenty minutes*

*a day for forty-six weeks*

*in order to master*

*920 new words and*

*almost 200 useful idioms*

# Introduction

After writing that *beauty is truth, truth beauty*, John Keats concluded: *That is all ye know on earth, and all ye need to know*. Naturally the poet's romantic philosophy must be appreciated on a lofty level while at the same time we concede that there are more specific things on this earth that we *need to know*.

To really come to grips with the question, one should be aware of his purposes, his aims in life. It is obvious that there are vital facts which a surgeon needs to know, just as there are essential knowledges and skills for butchers, bakers, and the manufacturers of candlesticks. The individual's life-style ultimately determines just how much he needs to know. There is a discipline, however, which cuts across every mode of living, and the mastery of it can bring all types of rewards. We are referring to the study of vocabulary.

Possessing a rich treasury of words assures one of personal pleasures, aside from material gains. The subtleties which we convey in our speech, the nuances we detect in our reading, the joys we derive from communicating effectively and from understanding precisely are priceless. Since assembling an extensive and practical vocabulary requires effort, we have tried to get the serious student started by selecting over 1100 useful words and idioms—*1100 Words You Need To Know*—and by teaching them through interest, variety, and repetition.

We believe that the reader who spends 15–20 minutes daily on our lessons will see a dramatic improvement in his word power. Aside from the higher grades and success on college entrance exams, he will be better able to send and receive ideas and to enrich his personal and professional relationships.

*Murray Bromberg*
*Melvin Gordon*

# FULL PRONUNCIATION KEY *

| | | | | | | |
|---|---|---|---|---|---|---|
| a | hat, cap | j | jam, enjoy | u | cup, butter |
| ā | age, face | k | kind, seek | ů | full, put |
| ã | care, air | l | land, coal | ü | rule, move |
| ä | father, far | m | me, am | ū | use, music |
| | | n | no, in | | |
| b | bad, rob | ng | long, bring | v | very, save |
| ch | child, much | | | w | will, woman |
| d | did, red | | | y | young, yet |
| | | o | hot, rock | z | zero, breeze |
| | | ō | open, go | zh | measure, seizure |
| e | let, best | ô | order, all | | |
| ē | equal, be | oi | oil, voice | ə | represents: |
| ėr | term, learn | ou | house, out | | a in about |
| | | | | | e in taken |
| f | fat, if | p | paper, cup | | i in April |
| g | go, bag | r | run, try | | o in lemon |
| h | he, how | s | say, yes | | u in circus |
| | | sh | she, rush | | |
| | | t | tell, it | | |
| i | it, pin | th | thin, both | | |
| ī | ice, five | ŦH | then, smooth | | |

* From *Thorndike-Barnhart High School Dictionary* by E. L. Thorndike and Clarence L. Barnhart. Copyright © 1968 by Scott, Foresman and Company.

**New Words:**  voracious   indiscriminate   eminent   steeped   replete
və rā′ shəs   in′ dis krim′ ə nit   em′ ə nənt   stēpt   ri′ plēt′

***Reading Wisely***  The youngster who reads *voraciously*, though *indiscriminately*, does not necessarily gain in wisdom over the teenager who is more selective in his reading choices. A young man who has read the life story of every *eminent* athlete of the twentieth century, or a coed who has *steeped* herself in every social-protest novel she can get her hands on, may very well be learning all there is to know in a very limited area. But books are *replete* with so many wonders that it is often discouraging to see bright young people limit their own experiences.

**Sample Sentences:**  On the basis of the above paragraph, try to use your new words in the following sentences. Occasionally it may be necessary to change the ending of a word; e.g., *indiscriminately* to *indiscriminate*.

1. A good library is ___replete___ with many different kinds of books.
2. The ___eminent___ author received the Nobel Prize for literature.
3. My cousin is so ___steeped___ in schoolwork that his friends call him a bookworm.
4. After skiing, I find that I have a ___voracious___ appetite.
5. Modern warfare often results in the ___indiscriminate___ killing of combatants and innocent civilians alike.

**Definitions:**  Now that you have seen and used the new words in sentences, and have the definitions "on the tip of your tongue," try to pair the words with their meanings.

6. voracious ___d___   a. of high reputation, outstanding
7. indiscriminate ___c___   b. completely filled or supplied with
8. eminent ___a___   c. choosing at random without careful selection
9. steeped ___e___   d. desiring or consuming great quantities
10. replete ___b___   e. soaked, drenched, saturated

***Today's Idiom***  *to eat humble pie*—to admit your error and apologize
    After his candidate had lost the election, the boastful campaign manager had *to eat humble pie*.

**ANSWERS ARE ON PAGE 231**

**New Words:**

| abound | technology | prognosticate | automaton | matron |
|--------|-----------|---------------|-----------|--------|
| ə bound′ | tek nol′ ə ji | prog nos′ tə kāt | ô tom′ ə ton | mā′ trən |

**Solving the Servant Problem**

The worlds of science-fiction *abound* with wonders. Yet modern *technology* progresses so rapidly that what may be today's wild dream may be next year's kitchen appliance. A British scientist has *prognosticated* that within ten years every suburban *matron* will have her own robot servant. One task this domesticated *automaton* will not have to contend with will be scouring the oven because even today the newest ranges can be "programed" to reduce their own baked-on grime to easily disposed of ashes.

**Sample Sentences:**

Now that you've seen the words used in context, and—hopefully—have an idea of their meanings, try to use them in the following sentences. Remember that a word-ending may have to be changed.

1. The mayor refused to ＿＿＿＿＿＿ as to his margin of victory in the election.

2. The time is approaching when human workers may be replaced by ＿＿＿＿＿＿.

3. A clever salesman will always ask a ＿＿＿＿＿＿ if her mother is at home.

4. The western plains used to ＿＿＿＿＿＿ with bison before those animals were slaughtered by settlers.

5. Man may be freed from backbreaking labor by the products of scientific ＿＿＿＿＿＿.

**Definitions:**

Test yourself now by matching the new words with the definitions. If you are sure of yourself, cover the top half of this page before you begin.

6. abound ＿＿＿  a. an older married woman

7. technology ＿＿＿  b. branch of knowledge dealing with engineering, applied science, etc.

8. prognosticate ＿＿＿  c. a robot; a mechanical "person"

9. automaton ＿＿＿  d. to exist in great numbers

10. matron ＿＿＿  e. to predict or foretell a future event

**Today's Idiom**

*a pig in a poke*—an item you purchase without having seen; a disappointment

The mail order bicycle that my nephew bought turned out to be *a pig in a poke*, and he is now trying to get his money back.

ANSWERS ARE ON PAGE 231

**New Words:**

| paradox | realm | annals | compound | tinge |
|---------|-------|--------|----------|-------|
| par' ə doks | relm | an' nəlz | kom' pound | tinj |

**It's a
Man's World**

How *paradoxical* that the world's greatest chefs have all been men! Cooking would clearly seem to be a field which lies exclusively within the ladies' *realm*, yet the *annals* of cookery are replete* with masculine names: Brillat Savarin, Ritz, Diat, Larousse. To *compound* the puzzle, there has rarely been a *tinge* of rumor or scandal casting doubts on the masculinity of these heroes of cuisine.

(* replete—if you've forgotten the meaning, see page 1)

**Sample Sentences:**

Try your hand now at using your new words by writing them in their correct form (change endings if necessary) in these sentences:

1. His gloom was now _____ by the failing mark on his geometry test.

2. The _____ of sports are replete* with the names of great Negro athletes.

3. One of the great _____ of American life is that though minority groups have suffered injustices, nowhere in the world have so many varied groups lived together so harmoniously.

4. A _____ of garlic is all that's necessary in most recipes.

5. The cruel king would not allow the prince to enter his _____, restricting him to the forest which abounded* with wild animals.

(* abounded—studied previously, see page 2)

**Definitions:**

If you are having trouble in picking the right definitions, it may be best *not* to do them in the order given, but to do the ones you are surest of first.

6. paradox _____  a. a trace, smattering, or slight degree

7. realm _____  b. a statement which at first seems to be absurd or self-contradictory but which may in fact turn out to be true

8. annals _____  c. to increase or add to

9. compound (v.) _____  d. historical records

10. tinge (n.) _____  e. special field of something or someone; kingdom

**Today's Idiom**

*a flash in the pan*—promising at the start but then disappointing

The rookie hit many home runs in spring training, but once the season began he proved to be *a flash in the pan*.

**ANSWERS ARE ON PAGE 231**

3

**New Words:**

| badger | implore | drudgery | interminable | perceive |
|--------|---------|----------|--------------|----------|
| baj′ ər | im plôr′ | druj′ ər ē | in ter′ mə nə bəl | pər sēv′ |

**How Not To Get Your Way**

It is difficult to change someone's opinion by *badgering* him. The child who begs his mother to "get off his back" when she *implores* him for some assistance with the household *drudgery,* may very well plead *interminably* for some special privilege when he wants something for himself. How paradoxical * that neither is able to *perceive* that no one likes being nagged.

( * paradoxical—studied previously, see page 3)

**Sample Sentences:**

Getting the hang of it? Now go on to use the five new words in the following sentences:

1. She does her homework on Fridays to save herself from the _____ of having to do it during the weekend.

2. The teacher continually _____ the pupil for the missing assignments.

3. The eminent scientist _____ difficulties in putting the invention into practice.

4. The sick child's mother _____ the doctor to come immediately.

5. I listened to the boring lecture for what seemed an _____ fifty minutes.

**Definitions:**

Pick the letter of the definition that matches your new word and write it in the answer space.

6. badger (v.) _____    a. unpleasant, dull, or hard work

7. implore _____    b. unending

8. drudgery _____    c. to plead urgently for aid or mercy

9. interminable _____    d. to understand, know, become aware of

10. perceive _____    e. to pester, nag, annoy persistently

**Today's Idiom**

*to pour oil on troubled waters*—to make peace, to calm someone down

When I tried to *pour oil on troubled waters,* both the angry husband and his wife stopped their quarrel and began to attack me.

ANSWERS ARE ON PAGE 231

You have accomplished something worthwhile this week. In learning twenty useful words and four idioms, you have taken a step towards a greater mastery of our language. As a result of today's lesson, you will become aware of those words which require greater study on your part for complete success in these first lessons.

Take the following quiz by matching the best possible definition with the word you have studied. Write the letter that stands for that definition in the appropriate answer space.

**REVIEW WORDS**

_____ 1　abound
_____ 2　annals
_____ 3　automaton
_____ 4　badger
_____ 5　compound
_____ 6　drudgery
_____ 7　eminent
_____ 8　implore
_____ 9　indiscriminate
_____10　interminable
_____11　matron
_____12　paradox
_____13　perceive
_____14　prognosticate
_____15　realm
_____16　replete
_____17　steeped
_____18　technology
_____19　tinge
_____20　voracious

**DEFINITIONS**

a. to be completely soaked in something
b. to be able to tell what will happen in the future
c. someone's special field
d. to continually nag
e. carelessly chosen
f. related to science of engineering
g. to add to
h. beg for assistance
j. of outstanding reputation
k. a mature woman
l. small amount of
m. dull, difficult work
n. desiring huge amount
o. existing in great number
p. historical records
r. to come to have an understanding of
s. completely filled with
t. machine that behaves like a person
u. seemingly self-contradictory situation
v. unending

**IDIOMS**

_____21　to eat humble pie
_____22　a pig in a poke
_____23　a flash in the pan
_____24　to pour oil on
　　　　　troubled
　　　　　waters

w. a blind item; poor purchase
x. admit to defeat
y. a star today, a flop tomorrow
z. to try to make peace

Now check your answers on page 231. Make a record below of those words you missed. You can learn them successfully by studying them and by using them in your own original sentences. If you neglect them, then the effort you have put into your vocabulary building campaign up to this point will have been wasted.

**WORDS FOR FURTHER STUDY**　　**MEANINGS**

1. _____　_____

2. _____　_____

3. _____　_____

4. _____　_____

5. _____　_____

**New Words:**

| laconic | throng | intrepid | accost | reticent |
|---|---|---|---|---|
| lə kon′ ik | thrông | in trep′ id | ə kôst′ | ret′ ə sənt |

**To the Point**

Calvin Coolidge, our thirtieth president, was named "Silent Cal" by reporters because of his *laconic* speech. One Sunday, after Mr. Coolidge had listened to an interminable* sermon, a *throng* of newsmen gathered around him. An *intrepid* reporter *accosted* the Chief Executive: "Mr. President, we know that the sermon was on the topic of sin. What did the minister say?" "He was against it," the *reticent* Coolidge replied.

(* interminable—See page 4. *Each review word will be followed by an asterisk—You will find the first use of the word by consulting the Index at the back of the book*).

**Sample Sentences:**   Use the new words in the following sentences.

1. His speech was usually rambling, but this time I found it brief and _____.
2. When _____ by a salesman, my mother always buys something.
3. Even under repeated questioning, the witness remained _____.
4. A howling _____ of teenage girls surrounded The Beatles.
5. The corporal received the Silver Star for his _____ deeds in combat.

**Definitions:**   Match the new words with their dictionary meanings.

6. laconic _____ a. expressing much in few words
7. throng _____ b. brave
8. intrepid _____ c. to approach and speak to
9. accost _____ d. crowd
10. reticent _____ e. silent

**Today's Idiom**

*the sword of Damocles*—any imminent danger (a king seated one of his subjects underneath a sword which was hanging by a hair, in order to teach him the dangers a king faces)

Although the president of the company seemed quite secure, he always complained that there was a *sword of Damocles* hanging over his head.

**ANSWERS ARE ON PAGE 231**

**New Words:**

| furtive | felon | plethora | hapless | irate |
|---------|-------|----------|---------|-------|
| fėr′ tiv | fel′ ən | pleth′ ə rə | hap′ lis | i′ rāt or i rāt′ |

**If I Had the Wings of an Angel**

Casting a *furtive* glance over his shoulder, the *felon* slipped out the main prison gate to be swallowed up in the British fog. A *plethora* of escapes from supposedly secure prisons embarrassed the *hapless* wardens. To compound * their problems, the officials were badgered * by *irate* citizens who accused the guards of accepting bribes from convicts whose motto was: "Stone walls do not a prison make, nor iron bars a cage."

( * compound—see page 3; * badgered—see page 4)

**Sample Sentences:** Use the new words in the following sentences.

1. The _____ contest winner was unable to locate the lucky ticket.

2. My uncle was _____ when the drunken driver swerved in front of us.

3. In a _____ manner she removed her shoes and tiptoed up to her room.

4. When the teacher asked why the homework had not been done, he was greeted by a _____ of incredible alibis.

5. Since the boss learned that Bob associated with a known _____, he fired him.

**Definitions:** Match the new words with their meanings.

6. furtive _____ a. angry, incensed

7. felon _____ b. a person guilty of a major crime

8. plethora _____ c. unfortunate

9. hapless _____ d. excess

10. irate _____ e. secret, stealthy

**Today's Idiom**

*Pyrrhic victory*—a too costly victory (King Pyrrhus defeated the Romans but his losses were extremely heavy)

In heavy fighting the troops managed to recapture the hill, but it could only be considered a *Pyrrhic victory*.

ANSWERS ARE ON PAGE 231

**New Words:**

| pretext | fabricate | adroit | gesticulate | vigilant |
|---------|-----------|--------|-------------|----------|
| pre′tekst | fab′ rə kāt | ə droit′ | jes tik′ ū lāt | vij′ ə lənt |

**Dr. Jekyll or Mr. Hyde?**

Under the *pretext* of being a surgeon he gained entry to the hospital. When interviewed by the director, he had to *fabricate* a tale of his medical experience, but he was so *adroit* at lying that he got away with it. It was not until the phony "doctor" began to *gesticulate* wildly with his scalpel, that a *vigilant* nurse was able to detect the fraud. In the annals* of medical history there have been a number of such cases.

**Sample Sentences:** Use the new words in the following sentences.

1. Because the teacher was extremely _____, no one could cheat on a test.
2. My nephew is quite _____ at making model airplanes.
3. Most fishermen can _____ a story about the size of the one that got away.
4. Her _____ of being tired did not fool us for an instant.
5. I often marvel as I watch the traffic policeman _____ at the onrushing cars.

**Definitions:** Pick the letter of the definition that matches your new word and write it in the answer space.

6. pretext _____ a. to lie; to construct
7. fabricate _____ b. skillful
8. adroit _____ c. an excuse
9. gesticulate _____ d. watchful
10. vigilant _____ e. move the arms energetically

**Today's Idiom**

*a wet blanket*—one who spoils your fun

Everyone wanted the party to go on, but Ronnie, *the wet blanket,* decided to go home to bed.

ANSWERS ARE ON PAGE 231

**New Words:**

| avid | cajole | rudimentary | enhance | nuance |
|------|--------|-------------|---------|--------|
| av′ id | kə jōl′ | rü′ də men′ tə rē | in hans′ | nü äns′ |

***You've Got To Be a Football Expert***

As an *avid* football fan, I try to see every game the Jets play. Whenever I can *cajole* my father into accompanying me, I try to do so. He has only a *rudimentary* knowledge of the game, and since I am steeped * in it, I enjoy explaining its intricate details to him. It certainly does *enhance* your appreciation of football when you are aware of every *nuance* of the sport.

**Sample Sentences:** Use the new words in the following sentences. You may have to change the ending of a word.

1. Since my grasp of algebra is _____, I cannot solve the problem.

2. The parakeet refused to be _____ into entering her cage.

3. It will _____ your enjoyment of an opera if you know what the plot is about in advance.

4. In reading the satires of Jonathan Swift, one must be vigilant* in order to catch each _____.

5. Franklin D. Roosevelt was an _____ reader of mystery stories.

**Definitions:** Match the new words with their meanings.

6. avid _____    a. eager

7. cajole _____    b. slight variation in meaning, tone, etc.

8. rudimentary _____    c. coax

9. enhance _____    d. intensify, heighten

10. nuance _____    e. elementary

**Today's Idiom**    *to beard the lion in his den*—to visit and oppose a person on his own grounds

     Having decided *to beard the lion,* I stormed into the manager's office to ask for a raise.

ANSWERS ARE ON PAGE 231

Keep adding to your vocabulary, as it is one of the most useful tools a student can possess. Let's go over the twenty new words and four idioms you studied during this week.

In the following quiz, match the best possible definition with the word you have studied. Write the letter that stands for that definition in the appropriate answer space.

| REVIEW WORDS | | DEFINITIONS | |
|---|---|---|---|
| f | 1 accost | a. | uncommunicative |
| a | 2 adroit | b. | enthusiastic |
| c | 3 avid | c. | alert |
| u | 4 cajole | d. | overabundance |
| v | 5 enhance | e. | courageous |
| n | 6 fabricate | f. | to greet first |
| k | 7 felon | g. | an excuse |
| d | 8 furtive | h. | unlucky |
| r | 9 gesticulate | j. | angry |
| h | 10 hapless | k. | criminal |
| e | 11 intrepid | l. | basic, elementary |
| j | 12 irate | m. | clever |
| b | 13 laconic | n. | to make up a lie |
| s | 14 nuance | o. | great number of people |
| m | 15 plethora | p. | concise, pithy |
| t | 16 pretext | r. | to use lively gestures |
| e | 17 reticent | s. | shade of difference |
| l | 18 rudimentary | t. | sly |
| o | 19 throng | u. | coax, wheedle |
| e | 20 vigilant | v. | to make greater |

**IDIOMS**

| | | | |
|---|---|---|---|
| | 21 the sword of Damocles | w. | an expensive conquest |
| | 22 Pyrrhic victory | x. | spoilsport |
| | 23 a wet blanket | y. | defy an opponent in his home |
| | 24 to beard the lion | z. | any threatening danger |

Now check your answers on page 231. Make a record below of those words you missed. You can learn them successfully by studying them and using them in your own original sentences. If you neglect them, then the effort you have expended in building up your vocabulary may be wasted.

**WORDS FOR FURTHER STUDY**     **MEANINGS**

1. _____    _____

2. _____    _____

3. _____    _____

4. _____    _____

5. _____    _____

**New Words:** loathe   reprimand   lackluster   caustic   wrest
lōth   rep′ rə mand   lak′ lus′ tər   kôs′ tik   rest

**The Pep Talk**   "If there's one thing I *loathe*," the coach said, "it's a quitter." He had good reason to *reprimand* us at half-time, because the scoreboard revealed that we were losing, 45–20. Our *lackluster* performance indicated to him that we had forgotten the rudimentary* aspects of basketball. His *caustic* remarks fired us up, however, and we dashed out, determined to *wrest* control of the game from our rivals.

**Sample Sentences:**   Use the new words in the following sentences.

1. With the help of his brothers he was able to _____ the leadership of the company from his partner.

2. Speaking in a monotone, the politician was booed for his _____ address.

3. In a _____ article, the drama critic slaughtered the hapless* actors.

4. I _____ spinach but I love other green vegetables.

5. When he arrived late, he knew that the grocer would _____ him.

**Definitions:**   Match the new words with their dictionary definitions.

6. loathe   _____   a. dull

7. reprimand
   (v.)   _____   b. to hate

8. lackluster   _____   c. sarcastic, biting

9. caustic   _____   d. take by force

10. wrest   _____   e. to show sharp disapproval

**Today's Idiom**   *crocodile tears*—insincere tears (crocodiles were said to cry while eating their prey)
   When the football player broke his leg, his substitute wept *crocodile tears*.

ANSWERS ARE ON PAGE 231

**New Words:**

| infamous | jostle | dupe | incipient | inadvertent |
|---|---|---|---|---|
| in′ fə məs | jos′ l | düp or dūp | in sip′ i ənt | in əd vûr′ tənt |

**The Handcuff Is Quicker Than the Eye**

Slippery Eddie, the *infamous* pickpocket, was back at work, and every detective had to be especially vigilant*. Eddie's technique was to *jostle* a victim toward a confederate who would then slip the man's wallet out of his back pocket while Eddie was stammering an apology to the confused *dupe*. Within a week the *incipient* crimewave came to an end when Slippery Eddie *inadvertently* chose the chief of police for his victim. Although Eddie loathes* Sing Sing, it's his permanent address now.

**Sample Sentences:** Can you put the new words in the right sentences?

1. By telling the truth, we stopped the _____ rumor from spreading.
2. The bombing of Pearl Harbor was referred to as an _____ deed.
3. The wealthy _____ consented to buy the often-sold Brooklyn Bridge.
4. When he attempted to _____ the old lady, she struck him with her umbrella.
5. Through an _____ error, the guided missile sped out of control.

**Definitions:** Match the new words with their meanings.

6. infamous _____ a. having a bad reputation
7. jostle _____ b. just beginning to exist
8. dupe (n.) _____ c. to shove hard
9. incipient _____ d. a person easily tricked
10. inadvertent _____ e. heedless, not attentive

**Today's Idiom**

*to carry the day*—to win the approval of the majority
The secretary's motion that we adjourn for lunch *carried the day*, and we headed for the restaurant.

ANSWERS ARE ON PAGE 231

**New Words:**

| ominous | tremulous | repudiate | cessation | bristle |
|---|---|---|---|---|
| om′ ə nəs | trem′ yə ləs | ri pū′ dē āt | se sā′ shən | bris′ l |

**Courtroom Drama**

There was an *ominous* silence when the jittery defendant rose in court. He explained in a *tremulous* voice what had led him to *repudiate* his confession made at the police station on the night of the crime. The audience began to buzz excitedly until the judge demanded a *cessation* of the noise. Although the district attorney *bristled* with anger, the defendant kept insisting that his rights had been violated because he had not been told that he could see a lawyer before confessing.

**Sample Sentences:** Fit the new words into the blanks.

1. After the weatherman had seen the _____ clouds, he prognosticated* rain.
2. The general attempted to _____ the testimony of the lieutenant, claiming that the young officer was not an authority on low level bombing.
3. Upon seeing the snake, the cat began to _____ with fear.
4. The widow's _____ hands revealed her nervousness.
5. The _____ of the shooting was replete* with benefits for both sides.

**Definitions:** Match the new words with their meanings.

6. ominous _____ a. a stopping
7. tremulous _____ b. to reject, decline
8. repudiate _____ c. stiffen with fear or anger
9. cessation _____ d. threatening
10. bristle (v.) _____ e. quivering

**Today's Idiom**

*Skid Row*—disreputable part of town, inhabited by derelicts and people "on the skids."

The presence of so many bars has turned our neighborhood into another *Skid Row*.

ANSWERS ARE ON PAGE 231

**New Words:** euphemism mundane incongruous condolence stipulate
ū′ fə miz əm mun′ dān in kong′ grü əs kən dō′ ləns stip′ ū lāt

**Call Me By My Right Name**

My cousin refers to himself as a "sanitary engineer"—a *euphemism* for garbage collector. There are any number of people who try to find more respectable or glamorous titles for the *mundane* jobs they hold. It may seem *incongruous* to call an undertaker a "*condolence* counselor," or to refer to a taxi driver as a "transportation expediter," but some prefer those titles. As a matter of fact, our butcher has *stipulated* that from now on he wants to be known as a "meat co-ordinator." He became irate* when I inadvertently* called him "Butch."

**Sample Sentences:** Into which blanks do the new words belong?

1. We repudiated * the contract because it did not _____ a cost of living bonus.

2. The word "expired" is a _____ for "died."

3. When my neighbor's dog was run over, we sent a _____ card.

4. The philosopher dealt with spiritual things, ignoring the _____ ones.

5. The play was so _____ that it seemed to be the work of several authors.

**Definitions:** Match the new words with their meanings.

6. euphemism _____    a. worldly

7. mundane _____    b. use of a less offensive term

8. incongruous _____    c. to specify a condition

9. condolence _____    d. inappropriate

10. stipulate _____    e. pity

**Today's Idiom**

*to go up in smoke*—to come to no practical result (kindling smokes but it will not light a fire)

    The mayor's plans to get the gubernatorial nomination *went up in smoke* when he couldn't end the costly strike.

ANSWERS ARE ON PAGE 231

The word "review" means "to view again" and that is the purpose of our weekly review. You will have noticed, of course, that many of the words which appear as new words are repeated in subsequent lessons. Sometimes they are in the paragraph, sometimes in the sample sentences, and occasionally in the idioms or directions. This continued emphasis on "viewing again" will help you to become familiar with the vocabulary.

In the following quiz, match the best possible definition with the word you have studied. Write the letter that stands for that definition in the appropriate answer space.

**REVIEW WORDS**

|        |    |              |
|--------|----|--------------|
| _____ | 1  | bristle      |
| _____ | 2  | caustic      |
| _____ | 3  | cessation    |
| _____ | 4  | condolence   |
| _____ | 5  | dupe         |
| _____ | 6  | euphemism    |
| _____ | 7  | inadvertent  |
| _____ | 8  | incipient    |
| _____ | 9  | incongruous  |
| _____ | 10 | infamous     |
| _____ | 11 | jostle       |
| _____ | 12 | lackluster   |
| _____ | 13 | loathe       |
| _____ | 14 | mundane      |
| _____ | 15 | ominous      |
| _____ | 16 | reprimand    |
| _____ | 17 | repudiate    |
| _____ | 18 | stipulate    |
| _____ | 19 | tremulous    |
| _____ | 20 | wrest        |

**DEFINITIONS**

a. despise
b. menacing
c. evil
d. a pause
e. just starting
f. trembling
g. to have one's hair stand up
h. stinging
j. earthly
k. due to an oversight, negligent
l. make a specific demand
m. to push, to elbow
n. an easily-fooled person
o. expression of sympathy
p. to scold severely
r. seize
s. having inconsistent elements
t. disown, refuse to accept
u. lacking brightness
v. saying something in a less direct way

**IDIOMS**

|        |    |                      |
|--------|----|----------------------|
| _____ | 21 | crocodile tears      |
| _____ | 22 | to carry the day     |
| _____ | 23 | Skid Row             |
| _____ | 24 | to go up in smoke    |

w. run down district
x. hypocritical sympathy
y. to win the honors
z. end fruitlessly

Now check your answers on page 231. Make a record below of those words you missed. You can learn them successfully by studying them and using them regularly in speech and in your writing.

**WORDS FOR FURTHER STUDY          MEANINGS**

1. _____   _____

2. _____   _____

3. _____   _____

4. _____   _____

5. _____   _____

15

**New Words:**  alacrity    disdain    belligerent    intimidate    feint
ə lak′ rə ti    dis dān′    bə lij′ ər ənt    in tim′ ə dāt    fānt

**Mullins a K.O. Victim**    When the bell sounded, K.O. Mullins responded with *alacrity*. He sprang from his stool and charged across the ring, showing *disdain* for the champion's strength. Although this *belligerent* attitude impressed the referee, it failed to *intimidate* the champ. That intrepid * battler laid the hapless* Mullins low with an adroit* *feint* and an uppercut.

**Sample Sentences:**  Use the new words in the following sentences.

1. The motorist tried to _____ the police officer, telling him of his eminent* friends in high places.
2. The Germans were duped * by the Allies' _____ toward the south, leaving the way open for the Normandy invasion.
3. The waiter moved with _____ because he perceived * they were big tippers.
4. His _____ manner caused him to lose one friend after another.
5. When the curtain came down, the critic's face registered the _____ he felt for the lackluster* play.

**Definitions:**  Match the new words with their meanings.

6. alacrity ____    a. contempt
7. disdain (n.) ____    b. a false show
8. belligerent ____    c. warlike
9. intimidate ____    d. to overawe
10. feint ____    e. briskness, lively action

**Today's Idiom**    *to throw down the gauntlet*—to challenge someone (when the gauntlet, or medieval glove, was thrown down, the challenger was required to pick it up)

The principal of our rival school *threw down the gauntlet*, and we had no choice but to accept the challenge.

**ANSWERS ARE ON PAGE 231**

**New Words:**  pugnacious   promulgate                    brash  scoff  belittle
pug nā′ shəs   prō mul′ gāt  or  prom′ əl gāt   brash  skof   bi lit′ l

**Mullins Throws Down the Gauntlet\***   The *pugnacious* K.O. Mullins demanded a rematch. He took a full-page newspaper advertisement to *promulgate* his challenge. When the champ's manager saw the *brash* announcement, he accosted\* Mullins who was surrounded by a throng\* of newsmen. The manager openly *scoffed* at Mullins and *belittled* his fighting ability. Mullins then lost his temper and fearlessly punched the manager, knocking him from his wheelchair.

**Sample Sentences:**  Use the new words in the following sentences.

1. We implored\* the faculty advisor to _____ the requirements for the presidency of the club.

2. My mother liked the salesman's _____ personality, but he irritated most people.

3. I don't understand modern art, but I neither loathe\* nor _____ at it.

4. Since everyone can outpunch my cousin, he cannot afford to be _____.

5. Although Ralph can't play, he doesn't hesitate to _____ the efforts of our football team.

**Definitions:**  Match the new words with their meanings.

6. pugnacious  _____   a. quarrelsome

7. promulgate  _____   b. to make seem less important

8. brash      _____   c. to sneer at

9. scoff      _____   d. impudent

10. belittle  _____   e. to make known officially

**Today's Idiom**   *feeling no pain*—drunk
Although the party had just begun, after his first drink he was *feeling no pain*.

ANSWERS ARE ON PAGE 231

**New Words:**   tangible   laceration   castigate   sordid   octogenarian
tan′ jə bl   las ər ā′ shən   kas′ tə gāt   sôr′ did   ok′ tə jə nãr′ i ən

**Mullins Forced to Eat Humble Pie\***   The irate\* 80-year-old manager pressed charges against K.O. Mullins, suing him for assault. As *tangible* evidence of the attack, he pointed to a deep *laceration* over his eyebrow which had required ten stitches. When the case was brought before the court, the judge *castigated* Mullins for the *sordid* incident. In addition to a costly financial settlement, Mullins was required to make a public apology to the *octogenarian*.

**Sample Sentences:**   Use the new words in the following sentences.

1. The medic reached into his kit to find a bandage for the ugly _____.

2. Mr. Dixon belittled \* our request for _____ proof of his loyalty.

3. The kindly foreman was too reticent\* to openly _____ the clumsy new worker.

4. When the teenager announced her engagement to the _____, the public suspected it to be a publicity stunt.

5. Stories of their _____ youth poured forth from the unhappy felons.\*

**Definitions:**   Match the new words with their meanings.

6. tangible _____   a. having actual form
7. laceration _____   b. to correct by punishing
8. castigate _____   c. jagged wound
9. sordid _____   d. dirty, base
10. octogenarian _____   e. person in his eighties

**Today's Idiom**   *Hobson's choice*—to have no choice at all (Mr. Hobson owned a livery stable but he did not allow the customers to pick their own horses)

Despite all the talk about democracy in my family, my father usually gives the rest of us *Hobson's choice*.

**ANSWERS ARE ON PAGE 231**

**New Words:**

| solace | aspirant | dregs | frenzy | scurrilous |
|--------|----------|-------|--------|------------|
| sol′ is | əs pīr′ ənt | dregz | fren′ zē | skėr′ ə ləs |

**The Decline of Mullins**

Mullins sought *solace* in whiskey. Once a highly-respected *aspirant* for the lightweight crown, he now found himself associating with the *dregs* of Skid Row.* He would work himself into an alcoholic *frenzy* in which he would trumpet *scurrilous* attacks on the champ, the old manager, and the judge. One avid * fight fan attributed Mullins' absence from the ring to sickness, saying that he was "recovering from a bad case of—SCOTCH."

**Sample Sentences:** Use the new words in the following sentences.

1. Vigilant* censors protect the public from listening to _____ language on television.

2. The publisher scoffed * at the reports that he was an _____ for the job of Secretary of State.

3. In a _____, the housewife overturned every drawer while searching for the car keys.

4. At the bottom of the beautiful wine bottle, only the _____ remained.

5. In trying to offer _____ to the pilot's wife, the reporter inadvertently* made the situation worse.

**Definitions:** Match the new words with their meanings.

6. solace    _____    a. most worthless part

7. aspirant   _____    b. coarse

8. dregs    _____    c. easing of grief

9. frenzy   _____    d. wild fit

10. scurrilous  _____    e. candidate for high position

**Today's Idiom**

*to rule the roost*—to be in charge, to be master (a roost is a perch where domestic birds can sleep)

    Although he is a lowly private in the army, at home he *rules the roost*.

ANSWERS ARE ON PAGE 231

Let's see how many of the new words studied during the course of this week you remember. Incidentally, try to keep a record of the many times you find your new words in magazines, newspapers, and books. Before you knew the meanings of those words you probably skipped right over them.

In the following quiz, match the best possible definition with the word you have studied. Write the correct letter in the appropriate answer space.

| REVIEW WORDS | | DEFINITIONS |
|---|---|---|
| _____ 1 | alacrity | a. scorn |
| _____ 2 | aspirant | b. to make afraid |
| _____ 3 | belligerent | c. frantic outburst |
| _____ 4 | belittle | d. man of eighty |
| _____ 5 | brash | e. to mock |
| _____ 6 | castigate | f. publish |
| _____ 7 | disdain | g. pretense, sham |
| _____ 8 | dregs | h. combative |
| _____ 9 | feint | j. candidate for better job |
| _____ 10 | frenzy | k. seeking war, hostile |
| _____ 11 | intimidate | l. speak of as unimportant |
| _____ 12 | laceration | m. vulgar, using indecent language |
| _____ 13 | octogenarian | n. insolent |
| _____ 14 | promulgate | o. punish, chastise |
| _____ 15 | pugnacious | p. comfort |
| _____ 16 | scoff | r. most worthless part |
| _____ 17 | scurrilous | s. able to be touched |
| _____ 18 | solace | t. rough cut |
| _____ 19 | sordid | u. filthy, ignoble |
| _____ 20 | tangible | v. quick willingness |

**IDIOMS**

| | | |
|---|---|---|
| _____ 21 | to throw down the gauntlet | w. be the boss, lay down the laws |
| _____ 22 | feeling no pain | x. under the influence of alcohol |
| _____ 23 | Hobson's choice | y. to offer a challenge |
| _____ 24 | to rule the roost | z. to have no say in a matter |

Check your answers on page 231. Make a record below of those words you missed. You can master them with additional review.

**WORDS FOR FURTHER STUDY**　　**MEANINGS**

1. _____ _____

2. _____ _____

3. _____ _____

4. _____ _____

5. _____ _____

**New Words:**  rampant  inane  ethics  concur  clandestine
ram′ pənt  in ān′  eth′ iks  kən kėr′  klan des′ tən

**Cheating**  During my first weeks at the new school I observed that cheating was *rampant*. I had always considered it rather *inane* to cheat on a test because of my code of *ethics*, and because so much was at stake. Apparently the other students didn't *concur*. In fact, even the presence of a proctor did not intimidate* them. Far from being a *clandestine* activity, the cheating was open and obvious.

**Sample Sentences:**  Use the new words in the following sentences.

1. When the plague was _____ on the island, Dr. Arrowsmith's wife died.
2. The spies thought their meeting was a _____ one, but a throng* of F.B.I. agents gathered outside the building.
3. A special management committee was asked to investigate business _____.
4. Orville Wright was criticized for his _____ desire to fly.
5. If I can get my parents to _____, I'll join the Peace Corps.

**Definitions:**  Match the new words with their meanings.

6. rampant  _____  a. secret, undercover
7. inane  _____  b. code of principles
8. ethics  _____  c. foolish
9. concur  _____  d. agree
10. clandestine  _____  e. going unchecked, widespread

**Today's Idiom**  *stock in trade*—the goods, tools and other requisites of a profession.
    A quick wit and a warm smile were the salesman's *stock in trade*.

ANSWERS ARE ON PAGE 232

**New Words:**

| flagrant | admonish | duress | culprit | inexorable |
|----------|----------|--------|---------|------------|
| flā′ grənt | ad mon′ ish | dü res′ or dū res′ | kul′ prit | in ek′ sə rə bəl |

**Cracking Down**

Mr. Dorsey, our new principal, determined to do something about the *flagrant* cheating at our high school. He issued bulletins and began to *admonish* those teachers who did not proctor alertly. Under *duress*, the faculty reported the names of the *culprits*. Several crib sheets were turned in as tangible* evidence of the cheating. Mr. Dorsey's *inexorable* campaign against the wrong-doers seemed to be paying off.

**Sample Sentences:** Into which sentences do the new words fit best?

1. The _____ was caught with his fingers in the cookie jar.
2. Batman and Robin were _____ in their pursuit of lawbreakers.
3. The confession was signed under _____, the attorney claimed.
4. I suspect that my father will _____ me for coming home late.
5. Parking in front of a hydrant is a _____ violation of the city's law.

**Definitions:** Match the new words with their meanings.

6. flagrant _____ a. inflexible, unrelenting
7. admonish _____ b. compulsion, force
8. duress _____ c. outrageous, glaringly bad
9. culprit _____ d. the guilty person
10. inexorable _____ e. to warn, to reprove

**Today's Idiom**

*to take down a peg*—to take the conceit out of a braggart (ships' colors used to be raised or lowered by pegs—the higher the colors, the greater the honor)

The alumni thought they had a great basketball team, but our varsity *took them down a peg.*

ANSWERS ARE ON PAGE 232

22

**New Words:**

| egregious | distraught | duplicity | acrimonious | paucity |
|---|---|---|---|---|
| i grē′ jəs | dis trôt′ | dü plis′ ə ti | ak′ rə mō′ ni əs | pô′ sə ti |

**Star Player Is Caught**

The cheating scandal came to a head when Art Krause, our football captain, made the *egregious* mistake of getting caught cheating on a midterm exam. If Art were suspended for his part in that sordid* affair, our chances for winning the city championship would go up in smoke.* The *distraught* coach asked the principal to overlook Art's *duplicity,* but Mr. Dorsey replied in an *acrimonious* fashion that the players had been given "a plethora* of athletic instruction but a *paucity* of moral guidance."

**Sample Sentences:** Use the new words in the following sentences.

1. The bank teller's _____ error was difficult to correct.

2. We tried to ignore her _____ comments, but that took considerable restraint.

3. _____ is the stock in trade of all adroit* counterspies.

4. Although it was a creative writing class, the teacher complained about the _____ of talent there.

5. The soldiers were _____ to learn that their furloughs had been canceled.

**Definitions:** Match the new words with their meanings.

6. egregious _____    a. scarcity

7. distraught _____    b. cunning, trickery

8. duplicity _____    c. mentally confused, crazed

9. acrimonious _____    d. remarkably bad

10. paucity _____    e. bitter

**Today's Idiom**

*to pass the buck*—to evade responsibility (the "buck" may have been a piece of buckshot passed from one poker player to another to keep track of whose turn it was to deal)

He always gives me a straight answer and never tries to *pass the buck.*

ANSWERS ARE ON PAGE 232

**New Words:**

| elicit | pernicious | tolerate | construe | impunity |
|--------|-----------|----------|----------|----------|
| i lis' it | pər nish' əs | tol' ər āt | kən strü' | im pū' nə ti |

**Our Pyrrhic Victory\***

Mr. Dorsey summoned a representative group of teachers and student leaders to his office in order to *elicit* their reactions to the suspension of the football captain. He told them that cheating was a *pernicious* disease which could not be *tolerated* at our school. He loathed * having to discipline Art Krause so severely, but unless strict measures were taken, the student body would *construe* the incident as an open invitation to cheat with *impunity*. "We may lose a football game," the principal said, "but we can salvage our self-respect."

**Sample Sentences:** Use the new words in the following sentences.

1. The border guards allowed the doctor to cross the frontier with _____.

2. It isn't easy to _____ answers from a sleepy class on Monday morning.

3. Dentists appreciate patients who can _____ pain.

4. He hoped that we would not _____ his decision to run for office as a thirst for power.

5. The dictator's _____ rules failed to intimidate* the leaders of the underground.

**Definitions:** Place the letter of the correct definition in the blank next to the new vocabulary word.

6. elicit _____    a. freedom from punishment

7. pernicious _____    b. to make a deduction, to infer

8. tolerate _____    c. to put up with, to bear

9. construe _____    d. to draw forth

10. impunity _____    e. harmful, causing injury

**Today's Idiom**

*to lionize a person*—to make a big fuss over someone (the lions at the Tower of London were considered its main attraction)

When the famous poet Dylan Thomas visited the United States, he was *lionized* wherever he lectured.

ANSWERS ARE ON PAGE 232

Congratulations! You have covered the first one-hundred words in the book. With the same diligence you should be able to tackle the remaining work and to master most of the challenging words.

Take the following quiz by matching the best possible definition with the word you have studied. Write the letter that stands for that definition in the appropriate answer space.

**REVIEW WORDS**

_____ 1 acrimonious
_____ 2 admonish
_____ 3 clandestine
_____ 4 concur
_____ 5 construe
_____ 6 culprit
_____ 7 distraught
_____ 8 duplicity
_____ 9 duress
_____ 10 egregious
_____ 11 elicit
_____ 12 ethics
_____ 13 flagrant
_____ 14 impunity
_____ 15 inane
_____ 16 inexorable
_____ 17 paucity
_____ 18 pernicious
_____ 19 rampant
_____ 20 tolerate

**DEFINITIONS**

a. double-dealing
b. cannot be moved by persuasion, inflexible
c. silly
d. flourishing
e. to scold, warn
f. harassed
g. to permit, to put up with
h. extract
j. damaging, harmful
k. outstanding for undesirable quality
l. notorious
m. force, coercion
n. exemption
o. moral philosophy
p. agree
r. hidden, secret
s. to interpret
t. one who commits a crime
u. shortage
v. caustic, bitter

**IDIOMS**

_____ 21 stock in trade
_____ 22 to take down a peg
_____ 23 pass the buck
_____ 24 to lionize a person

w. to idolize
x. to humiliate

y. the necessary equipment
z. to refuse to take responsibility

Now check your answers on page 232. Make a record below of those words you missed. You can learn them successfully by studying them and by using them in original sentences. Use a word three times and it is yours forever, a wise man once said.

**WORDS FOR FURTHER STUDY**       **MEANINGS**

1. _____ _____

2. _____ _____

3. _____ _____

4. _____ _____

5 _____ _____

**New Words:**

| affluent | feasible | discern | sally | consternation |
|---|---|---|---|---|
| af' lü ənt | fē' zə bəl | də zėrn' | sal' i | kon' stər nā' shən |
| | | or də sėrn' | | |

**The Newspaper Umbrella**

Our neighbor is an *affluent* inventor whose latest brainstorm, a *feasible* umbrella substitute, has been featured in many magazines. As simply as the eye can *discern*, it is a hard plastic strip, about the size of a ruler, which fits comfortably into a woman's handbag or a man's suit jacket. If a person is caught in a sudden rainstorm, he swings the plastic open in the shape of a cross. Attached to each arm is a clip-like device. Next, he takes the newspaper he is carrying and slides it under each of the four clips. Now, equipped with a rigid head covering he can *sally* forth to face the elements. To the *consternation* of the umbrella manufacturers, it has been enjoying a brisk sale, especially among commuters. If it continues to do well, it could have a pernicious* effect upon the umbrella industry.

**Sample Sentences:** Fit the new words into the proper blanks.

1. Some prisoners planned a disturbance while others would _____ toward the gate.

2. Under duress* from the tax officer, the beggar admitted that he was truly _____.

3. To the _____ of the sergeant, there was a paucity* of volunteers for the dangerous mission.

4. It's _____ to build an electric auto, but wouldn't you need a terribly long extension cord?

5. When we could _____ the city lights, we knew we were safe at last.

**Definitions:** Match the new words with their meanings.

6. affluent   _____   a. suddenly rush forth

7. feasible   _____   b. possible

8. discern   _____   c. dismay

9. sally (v.)   _____   d. rich

10. consternation   _____   e. perceive*

**Today's Idiom**

*I'm from Missouri*—a skeptic, one who is not easily convinced

    *You* might swallow his promises, but *I'm from Missouri.*

**ANSWERS ARE ON PAGE 232**

**New Words:**

| precocious | perfunctory | chagrin | perverse | deride |
|---|---|---|---|---|
| pri kō′ shəs | pər fungk′ tə ri | shə grin′ | pər vẻrs′ | dĭ rīd′ |

**Patent Pending**

My buddy Verne, a *precocious* automotive wizard, and I were inspired to do some inventing on our own. We thought it might be feasible* to park a car parallel to a space on the street. Then, by pressing a button, we could raise the four tires off the ground slightly, while dropping two special wheels perpendicular to the curb. It would then be child's play to roll into the narrowest of parking spaces. We took the idea to Ed Greene who runs the Ford agency in order to elicit* his reaction. After a *perfunctory* glance at our plans, to our *chagrin* Ed snorted that our idea was inane,* but we decided that he was just jealous of our brilliance. Tomorrow we are going to start on a computer which will enable us to measure the intelligence of *perverse* automobile dealers who like to *deride* the efforts of junior geniuses.

**Sample Sentences:**  Use the clues above to help find the proper words.

1. The children in Shakespeare's plays are so _____ that they all sound like grandparents.

2. I construed * the doctor's _____ examination to indicate that I was in good health.

3. The Wright brothers didn't become distraught* when a skeptic would _____ their work.

4. When I correct my kid brother's math errors, he is _____ enough to insist that he is right.

5. To the _____ of many taxpayers, some citizens seem to cheat the government with impunity.*

**Definitions:**  Match the new words with their meanings.

6. precocious _____  a. done without care, superficial

7. perfunctory _____  b. reaching maturity early

8. chagrin _____  c. feeling of disappointment, humiliation

9. perverse _____  d. contrary, persisting in error

10. deride _____  e. to ridicule, scoff * at

**Today's Idiom**

*red-letter day*—day of happiness, time for rejoicing (holidays are red-letter days on our calendars)

My *red letter day* came when I was chosen as senior class president.

ANSWERS ARE ON PAGE 232

**New Words:**

| disparage | laudable | fiasco | masticate | eschew |
|-----------|----------|--------|-----------|--------|
| dis par′ ij | lôd′ ə bəl | fi as′ kō | mas′ tə kāt | es chü′ |

**Hold That Nobel Prize!**

Speaking of inventions and discoveries, I just learned that an eminent* scientist in Ohio has developed a pill which contains all the nutritive value of three complete meals. In addition to providing us with the vitamins and minerals we need daily, this pill also gives a feeling of fullness. According to its sponsors, the pill will nourish and satisfy. I hate to *disparage* such a *laudable* achievement, but to me it seems like a most objectionable discovery. Rather than a scientific triumph, I'd be inclined to label it as an egregious* blunder, a scientific disaster, a laboratory *fiasco*. Is there anyone in his right mind who thinks that a pill can replace the pleasures of devouring hot corn bread, *masticating* on a thick steak, biting into crisp french fries, or attacking a chocolate sundae? I'm afraid that this is one pill I'll have to *eschew* from chewing.

**Sample Sentences:** Insert the new words in the following sentences.

1. The paradox* is that Javert's inexorable* pursuit of Jean Valjean was both _____ and despicable.

2. The affluent* storeowner _____ the efforts of his small competitor, saying that he could always tolerate* that kind of rivalry.

3. To aid in digestion, you must _____ each piece of meat one dozen times.

4. In an acrimonious* letter, her father described the project as a complete _____.

5. Once he sought the limelight, but now he _____ all interviews.

**Definitions:** Match the new words with their meanings.

6. disparage _____ a. to discredit, belittle*

7. laudable _____ b. avoid

8. fiasco _____ c. to chew up

9. masticate _____ d. praiseworthy

10. eschew _____ e. complete failure

**Today's Idiom**

*to let sleeping dogs lie*—to let well enough alone, to avoid stirring up old hostilities
    The lawyer wanted to open up the old case, but his partner advised him *to let sleeping dogs lie.*

ANSWERS ARE ON PAGE 232

**New Words:**

| quell | voluble | confidant | obsolescence | dubious |
|-------|---------|-----------|--------------|---------|
| kwel | vol′ ū bəl | kon′ fə dant′ | ob′ sə les′ əns | dü′ bi əs |

**Perfect Products**

I guess we'll never be able to *quell* those persistent rumors about the invention of auto tires which will never wear out, stockings which cannot tear, and pens which won't run dry. A *voluble* economist informed me that such products will never be marketed. "Can you imagine," he asked, "a manufacturer cutting his own throat? Why would he sell you an item which you will never have to replace? No," my *confidant* whispered, "it's part of their scheme of planned *obsolescence* to sell you merchandise with a limited life span in order to keep you coming back for more." I am *dubious* about the existence of those perfect products, but then I'm from Missouri.*

**Sample Sentences:** Use the new words in the proper blanks.

1. When the duplicity* was revealed, the jury became _____ about Ed's innocence.

2. In order to _____ the riot, the police sallied * forth with tear gas.

3. A teenage boy's father should be his true _____.

4. The _____ built into many products could be regarded as a flagrant* insult toward the duped * consumer.

5. I could not doze in the chair because of the _____ barber.

**Definitions:** Play the familiar matching game.

6. quell _____ a. one to whom you confide your secrets

7. voluble _____ b. talkative

8. confidant
   (e) _____ c. process of wearing out

9. obsolescence _____ d. put an end to

10. dubious _____ e. doubtful

**Today's Idiom**

*thumbs down*—signal of rejection (Roman emperors could condemn a gladiator who fought poorly by turning their thumbs down)

My father turned *thumbs down* on our plan to hitchhike to Florida during Easter.

ANSWERS ARE ON PAGE 232

After reading about these new ideas, you should be inventive enough to handle this review. If there is a necessity for it, you may turn back to the original lesson to check on the meaning of a word. As someone once remarked, "Necessity is the mother of invention."

Match the twenty words with their meanings. Write the letter that stands for the definition in the appropriate answer space.

**REVIEW WORDS**

| | | **DEFINITIONS** |
|---|---|---|
| _____ 1 | affluent | a. careless |
| _____ 2 | chagrin | b. dread, dismay |
| _____ 3 | confidant (e) | c. to chew |
| _____ 4 | consternation | d. complete failure |
| _____ 5 | deride | e. reaching maturity early |
| _____ 6 | discern | f. talkative |
| _____ 7 | disparage | g. practicable |
| _____ 8 | dubious | h. to make fun of |
| _____ 9 | eschew | j. contrary |
| _____ 10 | feasible | k. wealthy |
| _____ 11 | fiasco | l. keep away from |
| _____ 12 | laudable | m. recognize |
| _____ 13 | masticate | n. crush, stop |
| _____ 14 | obsolescence | o. to discredit |
| _____ 15 | perfunctory | p. person you tell your secrets to |
| _____ 16 | perverse | r. disappointment |
| _____ 17 | precocious | s. uncertain |
| _____ 18 | quell | t. commendable |
| _____ 19 | sally | u. sudden rushing forth |
| _____ 20 | voluble | v. process of wearing out |

**IDIOMS**

| | | |
|---|---|---|
| _____ 21 | I'm from Missouri | w. occasion for rejoicing |
| _____ 22 | red letter day | x. I have to be convinced |
| _____ 23 | let sleeping dogs lie | y. don't rake up old grievances |
| _____ 24 | thumbs down | z. to signal rejection |

Now check your answers on page 232. Make a record below of those words you missed. Study them, work on them, use them in original sentences. Amaze your friends at parties!

**WORDS FOR FURTHER STUDY**     **MEANINGS**

1. _____ _____

2. _____ _____

3. _____ _____

4. _____ _____

5. _____ _____

**New Words:**

| | | |
|---|---|---|
| implacable | paroxysm | reprehensible |
| im plak′ ə bəl | par′ ək siz əm | rep′ ri hen′ sə bəl |
| jurisdiction | skirmish | |
| jür′ is dik′ shən | sker′ mish | |

**Much Ado about a Haircut**

Perhaps you read about our school in the newspapers? We were one of the first to have a showdown on the topic of long hair for boys. Two honor students, Ron Harris and Len Chester, were sent to the principal by their French teacher, an *implacable* foe of non-conformists, who went into a *paroxysm* of anger when she spied the boys in the hall. At first it seemed like a simple case. The school would reprimand * the boys for their *reprehensible* appearance and order them to cut their hair or be suspended. But the boys' parents decided that the school had overstepped its *jurisdiction;* they took their case to the newspapers. What had started as a local *skirmish* now began to take on the appearance of a full-scale war.

**Sample Sentences:** Use the new words in the following sentences.

1. The detective was _____ in his search for the murder weapon.

2. Saying that it was beyond his _____, Judge Klein refused to rule on the case.

3. In a _____ of rage, the tenant stormed out of the landlord's office.

4. The precocious* boy enjoyed an intellectual _____ with his elders.

5. The brash* student was forced to apologize for his _____ conduct.

**Definitions:** Match the new words with their meanings.

6. implacable _____ a. a fit, sudden outburst

7. paroxysm _____ b. cannot be pacified, inexorable*

8. reprehensible _____ c. small fight, brief encounter

9. jurisdiction _____ d. worthy of blame

10. skirmish _____ e. power, range of authority

**Today's Idiom**

*cause célèbre*—a famous law case or controversy

It was a minor dispute, but the ambitious lawyer sought to turn it into a *cause célèbre.*

**ANSWERS ARE ON PAGE 232**

**New Words:**

| harass | monolithic | indigent | arbitrary | fray |
|--------|-----------|----------|-----------|------|
| har′ əs | mon′ ə lith′ ik | in′ də jənt | är′ bə trer′ i | frā |
| or hə rəs′ | | | | |

**The Tempest Spills Out of the Teapot**

Once the newspapers got the story, the case of the longhairs became a cause célèbre.* Ron and Len were interviewed, seen on T.V., and regarded by their fellow students as heroes. "These are not delinquents or hoods," one reporter wrote, "but clean-cut American boys who are being *harassed* by a *monolithic* school system." A caustic* editorial referred to the school's decision as *arbitrary* and inane.* A false story even circulated about the boys being rock-'n-roll performers whose *indigent* families needed their salaries. Finally, the Civil Liberties Union jumped into the *fray* with a court order stipulating* that the principal be required to show cause why the boys should not be allowed to return to class.

**Sample Sentences:** Use the new words in the following sentences.

1. After the _____, the feuding families agreed to patch up their differences.

2. The _____ client was surprised when she was accosted * by her social worker in the elegant restaurant.

3. To my mind the decision was unreasonable and _____.

4. George Orwell's *1984* depicts a frightening, _____ government.

5. If anonymous telephone callers _____ you, the phone company will give you an unlisted number.

**Definitions:** Match the new words with their meanings.

6. harass _____    a. based on whim, dictatorial

7. monolithic _____    b. poor, needy

8. indigent _____    c. massively solid

9. arbitrary _____    d. a fight

10. fray _____    e. to trouble, torment

**Today's Idiom**

*one swallow does not make a summer*—don't jump to conclusions based on incomplete evidence.

"Sure, the Yankees won their opening game, but *one swallow does not make a summer*."

ANSWERS ARE ON PAGE 232

**New Words:**

| stymie | effigy | flout | cognizant | turbulent |
|--------|--------|-------|-----------|-----------|
| stī′ me | ef′ ə ji | flout | kog′ nə zənt | tér′ bū lənt |

**Haircut Dilemma**

The school authorities were *stymied*. Public opinion had been marshaled against them. No longer was it a simple case of disciplining two wayward lads. Suddenly it had taken on the appearance of a nightmare in which the principal was either hanged in *effigy* or pictured in cartoons making a villainous swipe at the two innocent Samsons. But the officials could not allow Ron and Len to *flout* their authority with impunity.* Members of the school board concurred * with the principal's action but they were *cognizant* of the popular support for the boys. Clearly a compromise was called for to resolve the *turbulent* situation.

**Sample Sentences:**

Into which of the following newspaper headlines do the new words belong?

1. "COACH OF LOSING TEAM HANGED IN _____"
2. "CAUSE OF CANCER CONTINUES TO _____ DOCTORS"
3. "F.B.I. _____ OF CLANDESTINE * GANGLAND MEETING"
4. "MANY MOTORISTS _____ TRAFFIC LAWS, STUDY REVEALS"
5. "_____ ATMOSPHERE IN ANGRY SENATE CHAMBER"

**Definitions:**

Match the new words with their meanings.

6. stymie _____  a. unruly, agitated
7. effigy _____  b. to hinder, impede
8. flout _____  c. show contempt, scoff *
9. cognizant _____  d. aware
10. turbulent _____  e. a likeness (usually of a hated person)

**Today's Idiom**

*a bitter pill to swallow*—a humiliating defeat
It was a *bitter pill* for the famous billiard player to be overwhelmed by the 12-year-old girl.

ANSWERS ARE ON PAGE 232

**New Words:**

| terminate | forthwith | exacerbate | revert | oust |
|-----------|-----------|------------|--------|------|
| tèr′ mə nāt | fôrth′ with′ | eg zas′ ər bāt | ri vèrt′ | oust |

**Happy Ending?**

Following an executive session, the school board ordered the principal to *terminate* the suspension and to send the boys back to class *forthwith*. Unless it could be shown that their presence disrupted the learning process, there was no reason to bar the boys. It was a bitter pill * for the principal whose irritation was *exacerbated* by the ruling. But some of the sting was taken out of the victory when the boys appeared in school the next day with their hair clipped to a respectable length. Everyone breathed a sigh of relief. Just as things were about to *revert* to normalcy, however, the same French teacher then demanded that a girl be *ousted* from school for wearing a mini skirt.

**Sample Sentences:** Use the new words in the following sentences.

1. It seemed incongruous* to _____ his employment just when he was so successful.

2. Upon seeing the show, he called the T.V. studio _____ to protest.

3. The ushers moved with alacrity* to _____ the disorderly patrons.

4. After taking the drug, she began to _____ to the days of her childhood.

5. The arrest of the spy did much to _____ relations between the two countries.

**Definitions:** Match the new words with their meanings.

6. terminate _____    a. to drive out, eject

7. forthwith _____    b. return

8. exacerbate _____    c. to end

9. revert _____    d. immediately

10. oust _____    e. to irritate, make worse

**Today's Idiom**

*an ax to grind*—having a selfish motive in the background

    I am always dubious* about the motives of a man who tells me that he has no *ax to grind*.

**ANSWERS ARE ON PAGE 232**

Pupils want to be individuals these days, and many of them refuse to conform to regulations unless there are good reasons for such rules. In the area of vocabulary study, however, the only rule which makes sense to all is that true mastery derives from continuous practice.

Match the twenty words with their meanings. Write the letter that stands for the definition in the appropriate answer spaces. (Which two review words are almost synonymous?)

## REVIEW WORDS

_____ 1 arbitrary
_____ 2 cognizant
_____ 3 effigy
_____ 4 exacerbate
_____ 5 flout
_____ 6 forthwith
_____ 7 fray
_____ 8 harass
_____ 9 implacable
_____ 10 indigent
_____ 11 jurisdiction
_____ 12 monolithic
_____ 13 oust
_____ 14 paroxysm
_____ 15 reprehensible
_____ 16 revert
_____ 17 skirmish
_____ 18 stymie
_____ 19 terminate
_____ 20 turbulent

## DEFINITIONS

a. having a massive structure
b. to hinder
c. a conflict, fight
d. relentless, unappeasable
e. immediately
f. blameworthy
g. range of authority
h. to show contempt
j. poverty-stricken
k. to irritate
l. violent outburst
m. to end
n. a likeness
o. go back
p. to torment
r. riotous
s. eject
t. small battle
u. aware
v. based on whim

## IDIOMS

_____ 21 cause célèbre
_____ 22 one swallow doesn't make a summer
_____ 23 bitter pill
_____ 24 an ax to grind

w. having a selfish motive
x. a humiliating defeat
y. don't jump to conclusions
z. famous law case

Now check your answers on page 232. Make a record below of those words you missed.

## WORDS FOR FURTHER STUDY    MEANINGS

1. _____ _____

2. _____ _____

3. _____ _____

4. _____ _____

5. _____ _____

**New Words:**

| emaciated | surge | tranquil | sanctuary | ascend |
|---|---|---|---|---|
| i mā′ shi ā tid | sėrj | trang′ kwəl | sangk′ chü er′ i | ə send′ |

**Enter Dr. Thomas A. Dooley**

In 1956, LOOK magazine named Thomas Dooley as one of the year's ten most outstanding men. Just under thirty years of age at the time, Dr. Dooley had already distinguished himself by caring for a half-million sick and *emaciated* Vietnamese refugees. When fighting broke out in the divided country of Viet Nam, the northern Communist Viet Minh forces *surged* southward, scattering thousands of refugees before them. At the time, Dr. Dooley was a lieutenant, assigned to a *tranquil* naval hospital in Yokosuka, Japan. Forthwith* he volunteered for duty on a navy ship that had been chosen to transport the refugees to *sanctuary* in Saigon. The curtain was beginning to *ascend* on Dooley's real career.

**Sample Sentences:** Use the new words in the following sentences.

1. The _____ residents of the Warsaw Ghetto managed to win several skirmishes* from the Nazis.

2. A firecracker terminated * the _____ climate of the neighborhood.

3. When Richard III violated the _____ of the church to seize the princes, he exceeded his jurisdiction.*

4. Chicago put its heaviest players up front, but they were helpless as the Giants' line _____ toward them.

5. Inexorably* the determined climber began to _____ the Himalayan peak.

**Definitions:** Match the new words with their meanings.

6. emaciated _____ a. to rush suddenly

7. surge _____ b. shelter

8. tranquil _____ c. quiet

9. sanctuary _____ d. abnormally thin, wasted away

10. ascend _____ e. to rise

**Today's Idiom**

*sour grapes*—to disparage* something which you cannot have (from Aesop's fable about the fox who called the grapes sour because he could not reach them)

Marcia said that she didn't want to be on the Principal's Honor Roll anyway, but we knew that it was just *sour grapes* on her part.

**ANSWERS ARE ON PAGE 232**

**New Words:** malnutrition    afflict    besiege    privation    sinister
mal′ nü trish′ ən    ə flikt′    bi sēj′    prī vā′ shən    sin′ is tər

**Dooley's Mission**    Aboard the refugee ship, Dooley's destiny took shape. He became painfully cognizant* of the *malnutrition*, disease, ignorance, and fear that *afflicted* the natives. In addition, he discerned * how active the Communists had been in spreading their anti-American propaganda. Tom Dooley pitched in to build shelters in Haiphong, and to comfort the poor Vietnamese there before that *besieged* city fell to the powerful Viet Minh forces. He was seemingly unconcerned by the many *privations* he had to endure. For his services, Dooley received the U.S. Navy's Legion of Merit. He told the story of this exciting experience in DELIVER US FROM EVIL, a best-seller which alerted America to the plight of the Vietnamese, as well as to the *sinister* menace of Communism.

**Sample Sentences:**    Use the new words in the following sentences.

1. The stool pigeon, the detective's confidant,* told him about the _____ plot.
2. By running up a white flag, the _____ troops indicated their desire to withdraw from the fray.*
3. Citizens of several Kentucky mountain communities are _____ by the worst poverty in the nation.
4. The emaciated * prisoners were obviously suffering from advanced _____.
5. Albert Schweitzer endured considerable _____ as a jungle doctor.

**Definitions:**    Match the new words with their meanings.

6. malnutrition _____    a. lack of necessities
7. afflict _____    b. faulty or inadequate diet
8. besiege _____    c. evil, ominous
9. privation _____    d. to surround, hem in
10. sinister _____    e. to trouble greatly, to distress

**Today's Idiom**    *to swap horses in midstream*—to vote against a candidate running for re-election, to change your mind
     The mayor asked for our support, pointing out how foolish it would be *to swap horses in midstream*.

**ANSWERS ARE ON PAGE 232**

**New Words:**

| ubiquitous | remote | thwart | harbinger | malignant |
|---|---|---|---|---|
| ū bik′ wə təs | ri mōt′ | thwôrt | här′ bin jər | mə lig′ nənt |

**Stymied\* By Personal Sickness**

After an extensive lecture tour in 1956, Dr. Dooley returned to Laos to set up a mobile medical unit. Because the Geneva Agreement barred the entrance of military personnel to the country, he resigned from the Navy and went to work as a civilian. That story is told in THE EDGE OF TOMORROW. Next year, despite a growing illness, the *ubiquitous* Dooley turned up in the *remote* village of Muong Sing, attempting to *thwart* his traditional enemies—disease, dirt, ignorance, starvation—and hoping to quell \* the spread of Communism. But his trained medical eye soon told him that the pain in his chest and back was a *harbinger* of a *malignant* cancer.

**Sample Sentences:** Use the new words in the following sentences.

1. Sprinting all over the court, the _____ referee called one foul after another.
2. Ben's reprehensible\* table manners led his fraternity brothers to seat him in a _____ corner of the dining room.
3. The excellent soup was a _____ of the delicious meal to follow.
4. In an attempt to _____ the voracious\* ants, he surrounded his house with a moat of burning oil.
5. The surgeon finally located the _____ tumor which had afflicted \* his patient for many months.

**Definitions:** Match the new words with their meanings.

6. ubiquitous _____ a. distant, hidden away
7. remote _____ b. to be everywhere at the same time
8. thwart _____ c. likely to cause death
9. harbinger _____ d. to hinder, defeat
10. malignant _____ e. a forerunner, advance notice

**Today's Idiom**

*to cool one's heels*—to be kept waiting

The shrewd mayor made the angry delegates *cool their heels* in his outer office.

**ANSWERS ARE ON PAGE 232**

**New Words:**
excruciating respite reverberating fretful succumb
eks krü′ shi āt′ ing res′ pit ri vėr′ bər āt ing fret′ fəl sə kum′

**"Promises To Keep"**

From August, 1959 until his death in January, 1961, Dooley suffered almost continuous, *excruciating* pain. His normal weight of 180 was cut in half, and even the pain-killing drugs could no longer bring relief. Knowing that he did not have long to live, Dr. Dooley worked without *respite* on behalf of MEDICO, the organization he had founded to bring medical aid and hope to the world's sick and needy. The lines of Robert Frost kept *reverberating* in his mind during those *fretful* days: "The woods are lovely, dark and deep/ But I have promises to keep/ And miles to go before I sleep." When he finally *succumbed*, millions throughout the world were stunned and grief-stricken by the tragedy.

**Sample Sentences:** Use the new words in the following sentences.

1. With _____ slowness, the minute hand inched its way around the clock.
2. The rescue team heard the miner's voice _____ through the caves.
3. Around income tax time _____ faces are ubiquitous.*
4. The voluble* insurance salesman gave my father no _____.
5. Besieged * by debts, the corporation finally had to _____ to bankruptcy.

**Definitions:** Match the new words with their meanings.

6. excruciating _____   a. an interval of relief, delay
7. respite _____   b. worrisome, irritable
8. reverberat-ing _____   c. re-echoing, resounding
9. fretful _____   d. agonizing, torturing
10. succumb _____   e. to give way, yield

**Today's Idiom**

*a red herring*—something which diverts attention from the main issue (a red herring drawn across a fox's path destroys the scent)

We felt that the introduction of his war record was a *red herring* to keep us from inquiring into his graft.

ANSWERS ARE ON PAGE 232

39

Shortly before his death, Dr. Dooley was selected by the U.S. Chamber of Commerce as one of America's ten most outstanding young men. There may be no connection between success of that type and an expanded vocabulary—but one never knows.

Match the twenty words with their meanings. Write the letter that stands for the definition in the appropriate answer space.

**REVIEW WORDS**

_____ 1 afflict
_____ 2 ascend
_____ 3 besiege
_____ 4 emaciated
_____ 5 excruciating
_____ 6 fretful
_____ 7 harbinger
_____ 8 malignant
_____ 9 malnutrition
_____ 10 privation
_____ 11 remote
_____ 12 respite
_____ 13 reverberating
_____ 14 sanctuary
_____ 15 sinister
_____ 16 succumb
_____ 17 surge
_____ 18 thwart
_____ 19 tranquil
_____ 20 ubiquitous

**DEFINITIONS**

a. lack of necessities
b. inadequate diet
c. to be everywhere at once
d. to trouble greatly
e. agonizing
f. wasted away
g. distant
h. evil
j. to rush suddenly
k. place of protection
l. forerunner
m. to rise
n. to hinder
o. yield
p. postponement
r. to surround
s. becoming progressively worse
t. re-echoing
u. worrisome
v. peaceful

**IDIOMS**

_____ 21 sour grapes
_____ 22 swap horses in midstream
_____ 23 to cool one's heels
_____ 24 a red herring

w. a diversion
x. to be kept waiting
y. to change your mind
z. claiming to despise what you cannot have

Now check your answers on page 232. Make a record below of those words you missed.

**WORDS FOR FURTHER STUDY**     **MEANINGS**

1 _____ _____

2. _____ _____

3. _____ _____

4. _____ _____

5. _____ _____

**New Words:**

| impresario | extortion | adverse | asset | bigot |
|---|---|---|---|---|
| im′ prə sä′ ri ō | eks tôr′ shən | ad vėrs′ | as′ et | big′ ət |

**Just Spell the Name Correctly**

P. T. Barnum, the great circus *impresario*, was once accosted* by a woman who showed him a scurrilous* manuscript about himself, and said that unless he paid her, she would have the book printed. Barnum rejected the *extortion* attempt. "Say what you please," he replied, "but make sure that you mention me in some way. Then come to me and I will estimate the value of your services as a publicity agent." Barnum obviously felt that *adverse* criticism was an *asset* for a public figure. A man who seeks the limelight should not care what is written about him but should be concerned only when they stop writing about him. Barnum's philosophy suggests that we might do well to review the plethora* of publicity given to rabble-rousers and *bigots*.

**Sample Sentences:** Use the new words in the following sentences.

1. When the business manager was accused of _____, his colleagues sought to oust* him from the firm.

2. The eminent* _____ brought many cultural spectacles to our shores.

3. Attacked by the irate* crowd, the _____ asked the police for sanctuary.*

4. The childless man's will stipulated* that all the _____ of his company should revert* to the original owners.

5. It was excruciatingly* painful for the actors to read the _____ reviews which their performances had received.

**Definitions:** Match the new words with their meanings.

6. impresario _____  a. a narrow-minded, prejudiced person

7. extortion _____  b. unfavorable, harmful

8. adverse _____  c. one who presents cultural series, organizer

9. asset _____  d. a valuable thing to have·

10. bigot _____  e. getting money by threats

**Today's Idiom**

*to spill the beans*—to give away a secret

   Although he was naturally reticent,* when the felon* was intimidated* by the members of the rival gang, *he spilled the beans*.

ANSWERS ARE ON PAGE 233

**New Words:**

| blatant | entourage | virulent | venom | spew |
|---------|-----------|----------|-------|------|
| blā′ tənt | än′ tü räzh | vir′ ū lənt | ven′ əm | spū |

**Bigots\* Get Publicity**

Today, the *blatant* bigot, the leader of a lunatic fringe, and the hate-monger, each with his tiny *entourage,* find it relatively easy to attract publicity. Newspapers give space to the *virulent* activities of those agitators on the grounds that they are newsworthy. T.V. producers and radio executives, seeking for sensationalism, often extend a welcome to such controversial characters. "Yes," said the host of one such program, "we invite bigots, but it is only for the purpose of making them look ridiculous by displaying their inane\* policies to the public." Some civic-minded organizations have answered, however, that the hosts are not always equipped to demolish those guests, and even if they were, the audience would still be exposed to the *venom* they *spew* forth.

**Sample Sentences:** Use the new words in the following sentences.

1. The visiting dictator's ubiquitous\* _____ of bodyguards disturbed our tranquil \* city.

2. Europe's population was afflicted \* by a _____ plague known as the Black Death.

3. From each candidate's headquarters acrimonious\* charges would _____ forth daily.

4. Clym Yeobright's mother succumbed \* to the _____ of a snake bite.

5. With _____ discourtesy the reporters continued to harass\* the pilot's widow.

**Definitions:** Match the new words with their meanings.

6. blatant _____ a. group of attendants

7. entourage _____ b. disagreeably loud, very showy

8. virulent _____ c. poison, spite, malice

9. venom _____ d. throw up, vomit, eject

10. spew _____ e. full of hate, harmful

**Today's Idiom**

*to keep a stiff upper lip*—to be courageous in the face of trouble

It was admirable to see how the British managed *to keep a stiff upper lip* in spite of the German bombing.

**New Words:**

| loath | solicit | astute | advocate | ineffectual |
|-------|---------|--------|----------|-------------|
| lōth | sə lis′ it | əs tüt′ or as tūt′ | ad′ və kāt | in′ ə fek′ chü əl |

**Coping with Bigots**

Suppose a bigot wished to organize a meeting in your neighborhood. Since we cherish freedom of speech, we are *loath* to deny the request, even if he preaches hatred. As a result, hate-mongers are given the opportunity to rent halls, conduct meetings, publish abusive literature, and *solicit* contributions. What can be done about them? One *astute* observer, Prof. S. Andhil Fineberg, *advocates* the "quarantine method." His plan is to give such groups no publicity and to ignore them completely. Without the warmth of the spotlight, he feels that the bigot will freeze and become *ineffectual*. Debating with such warped minds is not feasible* and only tends to exacerbate* the situation.

**Sample Sentences:** Use the new words in the following sentences.

1. Since we felt that the ruling was arbitrary,* we were _____ to obey it.

2. Daily the volunteers went out to _____ funds for the indigent* families.

3. My neighbor was _____ enough to discern* the adverse* features of the mortgage.

4. The general was sure to _____ that we give the enemy no respite* from the bombings.

5. The play was so blatantly* bad that the impresario* fired its _____ director.

**Definitions:** Match the new words with their definitions.

6. loath _____ a. keen, shrewd

7. solicit _____ b. to be in favor of, to support

8. astute _____ c. not effective

9. advocate (v.) _____ d. unwilling, reluctant

10. ineffectual _____ e. to beg, seek earnestly

**Today's Idiom**

*to have cold feet*—to hesitate because of fear or uncertainty
My cousin was all set to join the paratroops, but at the last moment he got *cold feet*.

**ANSWERS ARE ON PAGE 233**

**New Words:**

| scrutinize | nefarious | amicable | vexatious | malady |
|---|---|---|---|---|
| skrü′ tə nīz | ni fãr′ i əs | am′ ə kə bəl | veks ā′ shəs | mal′ ə di |

**More Than Silence**

The quarantine method for handling bigots implies more than giving them the silent treatment. Prof. Fineberg urges community-relations organizations to *scrutinize* the *nefarious* activities of hate-mongers and to be prepared to furnish information about them to *amicable* inquirers. When a rabble-rouser is coming, those organizations should privately expose him to opinion-molders. In addition, constructive efforts should be taken to induce people to involve themselves in projects for improving intergroup relations. Bigger than the *vexatious* immediate problem is the need to find out the cause for such bigotry and to counteract this sinister* *malady* which afflicts a segment of our society.

**Sample Sentences:** Use the new words in the following sentences.

1. The _____ buzzing of the mosquitoes as they surged * about our heads nearly drove us insane.

2. Our _____ relations with Latin America are an asset* to hemispheric trade.

3. Once the virulent* _____ had run its course, my temperature dropped.

4. We were distraught* upon hearing the venom* spewed * forth by the _____ bigot.*

5. No sooner did the lawyer _____ the extortion* note than he called the police.

**Definitions:** Match the new words with their definitions.

6. scrutinize  _____   a. annoying

7. nefarious  _____   b. villainous, vicious

8. amicable  _____   c. examine closely

9. vexatious  _____   d. disease

10. malady  _____   e. friendly, peaceful

**Today's Idiom**

*to look a gift horse in the mouth*—to be critical of a present given to you (from the practice of judging a horse's age by his teeth)

Although I didn't have much use for Uncle Roy's present, I took it with a big smile since I have been taught never *to look a gift horse in the mouth.*

ANSWERS ARE ON PAGE 233

There is an excellent book entitled *How to Argue with a Conservative* which gives the reader the tools necessary for success in argumentation. At times you may have to engage in a verbal skirmish* with a bigot.* It would be to your advantage if you had the proper words at your fingertips.

Match the twenty words with their meanings. Write the letter that stands for the definition in the appropriate answer space.

**REVIEW WORDS**

| | | | **DEFINITIONS** |
|---|---|---|---|
| \_\_\_\_\_ | 1 | adverse | a. to support |
| \_\_\_\_\_ | 2 | advocate | b. keen, shrewd |
| \_\_\_\_\_ | 3 | amicable | c. something of value |
| \_\_\_\_\_ | 4 | asset | d. villainous |
| \_\_\_\_\_ | 5 | astute | e. seek earnestly |
| \_\_\_\_\_ | 6 | bigot | f. organizer |
| \_\_\_\_\_ | 7 | blatant | g. annoying |
| \_\_\_\_\_ | 8 | entourage | h. followers |
| \_\_\_\_\_ | 9 | extortion | j. disagreeably loud |
| \_\_\_\_\_ | 10 | impresario | k. examine closely |
| \_\_\_\_\_ | 11 | ineffectual | l. poison |
| \_\_\_\_\_ | 12 | loath | m. harmful |
| \_\_\_\_\_ | 13 | malady | n. not effective |
| \_\_\_\_\_ | 14 | nefarious | o. prejudiced person |
| \_\_\_\_\_ | 15 | scrutinize | p. unfavorable |
| \_\_\_\_\_ | 16 | solicit | r. friendly |
| \_\_\_\_\_ | 17 | spew | s. unwilling |
| \_\_\_\_\_ | 18 | venom | t. vomit |
| \_\_\_\_\_ | 19 | vexatious | u. disease |
| \_\_\_\_\_ | 20 | virulent | v. getting money by threats |

**IDIOMS**

| | | | |
|---|---|---|---|
| \_\_\_\_\_ | 21 | to spill the beans | w. to be critical of a present |
| \_\_\_\_\_ | 22 | stiff upper lip | x. hesitation because of fear |
| \_\_\_\_\_ | 23 | cold feet | y. courage in the face of trouble |
| \_\_\_\_\_ | 24 | look a gift horse in the mouth | z. give away a secret |

Now check your answers on page 233. Make a record below of those words you missed. Once again, use those words in original sentences.

**WORDS FOR FURTHER STUDY**     **MEANINGS**

1. _____ _____

2. _____ _____

3. _____ _____

4. _____ _____

5. _____ _____

**New Words:**

| inclement | peruse | premonition | desist | recoil |
|-----------|--------|-------------|--------|--------|
| in klem′ ənt | pə rüz′ | prē′ mə nish′ ən | di zist′ | ri koil′ |

**Jerry Hart's Sixth Sense**

An uneasy feeling had made Jerry Hart miserable all day long. It was difficult to explain, but the similar sensations in the past had been accurate—trouble was on the way. Just as some people can predict the onset of *inclement* weather because of an aching in their bones, so could Jerry detect incipient* disaster. He sat at his desk, trying to *peruse* a company report but his efforts were ineffectual.* The gnawing at his insides, the tinge* of uneasiness, the *premonition* of calamity which besieged * him would not *desist*. When the phone rang, he *recoiled* with fear—it was his wife and she was hysterical. Their son had been bitten by a mad dog!

**Sample Sentences:** Use the new words in the following sentences.

1. After being admonished * by his father, he began to _____ the want ads daily.

2. When the black cat crossed her path, Ellen had a _____ of disaster.

3. The pickets promulgated* a warning that they would not _____ in their efforts to enhance* their standard of living.

4. As the snake prepared to strike, the girls _____ in horror.

5. She blamed her absence from the game on the _____ weather, but we knew that was sour grapes.*

**Definitions:** Match the new words with their meanings.

6. inclement _____ a. unfavorable, stormy

7. peruse _____ b. to read carefully

8. premonition _____ c. cease

9. desist _____ d. forewarning

10. recoil _____ e. draw back

**Today's Idiom**

*to pay the piper*—to bear the consequences (from the story of the Pied Piper of Hamelin)

The cruel leader was doing well at the present time, but he knew that one day he might have *to pay the piper*.

**ANSWERS ARE ON PAGE 233**

**New Words:**

| pertinent | mastiff | obsess | doleful | wan |
|-----------|---------|--------|---------|-----|
| per' tə nənt | mas' tif | əb ses' | dōl' fəl | wän |

**Crisis!** As soon as Jerry Hart could get the *pertinent* facts from his wife, he dashed out of the office on his way home. He jostled * people in the hallway, implored * the elevator operator to hurry, and with flagrant* disregard for an elderly gentleman jumped into the cab he had hailed. The twenty-minute taxi ride seemed interminable* and all the while horrible thoughts occurred to Jerry. Visions of an ugly *mastiff* with foaming jaws *obsessed* him. A crowd of people had gathered in front of his house so that Jerry had to force his way through them. Little Bobby was on his bed, surrounded by a doctor, a policeman, Jerry's *doleful* wife, his two daughters, and a half-dozen *wan* neighbors.

**Sample Sentences:** Use the new words in the following sentences.

1. The stockbroker was _____ with the idea of becoming a painter.

2. My nervous neighbor bought a pugnacious* _____ to frighten burglars.

3. _____ expressions abounded * throughout headquarters on the night of the election.

4. During the trial the astute* lawyer was able to elicit* the _____ information from the key witness.

5. After the tension, his normally ruddy face was _____ and tired.

**Definitions:** Match the new words with their meanings.

6. pertinent _____ a. sad, melancholy

7. mastiff _____ b. to the point

8. obsess _____ c. sickly pale

9. doleful _____ d. to haunt, preoccupy

10. wan _____ e. large dog

**Today's Idiom** *on the carpet*—being scolded
 Because of her repeated lateness, Betty's boss called her *on the carpet*.

ANSWERS ARE ON PAGE 233

**New Words:**  histrionics    elusive    frustrate    symptomatic    interject
his′ tri on′ iks    i lü′ siv    frus′ trāt    simp′ tə mat′ ik    in′ tər jekt′

**A Time for Decision**

The doctor explained the situation calmly, avoiding *histrionics*. First of all, they didn't know whether the dog had rabies. Secondly, the *elusive* dog had *frustrated* all attempts to find him so far. Finally, the decision would have to be made whether Bobby was to undergo the painful vaccination administered daily for two weeks. Mrs. Hart said that a neighbor who had seen the dog claimed that it had been foaming at the mouth, barking, and growling constantly— all *symptomatic* of rabies. But the policeman *interjected* that there hadn't been a case of a mad dog in the county in over twenty years; he repudiated * the neighbor's report, advocating* that they do nothing for at least another day. Mr. and Mrs. Hart sat down to think about their next step.

**Sample Sentences:** Use the new words in the following sentences.

1. The warden ＿＿＿＿＿＿ the prisoners' attempt to escape by adding more guards.

2. Most viewers hate it when a commercial is ＿＿＿＿＿ into a suspense drama.

3. Saying that he would not tolerate* her ＿＿＿＿＿＿, the director fired the temperamental actress.

4. All his life he found happiness ＿＿＿＿＿＿, but wealth easy to come by.

5. The sordid * rioting was ＿＿＿＿＿ of the problems facing the large cities.

**Definitions:** Match the new words with their meanings.

6. histrionics ＿＿＿    a. having to do with signs or symptoms, indicative

7. elusive ＿＿＿    b. hard to grasp

8. frustrate ＿＿＿    c. insert, interrupt

9. symptomatic ＿＿＿    d. display of emotions

10. interject ＿＿＿    e. counteract, foil, thwart*.

**Today's Idiom**

*to show one's hand*—to reveal your intentions
When someone joined in bidding for the antique, the dealer was forced *to show his hand*.

**ANSWERS ARE ON PAGE 233**

**New Words:**

| inert | salient | imminent | squeamish | engrossed |
|-------|---------|----------|-----------|-----------|
| in ért′ | sā′ li ənt | im′ ə nənt | skwēm′ ish | en grōst′ |

**The Pertinent\* Facts About Rabies**

"Give me some of the rudimentary\* information about the disease, Doc," said Jerry, glancing toward the *inert* figure of his son. "Well, as you know, the malady\* used to be called 'hydrophobia' (fear of water) because one of the symptoms is an inability to swallow liquids. Actually, it is caused by a live virus from the saliva of an infected animal. If saliva gets into a bite wound, the victim may get rabies. The virus travels along the nerves to the spine and brain. Once the *salient* characteristics appear (ten days to six months) then death is *imminent*." "What are the symptoms?" asked Mrs. Hart. "Pain and numbness, difficulty in swallowing, headaches and nervousness. Also, muscle spasms and convulsions." The *squeamish* neighbors who were *engrossed* in the doctor's remarks gasped. "I think we should go ahead with the injections," the distraught\* Mrs. Hart said. "I've heard enough."

**Sample Sentences:** Use the new words in the following sentences.

1. The senator loathed \* it when people said that an atomic war was _____.

2. When his _____ partner complained about a lack of ethics,\* the businessman laughed at his innocence.

3. _____ in his crossword puzzle, he failed to notice the paucity\* of customers in the restaurant.

4. One of the _____ features of his poetry is a dependence upon euphemisms.\*

5. Seeing the _____ player, the manager dashed out onto the field.

**Definitions:** Match the new words with their meanings.

6. inert \_\_\_\_\_    a. outstanding, prominent

7. salient \_\_\_\_\_    b. without power to move

8. imminent \_\_\_\_\_    c. likely to happen, threatening

9. squeamish \_\_\_\_\_    d. absorbed

10. engrossed \_\_\_\_\_    e. easily shocked, over sensitive

**Today's Idiom**

*to tilt at windmills*—to fight imaginary enemies (from *Don Quixote*)

The vice-president told the committee, "We're really on your side, and if you fight us you'll be tilting at windmills."

ANSWERS ARE ON PAGE 233

At the end of this week's study, you will have covered 200 words and 40 idioms. In addition, you will have seen many of those words used several times in subsequent lessons. If you have been operating at only 75% efficiency, you have, nevertheless, added substantially to your arsenal of words.

Here's a thought—wouldn't it be wonderful if through genuine attention to the daily dosage you could move up to 80%—or even 90%? Start by matching the 20 words with their meanings. Write the letter that stands for the definition in the appropriate answer space. Did somebody say 100%?

**REVIEW WORDS**

_____ 1 desist
_____ 2 doleful
_____ 3 elusive
_____ 4 engrossed
_____ 5 frustrate
_____ 6 histrionics
_____ 7 imminent
_____ 8 inclement
_____ 9 inert
_____ 10 interject
_____ 11 mastiff
_____ 12 obsess
_____ 13 pertinent
_____ 14 peruse
_____ 15 premonition
_____ 16 recoil
_____ 17 salient
_____ 18 squeamish
_____ 19 symptomatic
_____ 20 wan

**DEFINITIONS**

a. sad
b. draw back
c. foil
d. cease
e. interrupt
f. stormy, harsh
g. indicative
h. appropriate
j. powerless to move
k. large dog
l. outstanding
m. read carefully
n. preoccupy
o. easily shocked
p. forewarning
r. about to happen
s. hard to grasp
t. pale
u. absorbed
v. display of emotions

**IDIOMS**

_____ 21 to pay the piper
_____ 22 on the carpet
_____ 23 to show one's hand
_____ 24 to tilt at windmills

w. to reveal your emotions
x. being scolded
y. fight imaginary enemies
z. to bear the consequences

Now check your answers on page 233. Make a record below of those words you missed.

**WORDS FOR FURTHER STUDY**     **MEANINGS**

1. _____  _____

2. _____  _____

3. _____  _____

4. _____  _____

5. _____  _____

**New Words:**

| poignant | inundate | fruitless | garbled | sanguine |
|---|---|---|---|---|
| poin′ yənt or | in′ un dāt | früt′ lis | gär′ bəld | sang′ gwin |
| poin′ ənt | | | | |

**The Search for the Dog (Continued)**

Meanwhile, the Harts had notified the local radio station to broadcast a *poignant* appeal for the dog's owner to come forward. The station was *inundated* with phone calls but all leads were *fruitless.* From what Bobby had told them, a huge dog had leaped out from a red stationwagon in the supermarket's parking lot. After biting Bobby it vanished. The six-year-old was too concerned with the bites he had received to see where the dog disappeared to. The boy's story was *garbled,* but he did remember that the animal was gray and had a collar. There was little tangible* evidence to go on, but the police remained *sanguine.*

**Sample Sentences:** Use the new words in the following sentences.

1. The sermon was _____ enough to bring tears to the brash* delinquent's eyes.

2. Although the message was _____, its salient* points were clear enough.

3. After a _____ attempt to wrest* control of the government, the traitors were incarcerated.*

4. Even though his boat was almost _____, the skipper was loath* to radio for help.

5. Because the malignancy* had gone unchecked, the surgeons were not _____ about the patient's chances.

**Definitions:** Match the new words with their definitions.

6. inundate _____ a. useless

7. fruitless _____ b. confused, mixed up

8. poignant _____ c. optimistic

9. garbled _____ d. to flood

10. sanguine _____ e. moving, painful to the feelings

**Today's Idiom**

to *feather one's nest*—grow rich by taking advantage of circumstances

While working as the tax collector, he adroitly* *feathered his own nest.*

ANSWERS ARE ON PAGE 233

**New Words:** 
phlegmatic   corroborate   comprehensive   zealous   coerce
fleg mat' ik   kə rob' ə rāt   kom' pri hen' siv   zel' əs   kō érs'

**No Relief**    The normally *phlegmatic* Jerry Hart was deeply upset. Twenty-four hours had passed without result, and even if the rabies could not be *corroborated*, Jerry was determined to see that his son received the vaccine. At the suggestion of some friends, he organized a *comprehensive* search party, *zealously* fanning out in circles around the supermarket. They knocked on every door, inspected every dog, and came back empty-handed. Although the Harts were sick with worry (they had to be *coerced* into going to sleep), little Bobby seemed to be in great spirits. The excruciating* vigil continued.

**Sample Sentences:**    Use the new words in the following sentences.

1. Harriet's egregious* error disturbed even her _____ employer.

2. The fund raiser was so _____ that he solicited * money from a Salvation Army Santa Claus.

3. In order to get the job, you had to go through the drudgery* of filling out a ten-page _____ questionnaire.

4. The elusive* fugitive was _____ by his attorney into surrendering.

5. Even the swindler's nefarious* accomplice refused to _____ his alibi.

**Definitions:**    Match the new words with their definitions.

6. phlegmatic _____    a. enthusiastic

7. corroborate _____    b. calm, hard to rouse to action

8. comprehensive _____    c. confirm, support

9. zealous _____    d. thorough

10. coerce _____    e. to force

**Today's Idiom**    *fair-weather friends*—unreliable, they fail you in time of distress.

     The general was chagrined * to learn that so many of his supposed supporters were actually *fair-weather friends*.

**ANSWERS ARE ON PAGE 233**

**New Words:**

| elapse | meticulous | domicile | lax | sporadic |
|---|---|---|---|---|
| i laps′ | mə tik′ ū ləs | dom′ ə səl | laks | spə rad′ ik |

**The Police Find the Dog**

Forty hours had *elapsed* before the police work and the publicity paid off. By *meticulously* checking the registrations of every red station wagon in the neighborhood and then cross-checking dog licenses, the police narrowed the search to four owners. After a few telephone calls, the apologetic owner was located and directed to bring her muzzled German shepherd to the Hart *domicile*. Bobby identified the dog, and the animal was taken to a veterinary's clinic to have the necessary tests performed. The *lax* owner, Mrs. McGraw, admitted that the dog had a *sporadic* mean streak, but she scoffed * at the idea of rabies. Jerry Hart noticed for the first time in two days that his uneasy feeling had departed.

**Sample Sentences:** Use the new words in the following sentences.

1. Inadvertently,* Emma had allowed two months to _____ before paying her rent.
2. The lackluster* battle was punctuated by _____ mortar fire.
3. A man's _____ is his castle.
4. Because the watchman was _____, thievery was rampant* at the warehouse.
5. The _____ musician had nothing but disdain* for his disorganized friends.

**Definitions:** Match the new words with their definitions.

6. elapse _____ a. careless, negligent
7. meticulous _____ b. to slip by
8. domicile _____ c. occasional
9. lax _____ d. home
10. sporadic _____ e. careful

**Today's Idiom**

*to sow one's wild oats*—to lead a wild, gay life.

During his teen years, the millionaire avidly* *sowed his wild oats*.

ANSWERS ARE ON PAGE 233

**New Words:**   rash      conjecture      obviate      lurid      quip
                 rash      kən jek′ chər   ob′ vi āt    lür′ id    kwip

***All's Well That Ends Well***   The Harts were greatly relieved to learn that the *rash conjecture* about the dog was not true. Because the German shepherd was not rabid, the necessity for the painful treatment was *obviated*. The police gave the dog's owner a summons for allowing the animal to go unmuzzled. Little Bobby was treated to an ice cream sundae and a Walt Disney double feature. The neighbors searched for other *lurid* happenings, and Jerry Hart went back to his office. "What kind of dog was that?" his secretary asked. "Oh, his bark was worse than his bite," *quipped* Jerry.

**Sample Sentences:**   Use the new words in the following sentences.

1. It was sheer _____ on the detective's part but it led to the arrest of the vexatious* counterfeiters.

2. The newspaper switched from mundane* coverage to _____ reporting.

3. It was exceedingly _____ of the lightweight to insult the belligerent* longshoreman.

4. The necessity for preparing sandwiches was _____ when the picnic was postponed.

5. Hamlet remembered that Yorick was always ready with a lusty _____.

**Definitions:**   Match the new words with their definitions.

6. rash (adj.)  _____   a. do away with, eliminate
7. conjecture  _____   b. joke
8. obviate  _____   c. guess
9. lurid  _____   d. sensational
10. quip  _____   e. too hasty, reckless

***Today's Idiom***   *windfall*—unexpected financial gain.
When the bankrupt company struck oil, the surprised investor received a *windfall* of $20,000.

ANSWERS ARE ON PAGE 233

Many teachers have jested about their students who confused *rabies* with *rabbis*, Jewish clergymen. We know that those who get the message of this book, true vocabulary mastery, will make few such errors.

Match the twenty words with their meanings. Write the letter that stands for the definition in the appropriae answer space.

| REVIEW WORDS | DEFINITIONS |
|---|---|
| _____ 1 coerce | a. to flood, to swamp |
| _____ 2 comprehensive | b. home |
| _____ 3 conjecture | c. painful to the feelings, moving |
| _____ 4 corroborate | d. useless |
| _____ 5 domicile | e. reckless |
| _____ 6 elapse | f. confirm |
| _____ 7 fruitless | g. calm, sluggish |
| _____ 8 garbled | h. sensational |
| _____ 9 inundate | j. hopeful |
| _____ 10 lax | k. do away with |
| _____ 11 lurid | l. confused, mixed up |
| _____ 12 meticulous | m. guess |
| _____ 13 obviate | n. to pass by |
| _____ 14 phlegmatic | o. careless |
| _____ 15 poignant | p. occasional |
| _____ 16 quip | r. thorough |
| _____ 17 rash | s. careful |
| _____ 18 sanguine | t. to force |
| _____ 19 sporadic | u. enthusiastic |
| _____ 20 zealous | v. to joke |

**IDIOMS**

| | |
|---|---|
| _____ 21 to feather one's nest | w. to lead a wild life |
| _____ 22 fair-weather friends | x. unexpected financial gain |
| _____ 23 to sow wild oats | y. unreliable acquaintances |
| _____ 24 windfall | z. provide for yourself at the expense of others |

Now check your answers on page 233. Make a record below of those words you missed. If you were able to get them all right, use the five spaces to create antonyms for numbers 7, 8, 10, 17, and 19.

**WORDS FOR FURTHER STUDY**　　　**MEANINGS**

1. _____  _____

2. _____  _____

3. _____  _____

4. _____  _____

5. _____  _____

**New Words:**

| diatribe | inhibition | fortuitous | incoherent | ilk |
|---|---|---|---|---|
| dī′ ə trīb | in′ ə bish′ ən | fôr tü′ ə təs | in′ kō hēr′ ənt | ilk |
| | or in′ hi bish′ ən | | | |

**Off Broadway**    When Monte Ziltch told his boss, Mr. Foy, that he was quitting as an accountant to become an actor, the man was convulsed with laughter. After Mr. Foy realized that Monte was obsessed * with the idea, he became quite serious, launching into a *diatribe* on the importance of responsibility in the younger generation. Monte confessed that he had been developing ulcers as an accountant, and when his psychiatrist suggested that the sickness was a result of *inhibitions*, Monte agreed. Now a *fortuitous* opportunity to get into show business required Monte to make an immediate decision. Mr. Foy stormed out of the office, muttering *incoherently* about hippies, beatniks, and others of that *ilk*.

**Sample Sentences:**    Use the new words in the following sentences.

1. When a large expenditure is imminent*, my father goes into a long _____ on the need for economy.

2. It is often fruitless* to argue with racists, bigots*, and others of that _____.

3. Since the patient's speech was garbled * and _____, we could only conjecture* as to his message.

4. The meeting was a _____ one, but the jealous husband construed * it as pre-arranged and clandestine.*

5. After two drinks the usually phlegmatic* dentist lost all his _____.

**Definitions:**    Match the new words with their meanings.

6. diatribe    _____    a. kind, sort

7. inhibition    _____    b. disjointed

8. fortuitous    _____    c. accidental

9. incoherent    _____    d. bitter criticism

10. ilk    _____    e. restraint

**Today's Idiom**    to *wear your heart on your sleeve*—to make your feelings evident

People who *wear their hearts on their sleeves* frequently suffer emotional upsets.

ANSWERS ARE ON PAGE 233

**New Words:** prestigious placard integral remuneration nominal
pres stij′ əs plak′ ärd in′ tə grəl ri mū′ nər ā shən nom′ ə nəl

**An All-Round Man**

The need for a decision came about when Monte was invited to join a *prestigious* summer stock company, starting in mid-June. As a mature "apprentice," he would be required to take tickets, paint scenery, prepare *placards*, assist with lighting, costumes, and props, and carry an occasional spear in a walk-on role. Since the company would stage five major plays during the summer, as well as a half-dozen shows for children, there was a chance that Monte might actually get a part before too many weeks had elapsed.* In addition, he would be attending the drama classes which were an *integral* part of the summer theatre. The *remuneration* would be *nominal* but at last Monte Ziltch would be fulfilling a life-long ambition.

**Sample Sentences:** Use the new words in the following sentences.

1. The police posted a _____ asking all citizens to desist* from looting.

2. A salient* feature of the _____ company's success was its fair treatment of employees.

3. Although the comedian's employment was seasonal and sporadic*, the _____ was great.

4. For allowing his ferocious mastiff* to appear on a commercial, the trainer was paid a _____ sum.

5. He seemed to be an unimportant member of the President's entourage* but actually he played an _____ role in White House affairs.

**Definitions:** Match the new words with their meanings.

6. prestigious _____    a. essential

7. placard _____    b. poster

8. integral _____    c. slight

9. remunera-
   tion _____    d. reward, pay

10. nominal _____    e. illustrious

**Today's Idiom**

*to wash dirty linen in public*—to openly discuss private affairs

"Let's talk about it privately," his uncle said, "rather than *wash our dirty linen in public.*

**ANSWERS ARE ON PAGE 233**

**New Words:**

| expunge | flamboyant | anathema | schism | utopia |
|---------|------------|----------|--------|--------|
| eks punj′ | flam boi′ ənt | ə nath′ ə mə | siz′ əm | ū tō′ pi ə |

**From Ledgers to Scripts**

During the first weeks of the summer, Monte Ziltch didn't even have time to consider whether he had made an egregious* mistake. He was too engrossed * with his work, performing a thousand and one odd jobs around the theatre. First there was the opening production of "South Pacific," then two weeks of "The Fantasticks," followed by a poignant* "Diary of Anne Frank" which did excellent business. All through those weeks, Monte painted, carried, nailed, collected, ran, studied, and perspired. He had *expunged* all traces of debits and credits from his mind, burying himself in the more *flamboyant* world of the theatre. Accounting became *anathema* to him as the *schism* between his present *utopia* and his former drudgery* widened.

**Sample Sentences:** Use the new words in the following sentences.

1. In *Lost Horizon* a character recoiled * at the idea of living in a _____.

2. A pernicious* _____ developed between the two sisters.

3. The traitor's name was _____ in his father's domicile.*

4. Our theatrical pages were inundated * with press releases from the _____ producer.

5. After having made the rash* statements, the senator wished that he could _____ them from the record.

**Definitions:** Match the new words with their meanings.

6. expunge  _____  a. split

7. flamboyant  _____  b. something greatly detested

8. anathema  _____  c. perfection

9. schism  _____  d. erase

10. utopia  _____  e. showy, colorful

**Today's Idiom**

*to save face*—to avoid disgrace
Instead of firing the corrupt executive, they allowed him to retire in order that he might *save face*.

ANSWERS ARE ON PAGE 233

**New Words:**  timorous   truncated   jaunty   fractious   ostentatious
tim′ ər əs   trung′ kāt id   jòn′ ti   frak′ shəs   os′ ten tā′ shəs

**Irony for Merryweather**

At last, Monte's chance to perform came. He had played the *timorous* Tin Man in a *truncated* version of "The Wizard of Oz" which the apprentices had staged. But now there was an open audition to cast the final show of the season. It was to be a *jaunty* original comedy, given a summer tryout prior to a Broadway opening. Monte, who by now had adopted the stage name of Monte Merryweather, read for the producers, hoping to get the part of the hero's *fractious* landlord. Unfortunately, the competition was too rough—but the director assigned Monte to a less *ostentatious* part. And so for the first two weeks in September the stage-struck accountant had a two-minute, two-line part. What was his role? The hero's accountant!

**Sample Sentences:**  Use the new words in the following sentences.

1. It is frustrating* to have one's lengthy remarks printed in _____ form.
2. With his cap set at a _____ angle, the amicable* sailor strutted down the street.
3. In an _____ display of histrionics* the actress broke many dishes.
4. Under duress* the normally _____ husband was coerced * into demanding a raise.
5. Roger's _____ behavior compounded * the bad relationship he had already had with his partner.

**Definitions:**  Match the new words with their meanings.

6. timorous _____ a. fearful
7. truncated _____ b. cut short
8. jaunty _____ c. sprightly, gay
9. fractious _____ d. showy
10. ostentatious _____ e. quarrelsome

**Today's Idiom**

*Indian summer*—warm autumn weather
Parts of the country were deep in snow, but the East was enjoying an *Indian summer*.

**ANSWERS ARE ON PAGE 233**

How many of the new words have now become a part of your "working vocabulary"? At first, their use may be conscious, even studied. However, the squeaks will soon disappear. Try a few this weekend.

Match the twenty words with their meanings. Write the letter that stands for the definition in the appropriate answer space. (Note the resemblance between *flamboyant* and *ostentatious*.)

**REVIEW WORDS**

| | | |
|---|---|---|
| _____ | 1 | anathema |
| _____ | 2 | diatribe |
| _____ | 3 | expunge |
| _____ | 4 | flamboyant |
| _____ | 5 | fortuitous |
| _____ | 6 | fractious |
| _____ | 7 | ilk |
| _____ | 8 | incoherent |
| _____ | 9 | inhibition |
| _____ | 10 | integral |
| _____ | 11 | jaunty |
| _____ | 12 | nominal |
| _____ | 13 | ostentatious |
| _____ | 14 | placard |
| _____ | 15 | prestigious |
| _____ | 16 | remuneration |
| _____ | 17 | schism |
| _____ | 18 | timorous |
| _____ | 19 | truncated |
| _____ | 20 | utopia |

**DEFINITIONS**

a. well-known
b. quarrelsome
c. kind, sort
d. poster
e. disjointed
f. sprightly
g. accidental
h. in name only, slight
j. restraint
k. reward
l. a curse
m. bitter criticism
n. erase
o. colorful
p. cut short
r. essential
s. fearful
t. showy
u. split
v. perfection

**IDIOMS**

| | | |
|---|---|---|
| _____ | 21 | wear your heart on your sleeve |
| _____ | 22 | wash dirty linen in public |
| _____ | 23 | save face |
| _____ | 24 | Indian summer |

w. make your feelings evident

x. warm autumn weather

y. to avoid disgrace

z. openly discuss private affairs

Now check your answers on page 233. Make a record below of those words you missed.

**WORDS FOR FURTHER STUDY**    **MEANINGS**

1. _____ _____

2. _____ _____

3. _____ _____

4. _____ _____

5. _____ _____

**New Words:**

| importune | incontrovertible | surreptitious | haven |
|-----------|------------------|---------------|-------|
| im′ pôr tün′ | in′ kon trə vėr′ tə bəl | sər′ əp tish′ əs | hā′ ven |

subjugate
sub′ jù gāt

### A Visit to the President

In the winter of 1941, Enrico Fermi and a number of other distinguished scientists *importuned* President Franklin Roosevelt for authorization to begin an all-out effort in atomic energy research. The scientists were alarmed by *incontrovertible* evidence of *surreptitious* German experiments, and they asked for speedy approval. Italian-born Enrico Fermi was the ideal man to lead the atomic research. Already in 1938 he had won the Nobel Prize for work with radioactive elements and neutron bombardment. Fermi had found a *haven* from the Fascists (his wife was Jewish) and he knew that if the Germans were the first to develop an atomic bomb it would mean that Hitler could *subjugate* the entire world. The international race for atomic supremacy was on.

**Sample Sentences:** Use the new words in the following sentences.

1. Although Eddie was not sanguine* about his chances, he continued to _____ his boss for a winter vacation.

2. In inclement* weather our barn is a _____ for many animals.

3. The dictator used duplicity* in order to _____ his rivals.

4. With a _____ movement, the meticulous* housewife emptied the ash tray in her neighbor's apartment.

5. The expert's _____ testimony corroborated * the police report.

**Definitions:** Match the new words with their meanings.

6. importune _____     a. undeniable

7. incontro-
   vertible _____     b. ask urgently

8. surreptitious _____     c. conquer

9. haven _____     d. place of safety

10. subjugate _____     e. stealthy, accomplished by secret

### Today's Idiom

*to take the bull by the horns*—to face a problem directly.

    After several days of delay, the minister decided *to take the bull by the horns,* and so he sent for the vandals.

ANSWERS ARE ON PAGE 234

**New Words:**

| ultimate | eventuate | emit | subterranean | viable |
|----------|-----------|------|--------------|--------|
| ul′ tə mit | i ven′ chü āt | i mit′ | sub′ tə rā′ ni ən | vī′ ə bəl |

**The Ultimate Weapon Takes Shape**

Enrico Fermi designed a device which could *eventuate* in a chain reaction. It consisted of layers of graphite, alternated with chunks of uranium. The uranium *emitted* neutrons, and the graphite slowed them down. Holes were left for long cadmium safety rods. By withdrawing those control rods Fermi could speed up the production of neutrons, thus increasing the number of uranium atoms which would be split (fission). When the rods were withdrawn to a critical point, then the neutrons would be produced so fast that the graphite and cadmium could not absorb them. In that manner a chain reaction would result. Slowly, Fermi's first atomic pile began to grow in a *subterranean* room at Columbia University. The big question remained—was it *viable?*

**Sample Sentences:** Use the new words in the following sentences.

1. A thorough investigation _____ in a comprehensive* report.

2. After two years of confinement in a _____ dungeon, the prisoner was thin and wan.*

3. The mayor issued a diatribe* against companies whose smokestacks _____ poisonous fumes.

4. Gaining better housing for all was the _____ goal of the zealous* reformer.

5. When the schism* in the company was healed, a _____ arrangement was worked out.

**Definitions:** Match the new words with their meanings.

6. ultimate _____    a. underground
7. eventuate _____    b. final
8. emit _____    c. practicable, workable
9. subterranean _____    d. to give off
10. viable _____    e. to result finally

**Today's Idiom**

*the lion's share*—the major portion
    Because the salesman was essential to the business, he demanded the *lion's share* of the profits.

ANSWERS ARE ON PAGE 234

**New Words:** premise  jeopardize  incredulous  permeate  propitious
prem′ is  jep′ ər dīz  in krej′ u ləs  pér′ mi āt  prə pish′ əs

**The Squash Court Experiment**

As the pile grew, so did the entire project. Fermi moved his materials to an abandoned squash court under a football stadium at the University of Chicago. His pace accelerated because they were proceeding on the *premise* that the Germans were close to atomic success. Six weeks after the pile had been started, its critical size was reached. Three brave young men *jeopardized* their lives by ascending* the pile, ready to cover it with liquid cadmium if anything went wrong. Almost fifty scientists and several *incredulous* observers mounted a balcony to watch. One physicist remained on the floor; it was his job to extract the final cadmium control rod. Unbearable tension *permeated* the atmosphere. Fermi completed his calculations, waited for a *propitious* moment, and then gave the signal.

**Sample Sentences:**  Use the new words in the following sentences.

1. Acting on the _____ that there were no burglars around, the police became quite lax.*

2. After I had perused * the Yankee lineup, I was _____ about their chances of winning.

3. The trapeze artist was squeamish* about having to _____ his life.

4. A terrible odor which was impossible to expunge* _____ the skunk handler's clothing.

5. At a _____ moment the flamboyant* movie star made her grand entrance.

**Definitions:**  Match the new words with their meanings.

6. premise _____ a. favorable

7. jeopardize _____ b. endanger

8. incredulous _____ c. to spread through

9. permeate _____ d. skeptical

10. propitious _____ e. grounds for a conclusion

**Today's Idiom**

*out of the frying pan*—to go from a difficult situation to a worse one
   I thought I had escaped, but actually I went *from the frying pan into the fire.*

ANSWERS ARE ON PAGE 234

**New Words:**

| surmise | curtail | repress | cryptic | inchoate |
|---------|---------|---------|---------|----------|
| sər mīz′ | kėr tāl′ | ri pres′ | krip′ tik | in kō′ it |

**The Italian Navigator Lands**

The chain reaction took place precisely as Enrico Fermi had *surmised*. After twenty-eight minutes he *curtailed* the experiment, giving the signal to replace the control rod. The normally reserved scientists, unable to *repress* their excitement, let out a tremendous cheer and gathered around Fermi to shake his hand. Although it was time to celebrate, some of the men remarked soberly that "the world would never be the same again." On December 2, 1942, the news of Fermi's achievement was relayed in a *cryptic* telephone message:

"The Italian Navigator has reached the New World."

"And how did he find the natives?"

"Very friendly."

The Atomic Age was *inchoate*—but truly here!

**Sample Sentences:** Use the new words in the following sentences.

1. Publication of the lurid * magazine was _____ by the district attorney.

2. Although his remarks appeared _____ at first, we began to see how really pertinent* they were.

3. I had to _____ my desire to interject* my criticism during the debate.

4. Edna had _____ that she would be charged a nominal * sum and so she was outraged when she got the bill.

5. The young couple was disappointed to see the _____ state of their new house.

**Definitions:** Match the new words with their meanings.

6. surmise _____ a. puzzling

7. curtail _____ b. guess

8. repress _____ c. to put down

9. cryptic _____ d. to cut short

10. inchoate _____ e. in an early stage

**Today's Idiom**

*to keep the pot boiling*—to see that interest doesn't die down.

Dickens *kept the pot boiling* by ending each chapter on a note of an uncertainty and suspense.

ANSWERS ARE ON PAGE 234

No matter what the theme, no matter what the source, we can expect that important concepts will require a mature vocabulary. This week's topic, scientific and biographical in nature, serves as a vehicle for teaching you twenty worthwhile words. You now have the chance to see whether you remember their definitions. Write the letter that stands for the definition in the appropriate answer space.

**REVIEW WORDS**

| | | |
|---|---|---|
| _____ | 1 | cryptic |
| _____ | 2 | curtail |
| _____ | 3 | emit |
| _____ | 4 | eventuate |
| _____ | 5 | haven |
| _____ | 6 | importune |
| _____ | 7 | inchoate |
| _____ | 8 | incontrovertible |
| _____ | 9 | incredulous |
| _____ | 10 | jeopardize |
| _____ | 11 | permeate |
| _____ | 12 | premise |
| _____ | 13 | propitious |
| _____ | 14 | repress |
| _____ | 15 | subjugate |
| _____ | 16 | subterranean |
| _____ | 17 | surmise |
| _____ | 18 | surreptitious |
| _____ | 19 | ultimate |
| _____ | 20 | viable |

**DEFINITIONS**

a. ask urgently
b. undeniable
c. guess
d. accomplished by secret
e. to put down
f. favorable
g. cut short
h. workable
j. underground
k. final
l. to result finally
m. to spread through
n. conquer
o. place of safety
p. endanger
r. a proposition for argument
s. skeptical
t. in an early stage
u. puzzling
v. to give off

**IDIOMS**

| | | |
|---|---|---|
| _____ | 21 | take the bull by the horns |
| _____ | 22 | the lion's share |
| _____ | 23 | out of the frying pan |
| _____ | 24 | keep the pot boiling |

w. to maintain interest

x. from bad to worse

y. the major portion

z. to face a problem directly

Now check your answers on page 234. Make a record below of those words you missed.

**WORDS FOR FURTHER STUDY**       **MEANINGS**

1. _____  _____

2. _____  _____

3. _____  _____

4. _____  _____

5. _____  _____

**New Words:**

| aspire | inveigh | nettle | overt | relegate |
|--------|---------|--------|-------|----------|
| əs pīr′ | in vā′ | net′ əl | ō′ vért | rel′ ə gāt |

**Sunday Morning at Pearl Harbor**

At breakfast time on Sunday morning, December 7, 1941, Dorie Miller was serving coffee aboard the battleship West Virginia. Dorie was a Negro, and the highest job to which he could then *aspire* in the U.S. Navy was that of messman. While Dorie was technically a member of a great fighting fleet, he was not expected to fight. Most Army and Navy officers *inveighed* against the Negro as a fighting man. Although Negroes were *nettled* by such *overt* prejudice, Dorie Miller apparently accepted being *relegated* to the role of a messhall servant. Now, as he poured the coffee, Dorie was wondering why the airplanes above were making so much noise on a peaceful Sunday morning.

**Sample Sentences:** Use the new words in the proper blanks.

1. Although the comic's quips* seemed to be mild, they began to _____ the nightclub's owner.

2. I had a premonition* that Eli would _____ to the position of captain.

3. The pickets agreed to _____ against the law which curtailed * their freedom.

4. _____ acts of violence by the prisoner jeopardized * his parole.

5. When they tried to _____ the star to a minor role she was furious.

**Definitions:** Match the new words with their meanings.

6. aspire _____    a. irritate

7. inveigh _____    b. open

8. nettle _____    c. assign to an inferior position

9. overt _____    d. to strive for

10. relegate _____    e. attack verbally

**Today's Idiom**

*to bury the hatchet*—to make peace
After not speaking to each other for a year, they decided *to bury the hatchet.*

ANSWERS ARE ON PAGE 234

**New Words:**

| supine | mammoth | repulse | havoc | raze |
|--------|---------|---------|-------|------|
| sü pīn′ | mam′ əth | ri puls′ | hav′ ək | rāz |

**The Infamous\* Attack**

The coffee cups suddenly went spinning as an explosion knocked Dorie Miller flat on his back. Jumping up from his *supine* position, the powerfully-built Negro messman from Waco, Texas headed for the deck. Everywhere that Dorie looked he saw smoke and *mammoth* warships lying on their sides. Overhead dozens of Japanese dive bombers controlled the skies without a U.S. plane to *repulse* their attack. The *havoc* was enormous. Without hesitating, Dorie joined a team which was feeding ammunition to a machine gunner who was making an ineffectual \* attempt to protect their battleship from being *razed* by the torpedo planes.

**Sample Sentences:** Use the new words in the proper blanks.

1. From a _____ position, the hunter emitted \* the animal's mating call.

2. Following the revolution, the people _____ the subterranean\* dungeons of the dictator.

3. Management is sure to _____ any request for increased remuneration.\*

4. _____ placards\* announced the opening of the new Jerry Lewis movie.

5. The virulent\* plague caused _____ among the populace.

**Definitions:** Match the new words with their meaning.

6. supine _____ a. ruin

7. mammoth _____ b. drive back

8. repulse _____ c. huge

9. havoc _____ d. lying on the back

10. raze _____ e. destroy

**Today's Idiom**

*Philadelphia lawyer*—a lawyer of outstanding ability
His case is so hopeless that it would take a *Philadelphia lawyer* to set him free.

**ANSWERS ARE ON PAGE 234**

**New Words:**

| lethal | scurry | incisive | precipitate | stereotype |
|--------|--------|----------|-------------|------------|
| lē′ thəl | skėr′ ē | in sī′ siv | pri sip′ ə tāt | ster′ i ə tīp′ |

**The Heroism of Dorie Miller**

Men all around Miller were succumbing* to the *lethal* spray of Japanese bullets. He dragged his captain to safety and turned back to see that the machine-gunner had been killed. Dorie took the big gun and trained it on the incoming bombers. Within the space of ten minutes he was credited with destroying four bombers while dodging the bullets of their fighter escorts. The enemy *scurried* away, having struck the *incisive* blow which *precipitated* U.S. entrance into World War II. Amidst the dead bodies and the ruined fleet were the heroes such as Dorie Miller. The Navy had told him that he did not have to fight but he hadn't listened. The Navy had attempted to *stereotype* him, but Dorie changed all that.

**Sample Sentences:** Use the new words in the proper blanks.

1. Our editor castigated * the proposal with his _____ commentary.

2. Poe's hero watched the rats _____ across his inert* body.

3. The jockey received a _____ kick from the fractious* horse.

4. A quarrel was _____ among the relatives after they heard the terms of the reprehensible* will.

5. The laconic* Gary Cooper was a _____ of the strong, silent Western hero.

**Definitions:** Match the new words with their meanings.

6. lethal _____ a. acute

7. scurry _____ b. run hastily

8. incisive _____ c. unvarying pattern

9. precipitate _____ d. deadly

10. stereotype _____ e. hasten

**Today's Idiom**

*to gild the lily*—to praise extravagantly

There was no need for the announcer *to gild the lily* because we could see how beautiful the model was.

**ANSWERS ARE ON PAGE 234**

**New Words:**

| stentorian | singular | valor | bias | sinecure |
|---|---|---|---|---|
| sten tô′ ri ən | sing′ gū lər | val′ ər | bī′ əs | sī′ nə kūr |

**"For Distinguished Devotion to Duty"**

Some months later Dorie Miller was serving on an aircraft carrier when Admiral Chester Nimitz, the Commander of the Pacific Fleet, came aboard to preside over a special awards ceremony. In *stentorian* tones the Admiral presented Miller with the prestigious* Navy Cross, commending him for a *singular* act of *valor* and "disregard for his own personal safety." Miller's heroism helped to shatter the *bias* against Negroes in the armed forces. Although he could have accepted a *sinecure* at a U.S. naval base, Dorie chose to remain in the combat zone where he was killed in action in December, 1943.

**Sample Sentences:** Use the new words in the proper blanks.

1. The director was ousted * from his _____ when he angered the mayor.

2. In his customary _____ tones, the sergeant reprimanded * those who thought the army was a haven* for incompetents.

3. The word "surrender" is anathema* to men of _____.

4. A viable* peace was brought about as a result of the diplomat's _____ contribution.

5. The bigot's* _____ precipitated * a fistfight.

**Definitions:** Match the new words with their meanings.

6. stentorian _____ a. prejudice
7. singular _____ b. soft job
8. valor _____ c. courage
9. bias _____ d. extraordinary
10. sinecure _____ e. loud

**Today's Idiom**

*to steal one's thunder*—to weaken a person's position by stating his argument before he does

I had planned to be the first to resign from the club, but my cousin *stole my thunder*.

ANSWERS ARE ON PAGE 234

Many people agree that a lawyer should be skillful with words. A Philadelphia lawyer,* it goes without saying, must have an extensive vocabulary in order to help him present his case.

Match the twenty words with their meanings. Write the letter that stands for the definition in the appropriate answer space.

## REVIEW WORDS

_____ 1 aspire
_____ 2 bias
_____ 3 havoc
_____ 4 incisive
_____ 5 inveigh
_____ 6 lethal
_____ 7 mammoth
_____ 8 nettle
_____ 9 overt
_____ 10 precipitate
_____ 11 raze
_____ 12 relegate
_____ 13 repulse
_____ 14 scurry
_____ 15 sinecure
_____ 16 singular
_____ 17 stentorian
_____ 18 stereotype
_____ 19 supine
_____ 20 valor

## DEFINITIONS

a. huge
b. evident, open
c. courage
d. to strive for
e. banish, assign to inferior position
f. deadly
g. soft job
h. prejudice
j. keen, acute
k. run quickly
l. hasten
m. remarkable, uncommon
n. attack verbally
o. drive back
p. lying on the back
r. destroy
s. conventional custom
t. irritate
u. ruin
v. loud

## IDIOMS

_____ 21 bury the hatchet
_____ 22 Philadelphia lawyer
_____ 23 gild the lily
_____ 24 steal one's thunder

w. to praise extravagantly
x. outstandingly able
y. to beat someone to the punch
z. make peace

Now check your answers on page 234. Make a record below of those words you missed.

**WORDS FOR FURTHER STUDY**   **MEANINGS**

1. _____ _____
2. _____ _____
3. _____ _____
4. _____ _____
5. _____ _____

**New Words:**
complicity    liquidation    accomplice    recant    culpable
kəm plis′ ə ti    lik′ wə dā′ shən    ə kom′ plis    ri kant′    kul′ pə bəl

**Danny Escobedo Goes to Jail**
In 1960, a young Chicagoan, Danny Escobedo, was given a 20-year jail sentence for first-degree murder. Danny had confessed to *complicity* in the killing of his brother-in-law after the police had refused to allow him to see his lawyer. Actually, Danny was tricked into blaming a friend for the *liquidation* of his sister's husband, thereby establishing himself as an *accomplice*. Despite the fact that Danny later *recanted* his confession, he was found *culpable* and jailed. Danny had been stereotyped * as a hoodlum and nobody raised an eyebrow over the hapless* felon's* troubles.

**Sample Sentences:**    Use the new words in the following sentences.

1. Proceeding on the premise* that the broker was guilty of _____ in the swindle, the detective followed him surreptitiously.*

2. After the _____ of the gang leader, a mammoth* conflict arose among his ambitious lieutenants who aspired * to be boss.

3. Once the incontrovertible* evidence was offered, the servant was held _____ in the theft of the jewels.

4. When the clergyman refused to _____, his superiors were so nettled * that they relegated * him to an isolated parish in Alaska.

5. Although he was judged as a minor _____, the driver had actually played an integral * part in planning the crime.

**Definitions:**    Match the new words with their meanings. Two of the words are very close in meaning.

6. complicity    _____    a. deserving blame

7. liquidation    _____    b. partnership in wrongdoing

8. accomplice    _____    c. an associate in crime

9. recant    _____    d. disposal of, killing

10. culpable    _____    e. withdraw previous statements

**Today's Idiom**    *woolgathering:*—absentmindedness or daydreaming
    When the young genius should have been doing his homework, he was frequently engaged in *woolgathering*.

**ANSWERS ARE ON PAGE 234**

**New Words:**

| abrogate | alleged | access | invalidate | preclude |
|---|---|---|---|---|
| ab′ rə gāt | ə lejdt′ | ak′ ses | in val′ ə dāt | pri klüd′ |

**Escobedo's Lawyer Appeals**

Barry Kroll, a Chicago lawyer, took an interest in Danny Escobedo's case. Kroll felt that his client's rights under the Constitution had been *abrogated*. Since the *alleged* accomplice,\* Escobedo, had been denied *access* to an attorney, Kroll asked the courts to *invalidate* the conviction. He proposed that lawyers be entitled to sit in when the police question a suspect but the Illinois courts rejected that on the grounds that it would effectively *preclude* all questioning by legal authorities. If such a law were upheld, the police felt that it would play havoc\* with all criminal investigations.

**Sample Sentences:** Use the new words in the following sentences.

1. The manager was distraught\* when he realized that the slugger's sickness would _____ a World Series victory.

2. It is symptomatic\* of some newspapers that an _____ criminal is regarded in print as a guilty man.

3. The wealthy uncle decided to _____ his inane\* nephew's sinecure.\*

4. The general was sure to _____ the court-martial's decision once he learned of the flagrant\* bias\* of the presiding officer.

5. Once the druggist had been duped \* into opening the store, the addict gained _____ to the pep pills.

**Definitions:** Match the new words with their meanings.

6. abrogate _____    a. admittance

7. alleged _____    b. reported, supposed

8. access _____    c. to deprive of legal force, to nullify

9. invalidate _____    d. prevent

10. preclude _____    e. abolish

**Today's Idiom**

*to whitewash*—to conceal defects, to give a falsely virtuous appearance to something

    Although a committee was appointed to investigate the corruption, many citizens felt that their report would be a *whitewash* of the culprits.\*

**ANSWERS ARE ON PAGE 234**

**New Words:**

| persevere | landmark | extrinsic | declaim | fetter |
|---|---|---|---|---|
| pėr′ sə vēr′ | land′ märk′ | eks trin′ sik | di klām′ | fet′ ər |

**An Historic Supreme Court Ruling**

Lawyer Kroll *persevered* in his defense of Danny Escobedo. The case was argued before the Supreme Court, and in 1964, in a *landmark* decision, the Court reversed Danny's conviction. Legal aid, said the judges, must be instantly available to a suspect. "A system of law enforcement which comes to depend on the confession," one Justice declared, "will, in the long run, be less reliable than a system which depends on *extrinsic* evidence independently secured through skilful investigation." A Justice who *declaimed* against the decision said, however, "I think the rule is ill-conceived and that it seriously *fetters* perfectly legitimate methods of criminal enforcement."

**Sample Sentences:** Use the new words in the following sentences.

1. Collectors avidly* sought the rare coin for its _____ value.

2. If we _____, we can overcome many of our inhibitions.*

3. The Battle of Midway was a _____ victory in the U.S. campaign for ultimate* victory over the Japanese.

4. I knew that my father would _____ against Mother's choice of ostentatious* fabrics.

5. The senator inveighed * against the policy because he felt it would _____ our Air Force.

**Definitions:** Match the new words with their meanings.

6. persevere _____  a. to hamper

7. landmark (adj.) _____  b. foreign, coming from outside

8. extrinsic _____  c. speak loudly

9. declaim _____  d. persist

10. fetter (v.) _____  e. historic, turning point of a period

**Today's Idiom**

*to break the ice*—to make a start by overcoming initial difficulties

The auto salesman had a poor week, but he finally *broke the ice* by selling a fully-equipped Cadillac.

ANSWERS ARE ON PAGE 234

**New Words:** paragon  nomadic  asperity  epithet  controversial
par′ ə gon  nō mad′ ik  as per′ ə ti  ep′ ə thet  kon′ trə ver′ shəl

## The Effects of the Escobedo Decision

After Danny Escobedo's release from prison, hundreds of inmates began suits for their freedom on the grounds that their rights had been violated, too. Each case is being heard on its merits, and in numerous instances people who had been convicted of serious offenses have been freed because of the new standards established in the Escobedo case. Since getting out, Danny has not been a *paragon* of virtue, according to the police. He has led a *nomadic* existence, drifting from job to job, and being arrested frequently. With *asperity*, and a few choice *epithets*, Danny refers to police harassment.* Although the Escobedo case is a *controversial* one, most agree that it will inspire better police training, better law enforcement procedures, and improved scientific crime detection.

**Sample Sentences:** Use the new words in the following sentences.

1. In the desert, _____ tribes wander back and forth, enduring much privation.*

2. The town planners looked upon their utopia* as a _____ for other communities.

3. Some school principals attempt to repress* the publication of _____ editorials.

4. We were amazed at the display of _____ from our normally phlegmatic* neighbor.

5. A bitter quarrel was precipitated * when both politicians hurled vile _____ at each other.

**Definitions:** Match the new words with their meanings.

6. paragon _____ a. harshness of temper

7. nomadic _____ b. model of excellence

8. asperity _____ c. wandering

9. epithet _____ d. debatable

10. controversial _____ e. descriptive name

**Today's Idiom**

*the grapevine*—a secret means of spreading information
    The *grapevine* has it that Ernie will be elected president of the school's student council.

**ANSWERS ARE ON PAGE 234**

Police who have resorted to wire-tapping have been able to get evidence which was useful in gaining convictions. In a sense, everyone who listens to you is wire-tapping your conversation. Are the "detectives" impressed with the extent of your vocabulary? By the end of this week you will have gained a greater familiarity with 300 words and 60 idioms—enough to educate a conscientious wire-tapper.

Match the twenty words with their meanings. Write the letter that stands for the definition in the appropriate answer space. (Numbers 1 and 13 are close in meaning.)

| REVIEW WORDS | | DEFINITIONS | |
|---|---|---|---|
| _____ 1 | abrogate | a. | descriptive name |
| _____ 2 | access | b. | coming from outside, foreign |
| _____ 3 | accomplice | c. | supposed, reported |
| _____ 4 | alleged | d. | deserving blame |
| _____ 5 | asperity | e. | destruction, disposal of |
| _____ 6 | complicity | f. | an associate in crime |
| _____ 7 | controversial | g. | model of excellence |
| _____ 8 | culpable | h. | bitterness of temper |
| _____ 9 | declaim | j. | persist |
| _____ 10 | epithet | k. | repeal by law |
| _____ 11 | extrinsic | l. | prevent |
| _____ 12 | fetter (v.) | m. | speak loudly |
| _____ 13 | invalidate | n. | partnership in wrongdoing |
| _____ 14 | landmark (adj.) | o. | to deprive of legal force, cancel |
| _____ 15 | liquidation | p. | renounce previous statements |
| _____ 16 | nomadic | r. | to hamper, to chain |
| _____ 17 | paragon | s. | admittance |
| _____ 18 | persevere | t. | wandering |
| _____ 19 | preclude | u. | historic |
| _____ 20 | recant | v. | debatable |

## IDIOMS

| | | | |
|---|---|---|---|
| _____ 21 | woolgathering | w. | a means of spreading information |
| _____ 22 | to whitewash | x. | absentmindedness |
| _____ 23 | break the ice | y. | to conceal defects |
| _____ 24 | the grapevine | z. | make a start |

Now check your answers on page 234. Make a record below of those words you missed.

**WORDS FOR FURTHER STUDY**     **MEANINGS**

1. _____  _____

2. _____  _____

3. _____  _____

4. _____  _____

5. _____  _____

**New Words:**

| indigenous | gregarious | habitat | cursory | interloper |
|---|---|---|---|---|
| in dij′ ən əs | grə gãr′ i əs | hab′ ə tat | ker′ sə ri | in′ tər lōp′ ər |

**Meet the Bees**

One of the most interesting inhabitants of our world is the bee, an insect which is *indigenous* to all parts of the globe except the polar regions. The honeybee is a *gregarious* insect whose *habitat* is a colony which he shares with as many as 80,000 bees. Although the individual bees live for only a few days, their colony can be operative for several years. A *cursory* study of the activities of these insects reveals an orderliness and a social structure which is truly amazing. For example, bees in a particular hive have a distinct odor; therefore, when an *interloper* seeks access* they can identify him quickly and repulse* his invasion.

**Sample Sentences:** Use the new words in the following sentences.

1. Sherlock Holmes took a _____ glance at the cryptic* message and decoded it instantly.

2. The forest was replete* with the kind of wildlife which is _____ to Africa.

3. Electric eyes, watchdogs, and other nuances* were there to keep out an _____.

4. The alcoholic was found supine* in his favorite _____—Ryan's Bar.

5. At the party, the _____ hostess scurried * from group to group, making friends and influencing people.

**Definitions:** Match the new words with their meanings.

6. indigenous _____    a. hasty, not thorough
7. gregarious _____    b. native
8. habitat _____    c. natural environment
9. cursory _____    d. sociable
10. interloper _____    e. an unauthorized person

**Today's Idiom**

*in a bee line*—taking the straightest, shortest route (that's the way a bee flies back to the hive after he has gathered food)
    When the couple left, the babysitter made a *bee line* for the refrigerator.

ANSWERS ARE ON PAGE 234

**New Words:**

| prolific | bulwark | sedentary | frugal | antithesis |
|----------|---------|-----------|--------|------------|
| prə lif′ ik | bùl′ wərk | sed′ ən ter′ i | frü′ gal | an tith′ ə sis |

**Queens, Workers, Drones**

Each colony of honeybees consists of three classes: a) the queen who is a *prolific* layer of eggs; b) the worker who is the *bulwark* of the colony; and c) the *sedentary* drone whose only function is to mate with a young queen. The queen lays the eggs that hatch into thousands of female workers; some queens live as long as five years and lay up to one million eggs. The *frugal* worker builds and maintains the nest, collects and stores the honey, and is the *antithesis* of the lazy drone, or male honeybee, who does no work and has no sting. When the drone is no longer needed, the workers, in effect, liquidate* him by letting him starve to death. It's a cruel, cruel world!

**Sample Sentences:** Use the new words in the following sentences.

1. The usually _____ novelist was frustrated* by his failure to come up with a good plot.

2. Len, the gregarious* twin, was the _____ of Lon, the reticent one.

3. The typist shook off the fetters* of her _____ life and joined a mountain climbing expedition.

4. _____ housewives occasionally badger* supermarket managers for bargains.

5. Some feel that the United States should be a _____ to the inchoate* democracies around the world.

**Definitions:** Match the new words with their meanings.

6. prolific _____ a. producing abundantly

7. bulwark _____ b. thrifty

8. sedentary _____ c. protection

9. frugal _____ d. exact opposite

10. antithesis _____ e. largely inactive, accustomed to sitting

**Today's Idiom**

*the world, the flesh, and the devil*—temptations which cause man to sin.

By entering the monastery he sought to avoid *the world, the flesh, and the devil.*

**ANSWERS ARE ON PAGE 234**

**New Words:**

| altruistic | embellish | cache | coterie | cupidity |
|---|---|---|---|---|
| al′ trü is′ tik | em bel′ ish | kash | kō′ tə ri | kū pid′ ə ti |

**Spotlight on the Worker**

Let us examine the activities of the *altruistic* workers in greater detail. After the workers have constructed a hive of waterproof honeycomb (made from beeswax), the queen begins to lay eggs in the first cells. While some workers *embellish* the hive, others fly out in search of nectar and pollen. With their long tongues they gather nectar and use their hind legs to carry the pollen from the flowers. They fly directly back to the hive and then dance around the honeycomb, their movements indicating the direction of the flowers. Meanwhile, other workers have been cleaning cells, caring for the young, and guarding the precious *cache* of nectar. Another special *coterie* is entrusted with heating or cooling the hive. Dedicated to the welfare of the queen and the entire insect community, all of these workers display a complete absence of *cupidity*.

**Sample Sentences:** Use the new words in the following sentences.

1. Through a fortuitous* remark, the _____ of the art thieves was discovered.

2. We warned him that his reprehensible* _____ would eventuate* in a loss of all his friends.

3. Dr. Albert Schweitzer went into the jungle purely for _____ reasons.

4. A _____ of bridge players made our clubroom their permanent habitat.*

5. Everytime the irate* motorist told about the accident he had a tendency to _____ the story.

**Definitions:** Match the new words with their meanings.

6. altruistic _____ a. secret hiding place

7. embellish _____ b. unselfish

8. cache _____ c. small group having something in common

9. coterie _____ d. adorn, touch up

10. cupidity _____ e. greed

**Today's Idiom**

*to make bricks without straw*—to attempt to do something without having the necessary materials (In the Bible we read that the Egyptians commanded the Israelites to do so.)

My uncle's business schemes always fail because he tries *to make bricks without straw.*

**ANSWERS ARE ON PAGE 234**

**New Words:**

| virtuosity | temerity | amorous | progeny | saturate |
|---|---|---|---|---|
| vėr′ chü os′ ə ti | tə mer′ ə ti | am′ ə rəs | proj′ ə ni | sach′ ü rāt |

**The Saga of the Queen Bee**

Although the *virtuosity* of the workers is remarkable, the queen bee is really the main story. Workers choose a few larvae to be queens, feeding them royal jelly, a substance rich in proteins and vitamins. While the queen is changing from a larva to a pupa, a team of workers builds a special cell for her. Soon the young queen hatches, eats the prepared honey, and grows strong. After she kills any rivals who have the *temerity* to challenge her, an *amorous* note is injected. She flies from the hive and mates with one or more drones on her first flight. Then the process of egg laying begins. When her *progeny saturate* the hive, scouts are dispatched to find a new location, and the bees swarm after their leader to begin the amazing cycle again.

**Sample Sentences:** Use the new words in the following sentences.

1. A landmark\* in the history of _____ drama is "Romeo and Juliet."

2. The eminent\* artist, noted for his _____, was admired by classicists and beatniks alike.

3. The Bantu chief and all his _____ were noted for their valor.\*

4. For having the _____ to declaim\* against the majority leader, the freshman senator was given the worst committee assignments.

5. We decided to _____ ourselves on French geography before making a tour of the country.

**Definitions:** Match the new words with their meanings.

6. virtuosity _____    a. descendants

7. temerity _____    b. full of love

8. amorous _____    c. soak, fill up completely

9. progeny _____    d. foolish boldness

10. saturate _____    e. great technical skill

**Today's Idiom**

*to have the upper hand*—to gain control
I had him at my mercy but now he has *the upper hand*.

ANSWERS ARE ON PAGE 234

Even if you are as busy as the proverbial bee, you can always manage the fifteen to twenty minutes which are required for these daily vocabulary sessions.

Match the twenty words with their meanings. Write the letter that stands for the definition in the appropriate answer space.

**REVIEW WORDS**

| | | |
|---|---|---|
| _____ | 1 | altruistic |
| _____ | 2 | amorous |
| _____ | 3 | antithesis |
| _____ | 4 | bulwark |
| _____ | 5 | cache |
| _____ | 6 | coterie |
| _____ | 7 | cupidity |
| _____ | 8 | cursory |
| _____ | 9 | embellish |
| _____ | 10 | frugal |
| _____ | 11 | gregarious |
| _____ | 12 | habitat |
| _____ | 13 | indigenous |
| _____ | 14 | interloper |
| _____ | 15 | progeny |
| _____ | 16 | prolific |
| _____ | 17 | saturate |
| _____ | 18 | sedentary |
| _____ | 19 | temerity |
| _____ | 20 | virtuosity |

**DEFINITIONS**

a. secret hiding place
b. thrifty
c. enjoying the company of others
d. exact opposite
e. adorn
f. unselfish
g. small exclusive group
h. greed
j. not thorough, hasty
k. descendants
l. an unauthorized person
m. native
n. largely inactive
o. natural environment
p. foolish boldness
r. fill up completely
s. protection
t. full of love
u. great technical skill
v. fertile

**IDIOMS**

| | | |
|---|---|---|
| _____ | 21 | in a bee line |
| _____ | 22 | the world, the flesh, and the devil |
| _____ | 23 | make bricks without straw |
| _____ | 24 | have the upper hand |

w. directly
x. gain control

y. attempt something without necessary materials

z. temptations

Now check your answers on page 234. Make a record below of those words you missed.

**WORDS FOR FURTHER STUDY**     **MEANINGS**

1. _____  _____

2. _____  _____

3. _____  _____

4. _____  _____

5. _____  _____

**New Words:**

| perpetrate | consummate | subterfuge | concoct |
|---|---|---|---|
| pér′ pə trāt | kon′ sə māt′ | sub′ tər fūj | kon kokt′ |

fallacious
fə lā′ shəs

**A Plan to Fool the Nazis**

One of the truly remarkable stories of World War II concerns a ruse* which was *perpetrated* with such *consummate* skill that it saved the lives of many Allied troops and helped to shorten the war. The simple, bold, and ingenious *subterfuge* which British officers *concocted* is the subject of Ewen Montagu's classic, THE MAN WHO NEVER WAS. In short, the idea was to plant *fallacious* documents concerning the Allied invasion of Europe upon a dead officer, have his body recovered by agents who would transmit the false information to Germany, and then observe the effects of the plan.

**Sample Sentences:** Use the new words in the following sentences.

1. Because the inspector had given only cursory* attention to the reports, I surmised * that his conclusion would be _____.

2. Clarence Darrow, the famous and controversial * lawyer, gave _____ attention to the preparation of every case.

3. It was necessary for the interloper* to _____ a convincing story in order to gain access* to the exhibit.

4. In order to _____ the swindle, the jaunty* confidence man adopted an amorous* approach toward the wealthy widow.

5. The experienced teacher realized that Ricky's stomach ache was merely a _____ to keep him from taking the French test.

**Definitions:** Match the new words with their meanings.

6. perpetrate _____   a. devise

7. consummate _____   b. complete, of the highest degree

8. subterfuge _____   c. commit

9. concoct _____   d. ruse,* trick

10. fallacious _____   e. misleading

**Today's Idiom**

*to draw in one's horns*—to check your anger, to restrain yourself

The performer *drew in his horns* when he saw that his critic was an eight-year-old boy.

**ANSWERS ARE ON PAGE 235**

**New Words:**

| manifold | assiduous | impeccable | fraught | resourceful |
|---|---|---|---|---|
| man′ ə fōld | ə sij′ ü əs | im pek′ ə bəl | frôt | ri sôrs′ fəl |

**"Major Martin" Goes to War**

After Commander Montagu and his colleagues had been given official approval for their dangerous escapade, they encountered *manifold* problems. First, they conducted an *assiduous* search for a body which looked as though it had recently been killed in an airplane disaster. Then, a detailed history of the man had to be invented which would be so *impeccable* that the enemy would accept its authenticity. This meant documents, love letters, personal effects, keys, photographs, etc. Each step was *fraught* with difficulty, but the schemers were unbelievably *resourceful*. As a result, in the late spring of 1942, "Major Martin" was prepared to do his part for his country.

**Sample Sentences:** Use the new words in the following sentences.

1. Burdened by his _____ responsibilities, the young executive was precluded * from enjoying his new wealth.

2. Fear permeated * the crippled airplane as the passengers realized that their situation was _____ with danger.

3. Although basically frugal,* his taste in clothing is _____.

4. The store owner was _____ enough to run a sale the day after his building had been razed * by the flames.

5. Florence Nightingale was a paragon* of mercy in her _____ care for the wounded soldiers.

**Definitions:** Match the new words with their meanings.

6. manifold _____    a. able to meet any situation

7. assiduous _____    b. faultless

8. impeccable _____    c. complex, many

9. fraught _____    d. devoted, attentive

10. resourceful _____    e. filled

**Today's Idiom**

*to put the cart before the horse*—to reverse the proper order, do things backwards

My assistant was so eager to get the job done that he often *put the cart before the horse*.

ANSWERS ARE ON PAGE 235

**New Words:**

| murky | components | hoax | labyrinth | evaluate |
|-------|-----------|------|-----------|----------|
| mér′ ki | kəm pō′ nənt | hōks | lab′ ə rinth | i val′ ū āt |

**The Plot Thickens**

A submarine took the body out to sea. Then, "Major Martin," the man who never was, was slid into the *murky* Atlantic waters off the coast of Huelva, Spain. Attached to this courier's coat was a briefcase which contained the *components* of the *hoax*. Shortly thereafter, the Spanish Embassy notified the British that the body had been recovered. But Commander Montagu learned that the important documents had already been scrutinized * and later resealed so that the British would not be suspicious. The secret information was transmitted to the German High Command, through a *labyrinth* of underground networks, to be *evaluated*. Now the true test of the months of assiduous* planning would come— the question remained, would the Germans swallow the bait?

**Sample Sentences:** Use the new words in the following sentences.

1. The practical joker had the temerity* to perpetrate* a _____ upon the Dean of Boys.

2. A good motion picture producer should be skilled in all the manifold * _____ of film-making.

3. After wandering through the _____, the young hero came face to face with the dragon who was indigenous* to the caves.

4. When I asked the English teacher to _____ my plan for the term paper, her incisive* comments were very helpful.

5. The _____ quality of the artist's latest painting is the antithesis* of her former style.

**Definitions:** Match the new words with their meanings.

6. murky _____    a. dark, obscure
7. component _____    b. element
8. hoax _____    c. deception
9. labyrinth _____    d. arrangement of winding passages
10. evaluate _____    e. appraise, find the value of

**Today's Idiom**

*to turn the tables*—to turn a situation to your own advantage
    The wrestler thought that he could pin me to the mat, but I quickly *turned the tables* on him.

ANSWERS ARE ON PAGE 235

**New Words:**

| exult | attest | gullible | deploy | enigma |
|-------|--------|----------|--------|--------|
| eg zult′ | ə test′ | gul′ ə bəl | di ploi′ | i nig′ mə |

**A Puzzle for His Majesty**

The conspirators had reason to *exult*, for all evidence *attested* to the fact that the German High Command was *gullible* about "Major Martin." Their defense troops were moved away from the true invasion sites and *deployed* to areas which were inconsequential. Subsequently, when the actual attack took place, Allied casualties were minimized. After the war, Commander Montagu received a medal from the King of England. At the presentation ceremony, the King politely inquired where the young officer had earned his citation. "At the Admiralty," Montagu replied, presenting the King with a genuine *enigma*.

**Sample Sentences:** Use the new words in the following sentences.

1. Explaining that the bookkeeper was merely a _____ dupe,* the judge freed him from complicity* in the crime.

2. As the audience watched Bobby Fischer _____ his chess pieces, they applauded his virtuosity.*

3. An expert was summoned to _____ to the authenticity of the Rembrandts found in the Nazi cache* of stolen masterpieces.

4. When the College Board scores were promulgated,* my sister had good cause to _____.

5. I could not solve the _____ of why an altruistic* person should exhibit such cupidity.*

**Definitions:** Match the new words with their meanings.

6. exult _____ a. to certify

7. attest _____ b. easily cheated or fooled

8. gullible _____ c. to position forces according to a plan

9. deploy _____ d. riddle

10. enigma _____ e. rejoice greatly

**Today's Idiom**

*a chip off the old block*—a son who is like his father (from the same block of wood).

When we saw the alcoholic's son enter the liquor store we assumed that he was a *chip off the old block*.

ANSWERS ARE ON PAGE 235

Major Martin, if he had lived, would have used the word "bonnet" to refer to the hood of his auto, and he might have referred to a truck as a "lorry." As you can see, there are differences between American and British English. But Major Martin, undoubtedly, would have known all the words below—do you?

Match the twenty words with their meanings. Write the letter that stands for the definition in the appropriate answer space. (Note the similarity between numbers 13 and 20.)

**REVIEW WORDS**

| | |
|---|---|
| _____ 1 | assiduous |
| _____ 2 | attest |
| _____ 3 | component |
| _____ 4 | concoct |
| _____ 5 | consummate |
| _____ 6 | deploy |
| _____ 7 | enigma |
| _____ 8 | evaluate |
| _____ 9 | exult |
| _____ 10 | fallacious |
| _____ 11 | fraught |
| _____ 12 | gullible |
| _____ 13 | hoax |
| _____ 14 | impeccable |
| _____ 15 | labyrinth |
| _____ 16 | manifold |
| _____ 17 | murky |
| _____ 18 | perpetrate |
| _____ 19 | resourceful |
| _____ 20 | subterfuge |

**DEFINITIONS**

a. spread out in battle formation
b. a trick
c. busy, attentive
d. confirm as accurate, vouch for
e. devise
f. a riddle, puzzle
g. element, part
h. able to meet any situation
j. perfect, complete
k. filled
l. misleading, false
m. rejoice greatly
n. faultless
o. easily fooled
p. winding passages
r. find the value of, review
s. many
t. deception
u. commit
v. dark, obscure

**IDIOMS**

| | |
|---|---|
| _____ 21 | draw in one's horns |
| _____ 22 | put the cart before the horse |
| _____ 23 | turn the tables |
| _____ 24 | chip off the old block |

w. restrain yourself

x. turn a situation to your own advantage

y. do things backwards
z. son who is like his father

Now check your answers on page 235. Make a record below of those words you missed.

**WORDS FOR FURTHER STUDY**     **MEANINGS**

1. _____ _____

2. _____ _____

3. _____ _____

4. _____ _____

5. _____ _____

**New Words:**

| abortive | modify | accommodate | spontaneous | innate |
|----------|--------|-------------|-------------|--------|
| ə bôr′ tiv | mod′ ə fi | ə kom′ ə dāt | spon tā′ nē əs | i nāt′ or in′ āt |

**Teaching Chimpanzees to Talk**

Two resourceful * psychologists at the University of Nevada have made splendid progress in vocabulary development in chimpanzees. Following a number of *abortive* attempts to teach French, German, or English to chimps, the researchers persevered * until they hit upon the American Sign Language system which is often used by deaf persons. They have had to *modify* the language somewhat in order to *accommodate* the animals' *spontaneous* gestures. With a mixture of *innate* movements and learned ones, some laboratory chimps now have an extensive vocabulary.

**Sample Sentences:** Use the new words in the following sentences. There is no reason to monkey around with these.

1. His _____ cunning allowed him to see through the spy's subterfuge.*

2. The divers made an _____ attempt to rescue the dog from the murky* waters.

3. Because Phil refused to _____ his philosophy, the directors were forced to invalidate* his appointment.

4. My English teacher admonished * me: "I realize that the speech was to be _____, but it was not supposed to be incoherent* or fraught* with fallacious* statements."

5. A quarrel was precipitated * when the dietician refused to _____ the patient's special needs.

**Definitions:** If vocabulary is getting to be your stock in trade,* you should have no trouble in matching the new words with their meanings.

6. abortive _____ a. fruitless,* useless, failing

7. modify _____ b. to make fit, adjust to

8. accommo-
   date _____ c. natural

9. spontaneous _____ d. without preparation, unrehearsed

10. innate _____ e. to change

**Today's Idiom** *under the wire*—to enter just on time

Hank hesitated about his term paper for two months and finally submitted it just *under the wire*.

**ANSWERS ARE ON PAGE 235**

**New Words:**

| veneer | myriad | urbane | crave | irrelevant |
|--------|--------|--------|-------|------------|
| və nēr′ | mir′ i əd | er bān′ | krāv | i rel′ ə vənt |

**Chimpanzees Are Surprisingly Smart**

Washoe, the chimpanzee, has more than a *veneer* of intelligence; she can signal her desire to eat, go in or out, be covered, or brush her teeth. In addition, she can make signs for "I'm sorry," "I hurt," "Hurry," "Give me," and a *myriad* of other terms which are familiar to young children. This *urbane* animal can indicate that she *craves* more dessert by putting her fingers together ("more") and then placing her index and second fingers on top of her tongue ("sweet"). It is *irrelevant* that Washoe cannot actually talk. What is important, however, is the consummate* ease with which she has mastered her daily assignments.

**Sample Sentences:**

No sour grapes* now! These blanks are easy to fill with the words you have learned from their use in context above.

1. Why did Silas Marner _____ wealth and practice cupidity*?

2. Once the hoax had been concocted*, a _____ of problems arose.

3. The defendant was alleged * to have been an army deserter, but the judge said that was _____ to the case.

4. By embellishing* his work with _____ humor, the sophisticated playwright succeeded on Broadway.

5. The lieutenant confessed to a _____ of ignorance in order to properly evaluate* his corporal's resourcefulness.*

**Definitions:**

Take the bull by the horns* and match the new words with their meanings.

6. veneer _____ a. to desire

7. myriad _____ b. countless

8. urbane _____ c. polished, witty

9. crave _____ d. thin covering

10. irrelevant _____ e. not related to the subject ·

**Today's Idiom**

*to be at large*—not confined or in jail

Since the dangerous criminal was *at large*, all the townspeople began to buy dogs for protection.

**ANSWERS ARE ON PAGE 235**

**New Words:**

| deem | inherent | buff | romp | latent |
|------|----------|------|------|--------|
| dēm | in hēr′ ənt | buf | romp | la′ tənt |

**Easy to Train**

The chimpanzees are *deemed* by scientists to be the closest to man of all the living apes; consequently, they are fairly easy to train. Several years ago, two married researchers embarked on an interesting project: they reared and trained a chimp in almost the same manner as they would have raised a child. The animal did beautifully, convincing the couple of the *inherent* ability of the chimpanzee. Cinema *buffs* who have seen Tarzan's clever monkey *romp* through the jungle also recognize the *latent* intelligence of those animals.

**Sample Sentences:** Use the new words in the following sentences.

1. Whom do you _____ to be the bulwark* of the Republican Party?

2. The firemen did not have to cajole* the enthusiastic _____ into helping them extinguish the blaze.

3. When the intercity competition began, our team was supposed to _____ over our hapless* rivals.

4. At the age of 42, the artist first became cognizant* of his _____ genius.

5. Certain mice have an _____ alertness which enables them to conquer the researchers' labyrinths.*

**Definitions:** Match the new words with their meanings.

6. deem _____ a. lying hidden

7. inherent _____ b. to move in a lively manner

8. buff (n.) _____ c. inborn

9. romp _____ d. a fan, follower

10. latent _____ e. believe, to judge

**Today's Idiom**

*to go against the grain*—to irritate
My uncle is in favor of some protests, but certain demonstrations *go against his grain*.

ANSWERS ARE ON PAGE 235

**New Words:**

| tortuous | itinerant | peregrination | conjugal |
|---|---|---|---|
| tôr′ chü əs | ī tin′ ər ənt | per ə gri nā′ shən | kon′ jŭ gəl |

barometer
bə rom′ ə tər

**More Facts About Chimps**

Chimps in the laboratory have demonstrated their ability to find their way out of the most *tortuous* maze. They can press buttons, manipulate levers, avoid shocks, etc. When food is placed out of reach, the animals can prepare a ladder of boxes to reach it. In his natural habitat* the chimpanzee is something of an *itinerant*. He goes his nomadic* way through the jungle, living on fruit, insects, and vegetables. With the aid of his long, powerful hands he can swing rapidly from tree to tree and cover considerable ground in his *peregrinations*. Chimps are loyal in their *conjugal* relationships, taking only one mate at a time. That may be another *barometer* of these animals' superior intelligence.

**Sample Sentences:** Use the new words in the following sentences.

1. The other drivers were nettled * about the ease with which our car ascended * the _____ road.

2. Arguments over money have often led to _____ havoc.*

3. The sedentary* twin was content to follow his brother's _____ on a map.

4. Signs were posted in the lobby to prevent _____ beggars and others of that ilk* from entering.

5. The warmth of Mr. Smythe's greeting each morning may be construed * as an excellent _____ of his health.

**Definitions:** Match the new words with their meanings.

6. tortuous _____ a. wandering

7. itinerant _____ b. winding

8. peregrination _____ c. travel

9. conjugal _____ d. relating to marriage

10. barometer _____ e. instrument for measuring change

**Today's Idiom**

*to wink at*—to pretend not to see

There was a plethora* of evidence to show that the border guards would *wink at* illegal shipments if they were paid in advance.

ANSWERS ARE ON PAGE 235

While it is true that scientists have had remarkable success in teaching chimpanzees to communicate, we can be certain that even super-monkeys would have difficulty with any of the words below. However, higher animals who apply themselves can master all of them.

Match the twenty words with their meanings. Write the letter that stands for the definition in the appropriate answer space. (Note the similarity between numbers 8 and 9.)

**REVIEW WORDS**

| | | | **DEFINITIONS** |
|---|---|---|---|
| _____ | 1 | abortive | a. not related to the subject |
| _____ | 2 | accommodate | b. thin covering |
| _____ | 3 | barometer | c. fruitless, failing |
| _____ | 4 | buff (n.) | d. natural |
| _____ | 5 | conjugal | e. polished, civilized |
| _____ | 6 | crave | f. to make fit, adjust to |
| _____ | 7 | deem | g. on the spur of the moment |
| _____ | 8 | inherent | h. move in a lively manner |
| _____ | 9 | innate | j. to desire |
| _____ | 10 | irrelevant | k. instrument for measuring change |
| _____ | 11 | itinerant | l. winding |
| _____ | 12 | latent | m. inborn |
| _____ | 13 | modify | n. believe, to judge |
| _____ | 14 | myriad | o. going from place to place |
| _____ | 15 | peregrination | p. a fan, follower, enthusiast |
| _____ | 16 | romp | r. travel (n.) |
| _____ | 17 | spontaneous | s. relating to marriage, connubial * |
| _____ | 18 | tortuous | t. countless |
| _____ | 19 | urbane | u. to change |
| _____ | 20 | veneer | v. lying hidden |

**IDIOMS**

| | | | |
|---|---|---|---|
| _____ | 21 | under the wire | w. pretend not to see |
| _____ | 22 | to be at large | x. enter just on time |
| _____ | 23 | go against the grain | y. to irritate |
| _____ | 24 | wink at | z. not confined or in jail |

Now check your answers on page 235. Make a record below of those words you missed.

**WORDS FOR FURTHER STUDY**      **MEANINGS**

1. _____   _____

2. _____   _____

3. _____   _____

4. _____   _____

5. _____   _____

**New Words:**

| megalomania | profligate | strife | legion | coup |
|---|---|---|---|---|
| meg′ ə lō mā′ nēə | prof′ lə git | strīf | lē′ jən | kü |

**Trouble in Ruritania**

King Andre of Ruritania was afflicted * with *megalomania*, and the people of his country suffered, as a result. After ten years of his *profligate* rule, the treasury was bankrupt, un- employment was rampant*, domestic *strife* was mounting, and the number of the King's opponents who were incarcer- ated * was *legion*. Following a bloodless *coup*, his nephew, Prince Schubert, took command of the poor nation.

**Sample Sentences:**

Based upon your understanding of the new words, as dis- covered from the context, place them in the spaces provided.

1. With a singular* disregard for his family, the _____ husband spent his salary on alcohol.

2. Each spouse said that the other was culpable* for their conjugal * _____.

3. "The numbers of my followers is _____," said the flamboyant* politician.

4. The necessity for executing the leaders of the abortive* _____ was ob- viated * when they committed suicide.

5. Hitler's _____ was a veneer* for his insecurity and feelings of inferiority.

**Definitions:**

Match the new words with their meanings.

6. megalo-
mania        _____    a. discord, disagreement

7. profligate   _____    b. revolution

8. strife       _____    c. wasteful

9. legion       _____    d. a large number

10. coup        _____    e. abnormal desire for wealth and power

**Today's Idiom**

*to play possum*—to try to fool someone; to make believe one is asleep or dead

   Sensing that his life was in jeopardy*, the hunter *played possum* until the irate* lion disappeared.

**ANSWERS ARE ON PAGE 235**

**New Words:**

| amnesty | expatriate | exonerate | fiat | mendacious |
|---------|-----------|-----------|------|------------|
| am′ nəs tē | eks pā′ tri it | eg zon′ ər āt | fī′ ət | men dā′ shəs |

**Prince Schubert in Action**

Prince Schubert's first move was to declare an *amnesty* for political prisoners and to invite home all Ruritanian *expatriates.* Those who had been jailed on false charges were *exonerated* by special tribunals. The young leader announced that he would abrogate* all of the oppressive *fiats* which his predecessor had promulgated.* Things began to look up temporarily for the citizens who perceived in Prince Schubert the sincerity, idealism, and honesty which had been lacking in the *mendacious* King Andre.

**Sample Sentences:** Use the new words in the following sentences.

1. The publisher's _____ claims led to a myriad * of law suits.

2. When the jury began to deliberate, they were prepared to _____ the culprit.*

3. The itinerant* poet, living abroad for twenty years, was a voluntary _____.

4. One cannot govern by _____, the sedentary* mayor quickly learned; it is necessary to get out and meet the citizens if you want their cooperation.

5. We recognized the dictator's _____ as an obvious feint* which would be withdrawn after Christmas.

**Definitions:** It will be a red letter day* for you if you can match the new words with their meanings.

6. amnesty _____    a. an exile

7. expatriate _____    b. lying, untrue

8. exonerate _____    c. a general pardon

9. fiat _____    d. to free from guilt

10. mendacious _____    e. an official order, a decree

**Today's Idiom**

*it's an ill wind that blows nobody good*—someone usually benefits from another person's misfortune.

When the star quarterback broke his leg, the coach gave the rookie his big chance and the youngster made good; the coach mumbled, *"It's an ill wind."*

**ANSWERS ARE ON PAGE 235**

**New Words:**

| parsimonious | pecuniary | dismantle | sumptuous |
|---|---|---|---|
| pär′ sə mō ni əs | pi kū′ ni er′ i | dis man′ təl | sump′ chü əs |

underwrite
un′ dər rīt′

**Reform Movement**

In order to improve Ruritania's financial position, an astute* but *parsimonious* treasurer was installed and given wide *pecuniary* powers. He tried to get the little country back on its feet by slashing all waste from its budget, *dismantling* King Andre's *sumptuous* palaces, and firing all incompetents. In addition, Prince Schubert was able to get the United States to *underwrite* a substantial loan which would enable him to start a program of public works. Even so, Ruritania was still in desperate trouble.

**Sample Sentences:** Prove that you are not a flash in the pan* by using the new words correctly in the following sentences.

1. I plan to _____ the stereo set and clean all the components.*

2. The _____ feast was prepared with impeccable* care.

3. Unless my boss modifies* his _____ attitude, a spontaneous* picket line is going to be erected.

4. Clarence Day deemed * that _____ matters are best handled by men.

5. When our rivals agreed to _____ the cost of our trip, a myriad * of suspicions began to form in my mind.

**Definitions:** If you made mistakes above, you can now save face* by matching the new words correctly with their meanings.

6. parsimonious ____  a. agree to finance

7. pecuniary ____  b. financial

8. dismantle ____  c. to strip of covering, take apart

9. sumptuous ____  d. miserly

10. underwrite ____  e. lavish

**Today's Idiom**

*to know the ropes*—to be fully acquainted with the procedures

The president of the senior class *knew the ropes* and quickly taught me my duties.

ANSWERS ARE ON PAGE 235

**New Words:**

| restrictive | balk | blunt | nostalgia | rife |
|---|---|---|---|---|
| ri strik′ tiv | bôk | blunt | nos tal′ jə | rīf |

**Disappointment and Dedication**

When Prince Schubert asked for additional *restrictive* measures, the people began to *balk*. Speaking on radio, the young reformer explained the reasons for higher taxes and food rationing; he was *blunt* when he stated the need for personal sacrifices. Nevertheless, the resistance to reform was great, and *nostalgia* for the "good old days" of King Andre began to grow. The people admitted that graft and corruption had been *rife* under Andre, but at least "everybody got his slice of the pie." Although Prince Schubert was tempted to quit, he determined that he would help the people in spite of themselves.

**Sample Sentences:** Don't pass the buck*! Use the new words in the following sentences yourself.

1. The rebel's innate* hatred of _____ decrees led him to crave* freedom all the more.

2. A string of caustic* epithets* was directed at the recruit by his _____ sergeant.

3. Although the former farm girl pretended to be urbane*, a feeling of _____ always came over her when she heard country music.

4. Criticism of the author was _____ among the coterie* of intellectuals who used to praise him.

5. Jimmy was a lawbreaker, but he would _____ at the idea of carrying a lethal* weapon.

**Definitions:** Match the new words with their meanings.

6. restrictive _____ a. widespread
7. balk (v.) _____ b. plain spoken
8. blunt _____ c. to refuse to move
9. nostalgia _____ d. yearning for the past
10. rife _____ e. harsh, confining

**Today's Idiom**

*behind the eight ball*—in trouble

Susan found herself *behind the eight ball* in chemistry when she failed to do the term project.

ANSWERS ARE ON PAGE 23

Ruritania is a mythical kingdom, impossible to find on a map and difficult to find in a dictionary. The words which you are about to review, however, are all legitimate, acceptable dictionary words.

Match the twenty words with their meanings. Write the letter that stands for the definition in the appropriate answer space.

**REVIEW WORDS**

| | | | **DEFINITIONS** |
|---|---|---|---|
| _____ | 1 | amnesty | a. revolution, overthrowal |
| _____ | 2 | balk | b. unrest, discord |
| _____ | 3 | blunt | c. take apart, disassemble |
| _____ | 4 | coup | d. lavish |
| _____ | 5 | dismantle | e. to free from guilt |
| _____ | 6 | exonerate | f. agree to finance |
| _____ | 7 | expatriate | g. false, lying |
| _____ | 8 | fiat | h. an exile |
| _____ | 9 | legion | j. abnormal desire for power |
| _____ | 10 | mendacious | k. plain spoken |
| _____ | 11 | megalomania | l. harsh, confining |
| _____ | 12 | nostalgia | m. to refuse to move |
| _____ | 13 | parsimonious | n. wasteful |
| _____ | 14 | pecuniary | o. an official order, a decree |
| _____ | 15 | profligate | p. widespread |
| _____ | 16 | restrictive | r. large number |
| _____ | 17 | rife | s. financial |
| _____ | 18 | strife | t. a general pardon |
| _____ | 19 | sumptuous | u. miserly |
| _____ | 20 | underwrite | v. yearning for the past |

**IDIOMS**

| | | | |
|---|---|---|---|
| _____ | 21 | to play possum | w. someone profits from another's misfortune |
| _____ | 22 | an ill wind | x. be fully acquainted with procedures |
| _____ | 23 | know the ropes | y. in trouble |
| _____ | 24 | behind the eight ball | z. try to fool someone |

Now check your answers on page 235. Make a record of those words you missed.

| WORDS FOR FURTHER STUDY | MEANINGS |
|---|---|
| 1. _____ | _____ |
| 2. _____ | _____ |
| 3. _____ | _____ |
| 4. _____ | _____ |
| 5. _____ | _____ |

**New Words:**   reviled      derogatory      indict      nebulous      pesky
                 ri vīld′     di rog′ ə tôr ē  in dīt′    neb′ ū ləs    pes′ ki

**La Cucharacha—** The poor cockroach has been called the "most *reviled* creature
**the Cockroach** on the face of the earth." Nobody loves him—except, perhaps, another cockroach. Fiction, non-fiction, and poetry are
replete* with *derogatory* references to these ubiquitous* bugs.
Public health officials are quick to *indict* the insects as carriers
of viruses that cause yellow fever and polio. Although past
evidence has been somewhat *nebulous,* recent studies also
show that an allergy to roaches may contribute significantly
to asthma. Little wonder, therefore, that the *pesky* cockroach
is under attack.

**Sample Sentences:** Use the new words in the following sentences.

1. Because the contract offer was a _____ one, the union leaders balked * at it.

2. Ezra Pound, the expatriate* poet, was _____ for his pro-Fascist remarks.

3. When the grand jury refused to _____ him, the mobster was exonerated.*

4. Everytime his accountant called with _____ pecuniary* problems, Ben was very blunt* with him.

5. The columnist was ordered to recant* his _____ statements.

**Definitions:** Match the new words with their meanings.

6. reviled      _____    a. annoying
7. derogatory   _____    b. belittling*, disparaging*
8. indict       _____    c. unclear, vague
9. nebulous     _____    d. scolded
10. pesky       _____    e. accuse

**Today's Idiom**   *left holding the bag*—to be left to suffer the blame
The profligate* businessman left his distraught* partner
*holding the bag.*

**ANSWERS ARE ON PAGE 235**

**New Words:**

| redolent | repose | omnivorous | disparate | abstemious |
|----------|--------|------------|-----------|------------|
| red′ ə lənt | ri pōz′ | om niv′ ə rəs | dis′ pə rit | ab stē′ mi əs |

**Waiter, Please Take This Bowl of Soup Back to the Kitchen**

In addition to menacing our health, cockroaches are smelly, filthy, and ugly. Upon entering a cellar which is *redolent* with their aroma, you are not likely to forget the odor. And when you spy the foul culprits* creating havoc* in your sugar bowl or in *repose* atop your chocolate cake, your disposition may be exacerbated.* Roaches are *omnivorous* and will feast upon such *disparate* items as wallpaper, upholstery, nylon stockings, and beer. No one can accuse the hungry and thirsty bugs of being *abstemious.*

**Sample Sentences:** The words above fit into the blanks below.

1. While the palace guards were in _____, the rebels' coup* began in earnest.
2. Coach Fischer issued a fiat* which required that his players be _____.
3. The _____ scent which came from the bakery created in Eloise a sense of nostalgia* for her grandmother's bread.
4. _____ eaters find the dietary laws in some hotels as being too restrictive.*
5. Regardless of how _____ their crimes were, all the prisoners were freed by the general amnesty.*

**Definitions:** Match the new words with their meanings.

6. redolent _____    a. different
7. repose (n.) _____    b. fragrant
8. omnivorous _____    c. moderate in eating or drinking
9. disparate _____    d. eating any kind of food
10. abstemious _____    e. state of rest

**Today's Idiom**

*a lick and a promise*—to do something in a hasty and superficial manner

    The meticulous* housewife was in so much of a hurry that she could only give the apartment *a lick and a promise.*

ANSWERS ARE ON PAGE 235

**New Words:**

| extant | vicissitudes | edifice | sultry | trenchant |
|--------|--------------|---------|--------|-----------|
| eks′ tənt or | və sis′ ə tüdz | ed′ ə fis | sul′ tri | tren′ chənt |
| eks tant′ | | | | |

**The Roach Lives On**

Cockroaches are the oldest *extant* winged insects, having been traced back over 350 million years. They have endured the *vicissitudes* of weather, natural disasters, war, and planned liquidation.* They reside comfortably in caves in South America, in transcontinental airplanes, on mountain tops, in Park Avenue *edifices*, and in television sets. The climate may be *sultry* or frigid but roaches persevere.* In the words of one writer, "The miraculous survival of the roach is explained by its inherent* adaptability." In fact, a *trenchant* analysis made the point that any forthcoming nuclear war will be won by roaches, not Russians, Chinese, or Americans.

**Sample Sentences:** Use the new words in the following sentences.

1. Hundreds of _____ copies of Shakespeare's signature came from the same prolific* forger.

2. The _____ of life in the Medical Corps are not for the squeamish.*

3. We originally planned on a skyscraper but had to settle for a truncated * _____.

4. When he learned that the movie was to be replete* with _____ scenes, the cautious banker refused to underwrite* its cost.

5. General Fox submitted a _____ report on the enemy's latent* strength.

**Definitions:** Match the new words with their meanings.

6. extant _____  a. keen, incisive*

7. vicissitudes _____  b. difficulties

8. edifice _____  c. extremely hot and moist, torrid

9. sultry _____  d. still existing

10. trenchant _____  e. a building

**Today's Idiom**

*tongue in cheek*—insincerely

Speaking with his *tongue in his cheek*, the parsimonious* employer promised to double everyone's wages.

ANSWERS ARE ON PAGE 235

**New Words:**

| puissant | unabated | maudlin | levity | lugubrious |
|---|---|---|---|---|
| pū′ ə sənt  or | un′ ə bā′ tid | môd′ lən | lev′ ə ti | lü gü′ bri əs |
| pwis′ ənt | | | | |

**Tongue in Cheek\*?**

The U.S. Public Health Service admits to frustration\* in its attempts to destroy the cockroach. As soon as the scientists devise a *puissant* chemical, some bugs succumb.\* But the hardy ones survive and breed a resistant strain. Since the average female produces close to three hundred descendants, little hope is held out for a final solution to the roach problem. Nevertheless, extermination campaigns continue *unabated*. Surprisingly, some sentimental souls become *maudlin* as they consider the persecution of the insects. A writer noted for his *levity* made a *lugubrious* plea for a crash program of aid for the cockroach, calling him "a victim of his slum environment."

**Sample Sentences:** Use the new words in the following sentences.

1. She advocated \* _____ music as appropriate background for the funeral scene.

2. Although the debater's rebuttal was _____, it was totally irrelevant.\*

3. The plague continued _____, and the hapless\* Friar John was unable to deliver the note to Romeo.

4. A good barometer\* of the reunion's success was the number of _____ songs which the alumni sang.

5. Dean Flanigan admonished \* us for our _____ at the graduation exercises.

**Definitions:** Match the new words with their meanings.

6. puissant _____    a. sentimental

7. unabated _____    b. very sad

8. maudlin _____    c. lightness of disposition

9. levity _____    d. without subsiding

10. lugubrious _____    e. powerful

**Today's Idiom**

*to take the wind out of one's sails*—to remove someone's advantage.

Although Edna was bristling\* with anger when she stormed in, I *took the wind out of her sails* by voicing my own displeasure at the way she had been treated.

ANSWERS ARE ON PAGE 235

There are many choice epithets* for cockroaches, and over the centuries man has been most resourceful * in concocting* adjectives to describe the insects. Whether you are going to get excited over a roach, write a poem, take a College Board examination, or compose a letter to a loved one, it helps to have a rich vocabulary.

Match the twenty words with their meanings. Write the letter that stands for the definition in the appropriate answer space.

## REVIEW WORDS

| | | |
|---|---|---|
| _____ | 1 | abstemious |
| _____ | 2 | derogatory |
| _____ | 3 | disparate |
| _____ | 4 | edifice |
| _____ | 5 | extant |
| _____ | 6 | indict |
| _____ | 7 | levity |
| _____ | 8 | lugubrious |
| _____ | 9 | maudlin |
| _____ | 10 | nebulous |
| _____ | 11 | omnivorous |
| _____ | 12 | pesky |
| _____ | 13 | puissant |
| _____ | 14 | redolent |
| _____ | 15 | repose |
| _____ | 16 | reviled |
| _____ | 17 | sultry |
| _____ | 18 | trenchant |
| _____ | 19 | unabated |
| _____ | 20 | vicissitudes |

## DEFINITIONS

a. different
b. sentimental
c. building
d. very sad
e. humor, lightness of disposition
f. vague, not clear
g. expressing a low opinion
h. eating any kind of food
j. accuse
k. state of rest
l. still existing
m. powerful
n. annoying
o. fragrant
p. moderate in eating or drinking
r. keen, sharp, biting
s. torrid
t. difficulties
u. without subsiding
v. scolded

## IDIOMS

| | | |
|---|---|---|
| _____ | 21 | left holding the bag |
| _____ | 22 | a lick and a promise |
| _____ | 23 | tongue in cheek |
| _____ | 24 | take the wind out of one's sails |

w. insincerely

x. left to suffer the blame

y. do something in a cursory* manner
z. remove someone's advantage

Now check your answers on page 235. Make a record of those words you missed.

## WORDS FOR FURTHER STUDY     MEANINGS

1. _____ _____

2. _____ _____

3. _____ _____

4. _____ _____

5. _____ _____

**New Words:**

| scion | indoctrinate | opulence | obsequious | fulsome |
|-------|--------------|----------|------------|---------|
| sī′ ən | in dok′ trə nāt | op′ ū ləns | əb sē′ kwi əs | fül′ səm |

**Locked in an Ivory Edifice***

Prince Siddhartha Gautama was the *scion* of a family of warrior-kings in northern India. He was being *indoctrinated* for the time when he would assume his father's throne. Growing up in an atmosphere of *opulence*, the young Prince was constantly shielded from the cruel realities of the world. An army of *obsequious* servants and tutors catered to his every desire, providing Siddhartha with instruction in riding, fencing, dancing, and painting—while lavishing *fulsome* praise upon him. It wasn't until the Prince was thirty that he took the first step which led to his becoming the Buddha, one of the world's greatest spiritual leaders.

**Sample Sentences:** Use the new words in the following sentences. (Which two words are almost synonymous?)

1. It was not until the wreckers began to dismantle* the old edifice* that they discovered its real _____.

2. As the _____ of a family of wealthy bankers, Rothschild never had to face the vicissitudes* of life.

3. Uriah Heep's _____ manner nettled * all but the most gullible.*

4. In order to _____ the captive, his jailers repeatedly reviled * capitalism while praising communism.

5. The actress received _____ compliments from her friends but trenchant* criticism from the reviewers.

**Definitions:** Match the new words with their meanings.

6. scion _____ a. seeking favor, fawning

7. indoctrinate _____ b. child, descendant

8. opulence _____ c. wealth, riches

9. obsequious _____ d. excessive, insincere

10. fulsome _____ e. to teach certain principles

**Today's Idiom**

*two strings to one's bow*—two means of achieving one's aim
The salesman had *two strings to his bow*—if a phone call didn't get results, he would appear in person.

**ANSWERS ARE ON PAGE 236**

**New Words:**
lush   destitution    ponder   supplication   decadence
lush   des′ tə tü′ shən   pon′ dər   sup′ lə kā′ shən   dek′ ə dəns

**Siddhartha's Eyes Are Opened**

One day, Prince Siddhartha expressed the desire to leave his *lush* surroundings and ride out among his people. He was profoundly shaken by the misery, *destitution,* disease, and excruciating\* pain with which his people were constantly afflicted.\* Retiring to his room to *ponder* over what he had seen, he remained there for several days, deaf to the *supplication* of those who pleaded with him to come forth. It seemed to Siddhartha that his life had been redolent\* with *decadence,* and he was determined to make amends.

**Sample Sentences:**   Use the new words in the following sentences.

1. The _____ stage setting drew applause from the theatre buffs.\*
2. In the hospital, the alcoholic had time to _____ over the need to be abstemious.\*
3. As the traveler followed the tortuous\* path up the Kentucky mountain, he was sickened by the _____ which he saw.
4. Through _____, the fraternity head hoped to end the strife\* among the members.
5. Rumors of Rome's _____ were rife\* among the barbarian tribes.

**Definitions:**   Match the new words with their meanings.

6. lush _____    a. decay
7. destitution _____    b. extreme poverty
8. ponder _____    c. to consider carefully
9. supplication _____    d. earnest prayer
10. decadence _____    e. luxurious, elaborate

**Today's Idiom**

*on tenter hooks*—in a state of anxiety (cloth used to be stretched or "tentered" on hooks)

The indicted \* clerk was kept *on tenter hooks* by the district attorney.

ANSWERS ARE ON PAGE 236

**New Words:** penance ascetic desultory disciple metamorphosis
pen′ əns ə set′ ik des′ əl tô′ ri də sī′ pəl met′ ə môr′ fə sis

**The Enlightened One**

Siddhartha exchanged his sumptuous* garments for a monk's yellow robe and went out into the world to do *penance* for what he considered to be his previous life of sin. First he would cleanse himself by becoming an *ascetic;* then he would study Hindu wisdom in order to be prepared to help his suffering people. After six years of *desultory* wandering and attracting only a handful of *disciples,* Siddhartha came to a huge tree near the Indian city of Gaya. For seven weeks he sat beneath its branches, seeking an answer for his personal torment. Finally, it is said, he underwent a *metamorphosis,* becoming the Enlightened One—the Buddha.

**Sample Sentences:** Use the new words in the following sentences.

1. Billy the Vampire is the only extant* _____ of Count Dracula.

2. In a remarkable _____, her lugubrious* mood changed to one of levity.*

3. Following a lengthy diatribe* against mendacity*, the priest imposed _____ upon the sinner.

4. The cave of the _____ lacked the opulence* and lush* decoration of his former mansion.

5. Larry's compositions proceed in a _____ manner despite the supplication* of his English teacher.

**Definitions:** Match the new words with their meanings.

6. penance _____ a. change

7. ascetic (n.) _____ b. atonement for sin

8. desultory _____ c. occurring by chance, disconnected

9. disciple _____ d. one who practices self-denial and devotion

10. metamorphosis _____ e. follower

**Today's Idiom** *the fat is in the fire*—the mischief is done.
We implored * him to desist* but he said that the *fat was already in the fire.*

**ANSWERS ARE ON PAGE 236**

**New Words:**

| bona fide | salvation | materialism | nurture | nirvana |
|---|---|---|---|---|
| bō′ nə fīd′ | sal vā′ shən | mə tēr′ i əl iz′ əm | nėr′ chər | nir vä′ nə |

**Love Over Hatred, Goodness Over Evil**

Buddha outlined the three paths which men might travel: worldly pleasure, self-torment, and the middle path. Only through the middle path could man achieve *bona fide* peace and *salvation*. One had to repudiate* *materialism*, keep his self-control, restrict speech, be open-minded, never lie or steal, reject selfish drives, *nurture* goodness, etc. Buddha continued to preach until the age of eighty, spreading the philosophy that man has the power to shape his own destiny. Through good deeds and pure thoughts man may reach *nirvana*. Interestingly enough, the man who objected to traditional religious worship was to become idolized by millions throughout the world.

**Sample Sentences:** Use the new words in the following sentences.

1. In order to _____ good will, the management will do anything to accommodate* its guests' special needs.

2. When we saw the hundreds of _____ petitions, we realized that the number of people who supported the candidate was legion.*

3. The megalomaniac* believed that he alone had the answer to mankind's _____.

4. Rosalie found solace* in the conviction that one day mankind would reach Shangrila, Utopia,*_____

5. Disciples* of _____ may know the price of everything but the value of nothing.

**Definitions:** Match the new words with their meanings.

6. bona fide _____    a. to nourish, support

7. salvation _____    b. attention to worldly things and neglect of spiritual needs

8. materialism _____    c. freedom from care and pain, Buddhist heaven

9. nurture _____    d. genuine

10. nirvana _____    e. deliverance from ruin

**Today's Idiom**

*like Caesar's wife*—above suspicion

Mrs. Drake would have to be like Caesar's wife so that no tinge* of scandal would embarrass her husband, our new mayor.

ANSWERS ARE ON PAGE 236

For the past twenty weeks, each of these review exercises has contained a bit of propaganda to point up the need for you to expand your vocabulary. This week is no exception.

Match the twenty words with their meanings. Write the letter that stands for the definition in the appropriate answer space.

**REVIEW WORDS**

_____ 1 ascetic
_____ 2 bona fide
_____ 3 decadence
_____ 4 destitution
_____ 5 desultory
_____ 6 disciple
_____ 7 fulsome
_____ 8 indoctrinate
_____ 9 lush
_____ 10 materialism
_____ 11 metamorphosis
_____ 12 nirvana
_____ 13 nurture
_____ 14 obsequious
_____ 15 opulence
_____ 16 penance
_____ 17 ponder
_____ 18 salvation
_____ 19 scion
_____ 20 supplication

**DEFINITIONS**

a. one who practices self-denial
b. wealth
c. concern with possessions
d. luxurious
e. decay
f. disconnected, random
g. deliverance from ruin
h. extreme poverty
j. to teach certain principles
k. excessive
l. nourish
m. heavenly place
n. descendant
o. earnest prayer
p. consider carefully
r. follower
s. atonement for sin
t. seeking favor
u. change
v. genuine

**IDIOMS**

_____ 21 two strings to one's bow
_____ 22 on tenter hooks
_____ 23 fat is in the fire
_____ 24 like Caesar's wife

w. in a state of anxiety
x. two means to achieve one's aim
y. above suspicion
z. the mischief is done

Now check your answers on page 236. Make a record of those words you missed.

**WORDS FOR FURTHER STUDY**          **MEANINGS**

1. _____  _____
2. _____  _____
3. _____  _____
4. _____  _____
5. _____  _____

**New Words:**

| juxtapose | plight | covert | cope | incompatibility |
|---|---|---|---|---|
| juks′ tə pōz′ | plīt | kōv′ ərt | kōp | in kəm pat′ ə bil′ ə tē |

*Female Alcoholics*

When we *juxtapose* the words "woman" and "alcoholic" many readers are surprised. However, the *plight* of America's female alcoholics (about one million) is increasing in its intensity. But the statistics are inexact because it is estimated that there are nine *covert* alcoholics for every one under treatment. Women drink to help themselves to *cope* with life's vicissitudes.* They drink because of financial pressures, *incompatibility*, frustration,* and related reasons.

**Sample Sentences:** Use the new words in the following sentences.

1. If we were to _____ our philosophies, your materialism* would conflict with my idealism.

2. Judge Felder commented with asperity* upon the wife's charge of _____.

3. Just how our club's president is able to _____ with so many disparate* personalities is something I'll never understand.

4. The _____ of the refugees who wandered about in a desultory* fashion moved us to tears.

5. Woodrow Wilson stated that he found _____ agreements to be reprehensible.*

**Definitions:** Match the new words with their meanings.

6. juxtapose _____    a. quality of being mismated, lack of harmony

7. plight _____    b. to place side by side

8. covert _____    c. predicament, dangerous situation

9. cope _____    d. secret, hidden

10. incompatibility _____    e. to be a match for, to be able to handle

*Today's Idiom*

*Barmecide feast*—pretended generosity, a feast with no food (An Arabian prince of the Barmecide family invited a beggar to a feast but set before him a series of empty dishes.)

The committee always boasts about its luncheon, but to my way of thinking it's a real *Barmecide feast*.

ANSWERS ARE ON PAGE 236

**New Words:**

| | | | |
|---|---|---|---|
| incapacitated | fabricate | connubial | demur |
| in′ kə pas′ ə tāt id | fab′ rə kāt | kə nü′ bi əl | di mer′ |
| appellation | | | |
| ap′ ə lā′ shən | | | |

*A Profile of the Woman Who Drinks to Excess*

The typical alcoholic woman is above average in intelligence, in her forties, married, with two children. She started drinking socially in high school or college. Although frequently *incapacitated*, she can *fabricate* a story skillfully and thus conceal her true physical condition. She often attributes her alcoholism to *connubial* stress, boredom, or depression. A large percentage of the women give family histories of alcoholism. Most female drinkers would *demur* at the *appellation* of "alcoholic"—and that makes their treatment all the more difficult.

IMPORTANT NOTE: How good a detective are you? Did you spot one of the *new* words which had been introduced earlier? It should be part of your vocabulary now. From time to time in the lessons that follow, your alertness will be tested as a previously learned word is re-introduced.

**Sample Sentences:** Use the new words in the following sentences.

1. Dave's metamorphosis* from an honest person to one who could _____ an alibi so adroitly* was amazing.

2. The widow grew maudlin* as she reminisced about her former _____ bliss.

3. I will have to _____ even if I receive a bona fide* invitation to run for the G.O. council.

4. Because he was the scion* of the richest family on our block, Lenny was given the _____ of "Rockefeller."

5. He was ashamed to admit that a pesky* skin rash _____ him for weeks at a time.

**Definitions:** Match the new words with their meanings.

6. incapaci-
   tated _____ a. to object

7. fabricate _____ b. a name

8. connubial _____ c. to lie, concoct*

9. demur _____ d. related to marriage

10. appellation _____ e. disabled, made unfit

*Today's Idiom*

*in apple-pie order*—in neat order, good condition.
   The house was in dreadful condition when Mrs. Maslow arrived, but when she left it was *in apple-pie order*.

ANSWERS ARE ON PAGE 236

**New Words:**

| | | | |
|---|---|---|---|
| escalation | indifference | potential | cumulative |
| es′ kə lā′ shən | in dif′ ər əns | pə ten′ shəl | kū′ mū lə tiv |
| recondite | | | |
| rek′ ən dīt | | | |

***Nefarious\* Effects of Alcohol***

Aside from the reasons offered earlier, doctors have other interesting reasons for the *escalation* in female drinking. They also indict* social acceptance and *indifference* to alcohol's *potential* danger as contributory factors. If women realized the harmful extent of the *cumulative* effect of alcohol, they might taper off in their public and *recondite* drinking. Forty-three percent of the female alcoholics in a survey showed evidence of liver damage, and a quarter of the whole group had a high white-blood-cell count. Almost five percent of the patients died shortly after their release from the hospital.

**Sample Sentences:** If you can still see clearly after all the references to liquor, use the new words in the following sentences.

1. Many derogatory* statements were heard from those who were opposed to further _____ in the conflict.

2. With complete _____ toward his personal safety, Lt. Regan openly challenged the puissant* forces of the enemy.

3. When destitution* grips an area, there is excellent _____ for trouble.

4. The _____ effect of the summer's sultry* weather was to shorten everyone's temper.

5. The poet's _____ language precluded * any understanding of his theme.

**Definitions:** Match the new words with their meanings.

6. escalation _____ a. possible

7. indifference _____ b. accumulated

8. potential (adj.) _____ c. secret, hidden, obscure

9. cumulative _____ d. an increase, intensification

10. recondite _____ e. lack of concern

***Today's Idiom*** *apple-polishing*—trying to gain favor by gifts or flattery

If the way to advancement in this company is through *apple-polishing*, I quit!

**ANSWERS ARE ON PAGE 236**

# 22nd Week / 4th Day

**New Words:**    palliate    delude    prelude    chimerical    acknowledge
pal′ i āt    di lüd′    prel′ ūd    kə mer′ ə kəl    ak nol′ ij

***Danger Signals***    Potential* female alcoholics should be cognizant* of certain danger signals:

    a. Using alcohol in an attempt to *palliate* one's problems.
    b. *Deluding* oneself about the extent of her drinking habits.
    c. Drinking at regular time periods, both day and night.
    d. Reliance upon alcohol as a *prelude* to a major social obligation.
    e. Making unrealistic promises about terminating* her drinking.
    f. Using alcohol as a medication for real or *chimerical* illnesses.

If in evaluating* her drinking, a woman *acknowledged* that several of the danger signals applied to her, she should see a physician.

**Sample Sentences:**    Use the new words in the following sentences.

1. Monte refused to _____ the extrinsic* pressures which were causing him to do poorly in his sophomore year.

2. We must not allow fulsome* praise to _____ us about our actual abilities.

3. The drugs could only _____ the symptoms, not provide the cure.

4. As a _____ to his performance, the bullfighter vowed to do penance* for his sins.

5. The scheme sounded _____, but we were indoctrinated* to believe that it could work.

**Definitions:**    Match the new words with their meanings.

6. palliate _____    a. visionary, imaginary, fantastic
7. delude _____    b. alleviate, relieve without curing
8. prelude _____    c. introduction
9. chimerical _____    d. to fool
10. acknowledge _____    e. admit

***Today's Idiom***    *the Draconian Code*—a very severe set of rules (Draco, an Athenian lawmaker of the 7th cent. B.C., prescribed the death penalty for almost every violation.)

    The head counselor ran our camp according to his own *Draconian Code.*

**ANSWERS ARE ON PAGE 236**

If you're driving, don't drink! Alcohol does not mix with gasoline! We have seen those slogans on many billboards. Here's a new one: "If you use words, use good ones!"

Match the twenty words with their meanings. Write the letter that stands for the definition in the appropriate answer space.

**REVIEW WORDS**

| | | | **DEFINITIONS** |
|---|---|---|---|
| _____ | 1 | acknowledge | a. accumulated |
| _____ | 2 | appellation | b. admit |
| _____ | 3 | chimerical | c. relieve without curing |
| _____ | 4 | connubial | d. to lie |
| _____ | 5 | cope | e. to fool |
| _____ | 6 | covert | f. a name |
| _____ | 7 | cumulative | g. predicament |
| _____ | 8 | delude | h. secret |
| _____ | 9 | demur | j. intensification |
| _____ | 10 | escalation | k. to be a match for |
| _____ | 11 | fabricate | l. obscure, hidden |
| _____ | 12 | incapacitated | m. imaginary, fantastic |
| _____ | 13 | incompatibility | n. related to marriage |
| _____ | 14 | indifference | o. possible |
| _____ | 15 | juxtapose | p. to place side by side |
| _____ | 16 | palliate | r. to object |
| _____ | 17 | plight | s. introduction |
| _____ | 18 | potential (adj.) | t. lack of concern |
| _____ | 19 | prelude | u. lack of harmony |
| _____ | 20 | recondite | v. disabled |

**IDIOMS**

| | | | |
|---|---|---|---|
| _____ | 21 | Barmecide feast | w. trying to gain favor |
| _____ | 22 | in apple-pie order | x. severe set of rules |
| _____ | 23 | apple-polishing | y. pretended generosity |
| _____ | 24 | Draconian Code | z. in good condition |

Now check your answers page 236. Make a record of words you missed.

**WORDS FOR FURTHER STUDY**      **MEANINGS**

1. _____  _____

2. _____  _____

3. _____  _____

4. _____  _____

5. _____  _____

**New Words:**

| heterogeneous | gamut | perspicacious | analogous |
|---|---|---|---|
| het′ ər ə jē′ ni əs | gam′ ət | pėr′ spə kā′ shəs | ə nal′ ə gəs |

maladjusted
mal′ ə jus′ tid

**From A to Z**  Ellis Sloane, a teacher of science at a large metropolitan high school, first paid little attention to the fact that his two biology classes were so disparate* in their performance. In most schools the classes are alphabetically *heterogeneous,* with youngsters' names running the *gamut* from Adams to Zilch. But Biology 121 had only A's and B's, whereas Biology 128 had T's, V's, W's, Y's, and Z's. Mr. Sloane, a *perspicacious* teacher, began to perceive* differences between the two groups: while their reading scores and I.Q.'s were roughly *analogous,* it was apparent that Biology 128 was replete* with *maladjusted* students, while Biology 121 had the normal ones.

**Sample Sentences:**  Use the new words in the following sentences.

1. The Bureau of Child Guidance has been the salvation* for some _____ children.

2. Our algebra class is a _____ one in which bright students are juxtaposed* with slower ones.

3. Senator Thorpe was _____ enough to realize that the scurrilous* charge would have little effect upon the voters.

4. Although the lawyer acknowledged* that the two cases were hardly _____, he still felt that he had a good precedent on his side.

5. The actress ran the _____ of emotions in a poignant* performance which thrilled the audience.

**Definitions:**  Match the new words with their meanings.

6. heteroge-
   neous _____    a. range

7. gamut _____    b. acutely perceptive, shrewd

8. perspica-
   cious _____    c. poorly adjusted, disturbed

9. analogous _____    d. comparable, similar

10. maladjusted _____    e. dissimilar

**Today's Idiom**  *the distaff side*—women (distaff was a staff used in spinning)
   The men had brandy on the porch, while the *distaff side* gathered to gossip in the kitchen.

ANSWERS ARE ON PAGE 236

111

**New Words:**  phenomenon  mortality  decade  susceptible  neurotic
fə nom′ ə non  môr tal′ ə ti  dek′ ād  sə sep′ tə bəl  nü rot′ ik

**What's In a Name?**  As Mr. Sloane pursued his investigation of the *phenomenon*, he discovered that a Dr. Trevor Weston of the British Medical Association had corroborated * his findings. Dr. Weston had studied British *mortality* rates over a *decade*, finding that people whose names began with letters ranging from "S" to "Z" had a life expectancy which averaged twelve years fewer than the rest of the population. Furthermore, those at the bottom of the alphabet tended to contract more ulcers, were more *susceptible* to heart attacks, and were more likely to be *neurotic* than those at the top of the alphabet.

**Sample Sentences:**  Use the new words in the following sentences.

1. Irritability is one of the salient* features of a _____ personality.

2. After a _____ of connubial * acrimony,* the couple decided to consult with a marriage counselor.

3. If a miner were to ponder* over the high _____ rate in his occupation, he might want to quit.

4. Ethan Frome soon learned that his querulous* wife was _____ to a variety of ailments.

5. There was no paucity* of witnesses to describe the _____ of the flying saucer.

**Definitions:**  Match the new words with their meanings.

6. phenomenon _____    a. death
7. mortality _____    b. suffering from a nervous disorder
8. decade _____    c. ten years
9. susceptible _____    d. unusual occurrence
10. neurotic _____    e. easily affected, unusually liable

**Today's Idiom**  *on the qui vive*—on the alert
My mother is always *on the qui vive* for bargains.

ANSWERS ARE ON PAGE 236

**New Words:**

| | | | |
|---|---|---|---|
| pedagogue | enunciate | inordinate | irascible |
| ped′ ə gog | i nun′ si āt | in ôr′ də nit | i ras′ ə bəl |
| introspective | | | |
| in′ trə spek′ tiv | | | |

**The Perils of the Alphabet**

Dr. Weston is convinced that the *pedagogue* is the culprit.* Since teachers seat their pupils in alphabetical order, the "S" to "Z" child is usually the last to receive his test marks, the last to eat lunch, the last to be dismissed, and so on. As they are the last to recite, these youngsters feel frustrated * because what they had to say had usually been *enunciated* earlier. The *inordinate* amount of waiting which this group has to do causes them to become *irascible* and jittery. "S" to "Z" people also become quite *introspective,* convinced that they are inferior to those at the top of the alphabet.

**Sample Sentences:** Use the new words in the following sentences.

1. Reporters were expecting the candidate to _____ his policy on the escalation* of the war.

2. His profligate* son made the parsimonious* old crank even more _____.

3. Since Alice is so gregarious* it surprised me to learn that she is also an _____ girl.

4. Mr. Ford is proud to be called a teacher, but he demurs at the title of _____.

5. In an attempt to show how assiduous* he was, the executive spent an _____ amount of time on his report.

**Definitions:** Match the new words with their meanings.

6. pedagogue _____    a. irritable

7. enunciate _____    b. excessive

8. inordinate _____    c. to utter, proclaim

9. irascible _____    d. looking into one's own feelings

10. introspective _____    e. teacher

**Today's Idiom**

*to get one's back up*—to become angry
    Every time his mother mentioned getting a haircut, the young guitarist *got his back up.*

ANSWERS ARE ON PAGE 236

**New Words:**

| | | | |
|---|---|---|---|
| perpetuate | mandate | compensatory | neutralize |
| pər pech′ ü āt | man′ dāt | kəm pen′ sə tô′ ri | nü′ trəl īz |
| catastrophic | | | |
| kat′ ə strof′ ik | | | |

**In the Nature of Educational Reform**

Mr. Sloane did not want to *perpetuate* the disorders which stemmed from the alphabetical arrangement. Not only did he reverse the seating in his other classes, but he began to badger* the school's administration for a *mandate* to bring about such changes throughout the building. He called it a *compensatory* factor to *neutralize* the *catastrophic* effects of the traditional policy. Soon, Mr. Sloane earned the appellation* of "Mr. Backwards."

**Sample Sentences:** Use the new words in the following sentences.

1. Don Ricardo hoped that his son would _____ the family business, but Manuel was too involved with chimerical * schemes to want to run a restaurant.

2. If the Draconian* regulations are to continue unabated,* they will have _____ results.

3. Dr. Meyers prescribed medication to _____ the acid condition which had incapacitated * my uncle.

4. As a prelude* to his victory speech, the mayor announced that he considered the large vote to be a _____ from the people.

5. _____ education may help minority groups to cope* with their plight.*

**Definitions:** Match the new words with their meanings.

6. perpetuate _____    a. serving to pay back

7. mandate _____    b. an authoritative order or command

8. compensatory _____    c. to counteract

9. neutralize _____    d. to cause to continue

10. catastrophic _____    e. disastrous

**Today's Idiom**

*to bring home the bacon*—to earn a living, to succeed

The man's inability *to bring home the bacon* was the actual reason for the couple's incompatibility.*

ANSWERS ARE ON PAGE 236

You may not know the alphabet from *aardvark* to *zymurgy*, but you can certainly cope\* with *analogous* to *susceptible*.

Match the twenty words with their meanings. Write the letter that stands for the definition in the appropriae answer space.

**REVIEW WORDS**

_____ 1   analogous
_____ 2   catastrophic
_____ 3   compensatory
_____ 4   decade
_____ 5   enunciate
_____ 6   gamut
_____ 7   heterogeneous
_____ 8   inordinate
_____ 9   introspective
_____ 10  irascible
_____ 11  maladjusted
_____ 12  mandate
_____ 13  mortality
_____ 14  neurotic
_____ 15  neutralize
_____ 16  pedagogue
_____ 17  perpetuate
_____ 18  perspicacious
_____ 19  phenomenon
_____ 20  susceptible

**DEFINITIONS**

a.  disastrous
b.  irritable
c.  teacher
d.  disturbed
e.  to cause to continue
f.  comparable, similar
g.  shrewd
h.  authoritative command
j.  dissimilar
k.  range
l.  counteract
m.  having a nervous disorder
n.  excessive
o.  looking into one's own feelings
p.  unusual occurrence
r.  death
s.  easily affected
t.  serving to pay back
u.  ten years
v.  to utter, proclaim

**IDIOMS**

_____ 21  the distaff side
_____ 22  on the qui vive
_____ 23  to get one's back up
_____ 24  bring home the bacon

w.  women
x.  on the alert
y.  become angry
z.  earn a living

Now check your answers on page 236. Make a record of those words you missed.

**WORDS FOR FURTHER STUDY** | **MEANINGS**

1.  _____   _____

2.  _____   _____

3.  _____   _____

YOU ARE NOW AT THE MID-POINT OF THE BOOK, AND YOU SHOULD PLAN TO DEVOTE SOME ADDITIONAL TIME TO A REVIEW OF THOSE WORDS WHICH YOU MISSED DURING THE PAST TWENTY-THREE WEEKS.

**New Words:**

| anthropologist | bizarre | inanimate | fetish | artifact |
|---|---|---|---|---|
| an' thrə pol' ə jist | ba zär' | in an' ə mit | fē' tish | är' tə fakt |

**Primitive Magic**

In the course of their studies of other cultures, *anthropologists* have reported numerous customs and practices which seem *bizarre* to the average American. Many primitive people believe that certain *inanimate* objects have a will of their own and possess some magical powers. These *fetishes* may be simple things like a particular feather of a bird or a unique pebble. The *fetish* might have derived its power, according to members of some tribes, from a god who lives within the object and has changed it into a thing of magic. *Fetishes* need not only be natural objects, however. An *artifact* such as a sculpture or carving is also believed to possess supernatural powers.

**Sample Sentences:** Now use your new words in the following sentences.

1. Stones are ＿＿＿＿＿＿ objects which have no life of their own.

2. It has been suggested that the man who builds a better mousetrap will find the world beating a path to his door to possess this ＿＿＿＿＿＿.

3. The explorers saw the golden statue and thought of how much money it would bring them. But their lives would be in danger if they moved it because it was a powerful ＿＿＿＿＿＿ to the natives.

4. Margaret Mead, the famous ＿＿＿＿＿＿, fascinated thousands of readers with her studies of South Seas islanders.

5. It would be rather ＿＿＿＿＿＿ for a young man to come to school wearing a dress.

**Definitions:** If you have studied the reading selection and the sample sentences, now try your hand at matching your new words with their definitions.

6. anthropologist ＿＿＿＿ a. an object made by hand, rather than a thing as it occurs in nature

7. artifact ＿＿＿＿ b. lifeless

8. bizarre ＿＿＿＿ c. an object that is thought to have magic powers

9. fetish ＿＿＿＿ d. an expert in the study of the races, beliefs, customs, etc. of mankind

10. inanimate ＿＿＿＿ e. odd, peculiar, strange, weird

**Today's Idiom**

*To get down off a high horse*—to act like an ordinary person

When Susan discovered that the young man who was trying to make conversation with her was the son of a millionaire, she immediately *got down off her high horse*.

ANSWERS ARE ON PAGE 236

**New Words:**

| taboo | imprudent | prohibition | imperative | taint |
|-------|-----------|-------------|------------|-------|
| tə bü′ | im prü′ dənt | prō′ ə bish′ ən | im per′ ə tiv | tānt |

**Forbidden**

An outgrowth of the idea of a fetish* is the closely related practice of *taboo.* Whereas the gods or supernatural powers merely inhabit an object that is a fetish and lend it magic, they will punish the *imprudent* native who violates their *prohibition* of an act or use of an object or word which has become *taboo.* If a *taboo* has been broken, it becomes *imperative* for the offender to be punished. In many cases, however, the *taint* on the community may be removed after the priests have performed a special ceremony. Often, the violator of the *taboo* will be punished or die merely through his own fears of the terrible thing he has done.

**Sample Sentences:**

Has the context in which your new words appear given you clues to their meaning? Try now to use them in these sample sentences.

1. Unsanitary conditions in the bottling factory caused hundreds of cases of soda to be _____ by dirt and foreign objects. The health department refused to allow the soda to be sold.

2. Although a New Jersey high school principal placed a _____ on boys wearing their hair long, one student fought in the courts and won his case.

3. The _____ fellow had saved none of his wages and had to accept charity after he was laid off from his job.

4. It is _____ for certain South Seas islanders to eat some foods before they marry.

5. In the nuclear age it has become _____ for the nations of the world to learn to live in peace.

**Definitions:**

Now is your chance to test your knowledge of your new words by matching them with their definitions.

6. imperative _____    a. contamination, undesirable substance that spoils something

7. imprudent _____    b. the act of forbidding certain behavior

8. prohibition _____    c. urgent, necessary, compulsory

9. taboo _____    d. forbidden by custom or religious practice

10. taint (n.) _____    e. unwise, not careful

**Today's Idiom**

*the first water*—of the best quality, the greatest
Kareem Jabbar is obviously a basketball player of *the first water* who would be of enormous value to any team.

ANSWERS ARE ON PAGE 236

**New Words:**

| universal | contemptuous | absurd | bigot | abhor |
|---|---|---|---|---|
| ū′nə ver′ səl | kon temp′ chü es | ab sérd′ | big′ ət | ab hôr′ |

**An Absurdity**

Although it is probably *universal* human behavior to be *contemptuous* of the bizarre* superstitions practiced by inhabitants of unfamiliar cultures, it seems to be somewhat imprudent* to laugh at others before one takes a good, hard look at the *absurd* taboos* and fetishes* he accepts as part of his everyday life. Isn't it somewhat *absurd* when the "dyed-in-the-wool" *bigot*, who illogically fears the taint* of close association with Negroes (behavior that resembles fear of a taboo), spends most of the summer lying in the sun trying to acquire the color he claims to *abhor?* Since doctors tell us that excessive sun-tanning may be a cause of skin cancer, our strange yearning for sun-darkened skin has all the qualities of a fetish.*

**Sample Sentences:**

Did the starred review words seem familiar to you? Yet, how many were totally foreign several days ago? Keep up the good work now by using your new words in the following sentences.

1. Bob felt _____ of his best friend after he saw him cheating during an exam.

2. The teacher felt like laughing after he heard Sally's _____ excuse for not having done her homework.

3. One Southern politician, a notorious _____, hopes to get support as a presidential candidate on the basis of his prejudices and intolerance.

4. I _____ people who fall asleep and snore in movie theaters.

5. Would relations between countries be simpler if a _____ language were spoken rather than hundreds of separate ones?

**Definitions:** Match your new words with their definitions.

6. abhor _____ a. ridiculous

7. absurd _____ b. present everywhere

8. bigot _____ c. expressing a feeling that something is worthless

9. contemptuous _____ d. a person who is intolerant of other people or ideas

10. universal _____ e. to detest, to despise

**Today's Idiom**

*dyed-in-the-wool*—set in one's ways

He was a *dyed-in-the-wool* Republican who would not consider voting for a Democrat.

ANSWERS ARE ON PAGE 236

**New Words:**   vulnerable   entreaty   tradition   originate   inviolable
vul′ nər ə bəl   en trēt′ i   tra dish′ ən   ə rij′ ə nāt   in vī′ ə lə bl

**Gesundheit!**   During the Middle Ages most people believed that the devil could enter a man's body easily when he sneezed, because at that propitious* moment he left his body *vulnerable*. However, this catastrophic* event could be avoided if another person immediately made an *entreaty* to God. This was how the practice began of saying "God bless you" after someone sneezes. Although the *tradition* continues today, few people are aware of its history. A superstition *originates* in ignorance —when people are unsure of the causes of events. But it continues *inviolable* over the years because it usually represents man's deepest fears.

**Sample Sentences:**   Use these new words in the following sentences.

1. Some bad habits _____ in adolescence and continue throughout a person's life.

2. The murderer made a(n) _____ to the Governor for a pardon.

3. Despite the inexorable* torture, 007 kept the _____ secret of the labyrinth* leading to the underground headquarters.

4. Armor protected the most _____ parts of the warrior's body.

5. Eskimos have a(n) _____ of rubbing noses to show affection.

**Definitions:**   Match the new words with the definition.

6. vulnerable   _____   a. begin, arise

7. entreaty   _____   b. capable of being injured

8. tradition   _____   c. custom that has been handed down

9. originate   _____   d. appeal, plea

10. inviolable   _____   e. safe (from destruction, etc.)

**Today's Idiom**   *on his own hook*—without others' help
   The soldier said he would investigate behind the enemy lines *on his own hook*.

**ANSWERS ARE ON PAGE 236**

And today it's time to strengthen your word knowledge again. You've noticed, of course, that the matching definitions are not always the definitions you may have been familiar with. This is the way language works. It is impossible to provide a one-word synonym or simple definition for a word that you will always be able to substitute for it. Therefore, in our weekly review we hope not only to check your learning, but also teach you closely related meanings.

Match the best possible definition with the word you studied. Write the letter that stands for that definition in the appropriate answer space.

### REVIEW WORDS

_____ 1 abhor
_____ 2 absurd
_____ 3 anthropologist
_____ 4 artifact
_____ 5 bigot
_____ 6 bizarre
_____ 7 contemptuous
_____ 8 entreaty
_____ 9 fetish
_____ 10 imperative
_____ 11 imprudent
_____ 12 inanimate
_____ 13 inviolable
_____ 14 originate
_____ 15 prohibition
_____ 16 taboo
_____ 17 taint
_____ 18 tradition
_____ 19 universal
_____ 20 vulnerable

### DEFINITIONS

a. a hand-made object
b. unwise
c. one who is not tolerant of others' ideas
d. completely protected
e. a magical object
f. widespread
g. begin, arise
h. person who studies mankind's customs
j. forbidden
k. long-standing practice
l. weird
m. able to be hurt
n. looking down on someone or something
o. to utterly hate
p. without life
r. forbidding of certain actions
s. necessary
t. ridiculous
u. plea, appeal
v. contaminate

### IDIOMS

_____ 21 to get off one's high horse
_____ 22 of the first water
_____ 23 dyed-in-the-wool
_____ 24 on one's own hook

w. the greatest
x. without others' help
y. to act like an ordinary person
z. set in one's ways

Check your answers on page 236. Record your errors and their correct meanings below. These words *must* be studied independently if you want to master them. Use them in original sentences. Also, study the several different definitions a good dictionary provides for each of these problem words.

### WORDS FOR FURTHER STUDY     MEANINGS

1. _____ _____

2. _____ _____

3. _____ _____

**New Words:**

| awesome | eruption | puny | debris | dispersed |
|---------|----------|------|--------|-----------|
| ô′ səm | i rup′ shən | pū′ ni | də brē′ | dis pirsd′ |

**The Explosion of Krakatoa**

There are few sights that are more impressive and *awesome* than the *eruption* of an active volcano. There are few natural events that so singularly* dwarf man's *puny* attempts to control his environment. Perhaps the greatest volcanic *eruption* of modern times took place in 1883 when the island of Krakatoa in Indonesia blew up as the result of a volcanic explosion. An enormous tidal wave resulted which proved catastrophic* to the nearby coasts of Java and Sumatra. New islands were formed by the lava that poured out, and *debris* was scattered across the Indian Ocean for hundreds of miles. Volcanic material, *dispersed* seventeen miles into the atmosphere, created startlingly beautiful sunsets for years afterwards.

**Sample Sentences:** Relying on the contextual clues in the paragraph above, use the new words in the following sentences:

1. Fred had been known for his gentle ways, so his friends were stunned by the _____ of angry words that issued from him.

2. We were surprised by the _____ resistance put up by the voracious* tiger to its capture.

3. After her house had burned to the ground, Mrs. Wiley searched through the _____ for her valuable jewelry.

4. Many of those who witnessed the first atomic explosion reported that it was an _____ sight.

5. The fluffy seeds of the milkweed are _____ by the wind.

**Definitions:** Now take the final step in learning the new words.

6. awesome _____ a. scattered, spread, broken up

7. debris _____ b. weak, unimportant

8. dispersed _____ c. inspiring terror, weird

9. eruption _____ d. ruins, fragments

10. puny _____ e. bursting out

**Today's Idiom**

*as broad as it is long*—it makes very little difference.

Since both jobs pay $1.75 an hour and are equally boring, it is about *as broad as it is long* whether I take one or the other.

ANSWERS ARE ON PAGE 237

**New Words:**   obliterate   deplorable   initiate   conflagration   rue
əb lit′ ər āt   di plôr′ ə bəl   i nish′ i āt   kon′ flə grā′ shən   rü

**A Universal\***
**Danger**

Man's ability to *obliterate* life on this planet has increased at a rapid rate. We are now faced with the *deplorable* prospect of new weapons that can cause destruction of life and property on a scale far beyond our imagination. No matter who takes the first step to *initiate* a conflict, the possibility exists that the *conflagration* will spread and envelop the world. Much thought has been given to ways and means of preventing this catastrophe.\* Some consider it mandatory\* that the nuclear powers seek agreement on methods of limiting and controlling these weapons, for in the absence of such an agreement, we may *rue* the day atomic energy was made practical.

**Sample Sentences:**   Complete the sentences by filling in the blanks.

1. Who could imagine a more bizarre\* story than the one having to do with a cow causing the _____ in Chicago?

2. When a dog buries a bone, he goes to a great deal of trouble to _____ its hiding place.

3. You will _____ that display of histrionics\* when I asked you to help.

4. She could not imagine how she was going to get him to _____ a conversation about marriage.

5. The home-town fans thought the umpire's decision was _____.

**Definitions:**   Let's put the new words together with their meanings.

6. obliterate   _____   a. regret
7. deplorable   _____   b. sad, pitiable
8. initiate   _____   c. erase, wipe out
9. conflagration _____   d. start, set going
10. rue   _____   e. great fire

**Today's Idiom**

*blow hot and cold*—swing for and against something
   I told Charlie to give up his summer job and come cross-country biking with us. He's *blowing hot and cold* on the deal at this point.

**ANSWERS ARE ON PAGE 237**

**New Words:**

| congenial | hoard | sage | aegis | detriment |
|-----------|-------|------|-------|-----------|
| kən jēn′ yel | hôrd | sāj | ē′ jis | det′ rə mənt |

**Taken for Granted**

The presence of an ever-flowing supply of fresh, clean water is taken for granted. Unfortunately, this *congenial* condition is fast disappearing. As our population increases, as industry consumes more water each year, the level of our underground water supply sinks measurably. There is no way to *hoard* water; there are many ways to conserve it. During a particularly dry spell, New York City found its reservoirs going dry. Only then did the residents begin to heed the *sage* advice to limit the wasteful uses of water. Under the *aegis* of the Water Commissioner, citizens were encouraged to develop habits that would save water. The continued imprudent* waste by each of us of this most basic resource will work to the *detriment* of all.

**Sample Sentences:** Here's your opportunity to use your new words.

1. Isn't it a pity we can't _____ the ideal days of autumn?

2. A man may be a _____ everywhere, but at home he's called a "square" by his youngsters.

3. The tree in front of my house has the dubious* honor of being the spot voted the most _____ by the dogs of the neighborhood.

4. It was fortuitous* that at the last moment the mayor offered the _____ of his office in finding a solution to the problem.

5. A settlement that causes _____ to neither side is imperative.*

**Definitions:** Remember, words may have many synonyms.

6. congenial _____    a. injury, damage, hurt

7. hoard (v.) _____    b. sympathetic, agreeable

8. sage _____    c. shield, protection, sponsorship

9. aegis _____    d. hide, store, accumulate

10. detriment _____    e. wise man, philosopher

**Today's Idiom**

*in the doldrums*—in a bored or depressed state
    Mary has been *in the doldrums* since her best friend moved away.

ANSWERS ARE ON PAGE 237

**New Words:**

| longevity | imbibe | virile | senile | doddering |
|---|---|---|---|---|
| lon jev′ ə ti | im bīb′ | vir′ əl | sē′ nĭl | dod′ ər ing |

**An Ageless Story**

Every so often we can read about a man or woman who has reached an age far beyond the limits we ordinarily expect. Reports of a man in Chile or a woman in Turkey who has celebrated the 105th or 110th birthday occur regularly. The natural question is, to what do these people owe their *longevity?* Frequently, the answer concerns the fact that the ancient one liked to *imbibe* regularly of some hard liquor. The photograph will show an apparently *virile* man or robust woman. Somehow, people who reach this advanced age seem to remain eternally sturdy. There are no signs that they have become *senile.* Smoking a pipe, or sewing on some garment, these rare specimens of hardy humanity are far from the *doddering* folk we expect to see.

**Sample Sentences:** Use the new words in these sentences.

1. Far from being _____, the old man was considered the sage* of the neighborhood.

2. He came from a family noted for its _____, and all four of his grandparents lived to the age of 90.

3. It was deplorable* for us to see him _____ around the house with the aid of a cane.

4. If you _____, don't drive!

5. The boys struck up _____ poses to attract the girls on the beach.

**Definitions:** Here's your chance to match the new words with their meaning.

6. longevity _____    a. long duration of life

7. imbibe _____    b. masterful, manly

8. virile _____    c. drink

9. senile _____    d. infirm, weak from old age

10. doddering _____    e. trembling, shaking

**Today's Idiom**

*burn the midnight oil*—study or work late into the night

    If I'm going to pass the test tomorrow, I will have to *burn the midnight oil* tonight.

ANSWERS ARE ON PAGE 237

Week by week your word-power is being built. It's like putting money in the bank. Remember, in our language there may be many synonyms and related meanings for each word. Knowing one synonym is good, but you will reap greater benefit from knowing several. Below is the matching review for this week.

**REVIEW WORDS**

_____ 1 aegis
_____ 2 awesome
_____ 3 conflagration
_____ 4 congenial
_____ 5 debris
_____ 6 deplorable
_____ 7 detriment
_____ 8 dispersed
_____ 9 doddering
_____ 10 eruption
_____ 11 hoard
_____ 12 imbibe
_____ 13 initiate
_____ 14 longevity
_____ 15 obliterate
_____ 16 puny
_____ 17 rue
_____ 18 sage
_____ 19 senile
_____ 20 virile

**DEFINITIONS**

a. trembling, shaking with old age
b. regret
c. bursting out
d. infirm, weak as a result of old age
e. wise man, philosopher
f. ruins, fragments
g. weak, unimportant
h. protection, sponsorship, shield
j. agreeable, sympathetic
k. broken up, scattered, spread
l. sad, pitiable
m. hurt, damage, injury
n. drink
o. great fire
p. manly, masterful
r. inspiring terror, weird
s. set going, start
t. accumulate, save, store up
u. long duration of life
v. wipe out, erase

**IDIOMS**

_____ 21 as broad as it is long
_____ 22 blow hot and cold
_____ 23 in the doldrums
_____ 24 burn the midnight oil

w. in a bored or depressed state
x. makes very little difference
y. swing for and against something
z. work late into the night

**WORDS FOR FURTHER STUDY**　　**MEANINGS**

1. _____  _____
2. _____  _____
3. _____  _____

Check your answers on page 237. Don't neglect words you fail to answer correctly. These problem words can be mastered quickly if you write them down, look up their meanings, and practice using them.

**New Words:**

| lethargic | prevalent | paramount | remiss | hostile |
|-----------|-----------|-----------|--------|---------|
| lə thär′ jik | prev′ ə lənt | par′ ə mount | ri mis′ | hos′ təl |

**Informing the Public**

Public opinion has an important place in a democracy. The public, often *lethargic*, is susceptible* to a wide variety of influences. The most *prevalent* of these is the mass media. These communications media—the press, radio, and television —have a *paramount* position in initiating,* influencing, and shaping public opinion. Bearing this responsibility, the mass media are often accused of being *remiss* in their duty to inform the public. There has been a great deal of *hostile* comment leveled against these opinion molders.

**Sample Sentences:** Based upon your understanding of the new words as discovered from the context, place them in the spaces provided.

1. The audience became extremely _____ when the bigot* began to attack minority groups.

2. Long hair among boys is so _____ today, there is no longer a prohibition against it in most schools.

3. We are all susceptible* to a _____ feeling after a heavy meal.

4. A good politician seeks the _____ issue in his community.

5. Parents are often _____ in not warning their children of the dangers of cigarette smoking.

**Definitions:** Matching words and definitions will prove you've learned them.

6. lethargic ___    a. prevailing, common, general

7. prevalent ___    b. lazy, indifferent

8. paramount ___    c. antagonistic, angry

9. remiss ___    d. supreme, foremost

10. hostile ___    e. careless, negligent

**Today's Idiom**

*to split hairs*—to make fine distinctions.
The mother and child spent a great deal of time arguing about the *hair-splitting* question of whether "going to bed" meant lights out or not.

ANSWERS ARE ON PAGE 237

| New Words: | rebuke | aversion | evince | vogue | superficial |
|---|---|---|---|---|---|
| | ri būk′ | ə ver′ zhan | i vins′ | vōg | sü′ pər fish′ əl |

**The Lack of Foreign News**

The critics *rebuke* the press for the fact that most newspapers devote somewhat less than 10 percent of their news space to foreign items. In many hundreds of papers this falls below 2 percent. Why is there this *aversion* to foreign news? Newsmen claim that readers *evince* no interest in foreign affairs. In order to increase reader interest in foreign news, the *vogue* among editors is to sensationalize it to the point of distortion. Many other papers do only the most *superficial* kind of reporting in this area.

**Sample Sentences:** Insert the new words in these sentences.

1. The female _____ to mice is considered absurd * by boys.

2. After a _____ examination of the injured motorist, the doctor said that hospitalization was imperative.*

3. Many a husband has been given a _____ for having imbibed * too fully at an office party.

4. The teacher could not get the little boy to _____ any interest in their project.

5. Good manners are always in _____.

**Definitions:** Match the new words with their definitions.

6. rebuke (v.) _____    a. on the surface, slight

7. aversion _____    b. criticize, reproach, reprimand

8. evince _____    c. strong dislike, opposition

9. vogue _____    d. fashion

10. superficial _____    e. show plainly, exhibit

**Today's Idiom**

*to strike while the iron is hot*—to take an action at the right moment

As soon as John heard that his father had won in the lottery, he *struck while the iron was hot* and asked for an increase in his allowance.

**ANSWERS ARE ON PAGE 237**

**New Words:**

| jettison | inevitable | lucrative | tussle | intrinsic |
|----------|------------|-----------|--------|-----------|
| jet′ ə sən | in ev′ ə tə bəl | lü krə tiv | tus′ əl | in trin′ sik |

**Playing It Safe**

The average newspaper office receives many times the amount of foreign news than it has space to print. The editor must include or *jettison* items as he sees fit. It is *inevitable* that his ideas of what the reader wants to know, or should know, are decisive. Because the newspaper owners do not want to endanger a *lucrative* business, there is the constant *tussle* between personal opinion and the desire not to offend too many readers or advertisers. It is *intrinsic* to the operation of all mass media that they avoid being extremist in their news coverage or editorials.

**Sample Sentences:** Insert the new words in these sentences.

1. Our conscience must always _____ against our yearning* for what we know is taboo.*

2. Man sets the price of gold; it has no _____ value.

3. The pilot decided it would be imprudent* to _____ his fuel over the populated area.

4. It is _____ that children question what their elders accept as tradition.*

5. In New York one can build a _____ business selling the most bizarre* items.

**Definitions:** Match the new words with their definitions.

6. jettison _____ a. sure, certain, unavoidable

7. inevitable _____ b. essential, natural, inborn

8. lucrative _____ c. a rough struggle

9. tussle (n.) _____ d. profitable

10. intrinsic _____ e. throw overboard, discard

**Today's Idiom**

*once in a blue moon*—on a very rare occasion
   His wife complained that they go out to dinner and a show *once in a blue moon*.

ANSWERS ARE ON PAGE 237

**New Words:**

| acute | gist | transient | terse | cogent |
|-------|------|-----------|-------|--------|
| ə kūt′ | jist | tran′ shənt | tèrs | ko′ jent |

**A Favorite News Source**

The electronic media—television and radio—have more *acute* problems than does the press when it comes to news reporting. A normal broadcast can cover only a small part of a news day. The object is to transmit the *gist* of a story without supplying its background. Another difficulty of electronic news broadcasting is its *transient* nature; the viewer or listener may miss an important story if his attention wanders. On the other hand, because radio and television present news in a more *terse* and exciting way, they are accepted as the most *cogent* presentation of news and are preferred and believed above newspapers by most people.

**Sample Sentences:** A slow and thorough study is needed today.

1. After the catastrophe,* there was an _____ need for emergency housing.

2. The young lover was susceptible* to _____ feelings of jealousy when he saw his sweetheart dancing with his best friend.

3. He had to get the _____ of his message into a 25-word telegram.

4. The mayor made a _____ statement in which he rebuked * his election opponent for making a contemptuous* accusation.

5. The best debator makes the most _____ presentation.

**Definitions:** This day's work requires careful study.

6. acute _____    a. forceful, convincing, persuasive

7. gist _____    b. concise, brief, compact

8. transient _____    c. essence, main point

9. terse _____    d. passing, short-lived, fleeting

10. cogent _____    e. sharp, keen, severe

**Today's Idiom**

*sleep on it*—postpone a decision while giving it some thought
     He didn't want to show his hand * immediately, so he agreed to *sleep on it* for a few more days.

ANSWERS ARE ON PAGE 237

If you've ever watched or played baseball, you know how important a base hit is to each batter. Before the game players spend as much time as possible taking their batting practice. During the game the batter concentrates on every pitch. In the same way, each day you are getting in your "batting practice," and the weekly review is your chance to build up your "batting average." Collect new words with the same concentration that baseball players collect base hits.

## REVIEW WORDS

| | | DEFINITIONS |
|---|---|---|
| _____ 1 | acute | a. show plainly, exhibit |
| _____ 2 | aversion | b. fleeting, passing, short-lived |
| _____ 3 | cogent | c. throw overboard, discard |
| _____ 4 | evince | d. forceful, convincing, persuasive |
| _____ 5 | gist | e. on the surface, slight |
| _____ 6 | hostile | f. a rough struggle |
| _____ 7 | inevitable | g. compact, brief, concise |
| _____ 8 | intrinsic | h. reprimand, reproach, criticize |
| _____ 9 | jettison | j. inborn, natural, essential |
| _____ 10 | lucrative | k. fashion |
| _____ 11 | paramount | l. main point, essence |
| _____ 12 | prevalent | m. severe, keen, sharp |
| _____ 13 | rebuke | n. lazy, indifferent |
| _____ 14 | remiss | o. negligent, careless |
| _____ 15 | superficial | p. unavoidable, certain, sure |
| _____ 16 | lethargic | r. opposition, strong dislike |
| _____ 17 | terse | s. foremost, supreme |
| _____ 18 | transient | t. general, common, prevailing |
| _____ 19 | tussle | u. angry, antagonistic |
| _____ 20 | vogue | v. profitable |

## IDIOMS

| | | |
|---|---|---|
| _____ 21 | to strike while the iron is hot | w. on a very rare occasion |
| _____ 22 | to split hairs | x. postpone a decision |
| _____ 23 | sleep on it | y. take action at the right moment |
| _____ 24 | once in a blue moon | z. to make a fine distinction |

Check your answers on page 237. Take that extra moment *now* to review and study the words you got wrong.

**WORDS FOR FURTHER STUDY**     **MEANINGS**

1. _____  _____

2. _____  _____

3. _____  _____

**New Words:**

| pinnacle | array | obscure | ardent | culminate |
|----------|-------|---------|--------|-----------|
| pin′ə kəl | ə rā′ | əb skūr′ | är′ dənt | kul′ mə nāt |

***A Musical World***   Music reached its *pinnacle* in the nineteenth century. Every leading nation produced its share of great composers. There was a bewildering *array* of national schools and musical styles as the once *obscure* musician came into his own. Music became a widespread and democratic art. The *ardent* music lover turned to Vienna as the music center at the beginning of the last century. However, Paris was not far behind, especially in the field of operatic music. As the century progressed, the Germans became paramount* in orchestral and symphonic music. The growth of German music can be said to have *culminated* with Ludwig van Beethoven.

**Sample Sentences:**   Take command of the new words in these sentences.

1. The President faced an imposing _____ of reporters.
2. The party will _____ with the award for the most original costume.
3. The _____ of fame and success is often a transient* stage.
4. He expressed his _____ love by writing poems.
5. The _____ artist waits for the inevitable* day of recognition.

**Definitions:**   Match-up time for new words and definitions.

6. pinnacle _____ a. passionate, eager
7. array _____ b. summit, peak, top, crown
8. obscure (adj.) _____ c. arrangement, system
9. ardent _____ d. unknown, lowly, unclear
10. culminate _____ e. reach the highest point

***Today's Idiom***   *to break the ice*—to make a beginning, to overcome stiffness between strangers

All after-dinner speakers *break the ice* by telling a story or joke at the start of their speeches.

ANSWERS ARE ON PAGE 237

131

**New Words:**  constrict   prodigy   bereft   falter   exultation
kən strikt'   prod' ə ji   bi reft'   fôl' tər   eg' zul tā shən

**A Giant Composer**   Beethoven was able to free music from the traditions* which had tended to *constrict* it. He was a child *prodigy* who held an important musical post at the age of 14. He was a successful concert pianist, but when his health began to fail he turned to composing. Even though *bereft* of hearing at the age of 49, he did not *falter* in his work. Some of his later compositions reflect his sadness with his physical condition, but they also evince* an *exultation* about man and life.

**Sample Sentences:**   Place the new words in these sentences.

1. The catastrophe* left him _____ of all his possessions.

2. When the hostile* forces were driven from the gates, the population was filled with _____.

3. It is imprudent* for a youngster to _____ her circle of friends so that there is no opportunity to meet new people.

4. There is universal * wonder when some _____ appears on the stage to perform at the age of 4 or 5.

5. Though he knew well the danger involved, the knight did not _____ as he entered the dragon's cave.

**Definitions:**   Your personal test follows through matching.

6. constrict   _____   a. triumphant joy
7. prodigy   _____   b. stumble, hesitate, waver
8. bereft   _____   c. deprived of
9. falter   _____   d. limit, bind, squeeze
10. exultation   _____   e. marvel, phenomenon

**Today's Idiom**   *loaded for bear*—to be well prepared
    When the enemy finally attacked the positions, the defenders were *loaded for bear.*

**ANSWERS ARE ON PAGE 237**

**New Words:**  vitriolic   invective   besmirch   voluminous   retrospect
vit′ ri ol′ ik   in vek′ tiv   bi smerch′   və lü′ mə nəs   ret′ rə spekt

**A Worthy Successor**  A successor to Beethoven was Johannes Brahms. Also a prodigy,* he was the object of *vitriolic* attacks by other composers because of the individuality of his work. They heaped *invective* upon him for the intensely emotional quality and Germanic style of his writings. However, it was impossible to *besmirch* his talents for long, and he was soon one of the most popular composers in Europe. He produced *voluminous* varieties of compositions. Today, in *retrospect*, his originality is appreciated, and he is placed among the top romantic composers.

**Sample Sentences:**   Complete the following sentences with the new words.

1. It is difficult to keep _____ out of our discussion about the enemy.

2. The anthropologist* came back with _____ material showing how life on this continent originated.

3. The candidate tried to _____ his opponent's record.

4. In the future we will, in _____, regard today's bizarre* behavior as quite ordinary.

5. The _____ language used by critics of the new play tended to obliterate* its good qualities.

**Definitions:**   Study the paragraph and sample sentences for the meanings.

6. vitriolic _____ a. insulting, abusive speech

7. invective _____ b. bulky, large

8. besmirch _____ c. soil, stain, dim the reputation

9. voluminous _____ d. biting, burning

10. retrospect _____ e. looking backward

**Today's Idiom**   *to bring down the house*—to cause great enthusiasm
    The ardent* Beatle fans could be counted on *to bring down the house* at every public performance.

**ANSWERS ARE ON PAGE 237**

133

**New Words:**

| egotist | humility | pungent | inveterate | adamant |
|---------|----------|---------|------------|---------|
| ē′ gə tist | hū mil′ ə ti | pun′ jənt | in vet′ ẽr it | ad′ ə mant |

**Gruff but Likeable**

In his private life Brahms was considered by his friends as an *egotist*. He had an extremely lofty opinion of himself and his talents. He was not noted for his *humility*. Along with this quality, Brahms was known for his *pungent* sense of humor. While his closest friends could accept his biting jokes, others found him difficult to warm up to. Brahms was an *inveterate* stay-at-home. Cambridge University conferred an honorary degree upon him, but he was *adamant* about staying at home and did not go to receive the honor. Despite the ardent* and romantic nature of his music, Brahms never found the right girl and remained single throughout his life.

**Sample Sentences:** Use the new words in these sentences.

1. Doctors agree that it is imperative* that _____ smokers give up that imprudent* habit.

2. The _____ odor of burning leaves marks the autumn season.

3. The umpire was _____ about his decision to call the runner out.

4. We all expect _____ from the actors and actresses who win the Academy Awards.

5. However, we are not surprised to find that the best performer is also an _____ about his ability.

**Definitions:** Make the new words yours through the match-ups.

6. egotist _____ a. humbleness, modesty, meekness

7. humility _____ b. a vain, conceited person

8. pungent _____ c. unyielding, inflexible

9. inveterate _____ d. sharply stimulating, biting

10. adamant _____ e. habitual, firmly established

**Today's Idiom**

*to pull one's weight*—to do a fair share of the work
Everyone in a pioneer family had to *pull his own weight*.

ANSWERS ARE ON PAGE 237

Another week to build your vocabulary. Words stand for "things." The more "things" you can recognize, the better able you are to deal with the complicated and changing world. New and unusual situations are more easily handled by those who can utilize the largest number of "things" we call words.

**REVIEW WORDS**

| | | |
|---|---|---|
| _____ | 1 | adamant |
| _____ | 2 | ardent |
| _____ | 3 | array |
| _____ | 4 | bereft |
| _____ | 5 | besmirch |
| _____ | 6 | constrict |
| _____ | 7 | culminate |
| _____ | 8 | egotist |
| _____ | 9 | exultation |
| _____ | 10 | falter |
| _____ | 11 | humility |
| _____ | 12 | invective |
| _____ | 13 | inveterate |
| _____ | 14 | obscure |
| _____ | 15 | pinnacle |
| _____ | 16 | prodigy |
| _____ | 17 | pungent |
| _____ | 18 | retrospect |
| _____ | 19 | vitriolic |
| _____ | 20 | voluminous |

**DEFINITIONS**

a. reach the highest point
b. inflexible, unyielding
c. triumphant joy
d. looking backward
e. peak, crown, summit
f. a conceited, vain person
g. bind, limit, squeeze
h. biting, burning
j. insulting, abusive speech
k. system, arrangement
l. modesty, meekness, humbleness
m. phenomenon, marvel
n. stain, soil, dim the reputation
o. sharply stimulating
p. deprived of
r. bulky, large
s. hesitate, waver, stumble
t. eager, passionate
u. firmly established, habitual
v. unclear, unknown, lowly

**IDIOMS**

| | | |
|---|---|---|
| _____ | 21 | to break the ice |
| _____ | 22 | to pull one's own weight |
| _____ | 23 | to bring down the house |
| _____ | 24 | loaded for bear |

w. to be well prepared
x. to cause great enthusiasm
y. to make a beginning
z. to do a fair share of the work

Check your answers on page 237. A word missed can now be made part of your vocabulary quite easily. Review the paragraph, sample sentence, definition, and then write your own sentence using the word.

**WORDS FOR FURTHER STUDY**     **MEANINGS**

1. _____ _____

2. _____ _____

3. _____ _____

**New Words:**   vulnerable   bedlam   cacophony   exploit   propinquity
vul′ nər ə bəl   bed′ ləm   kə kof′ ə ni   eks′ ploit   prō ping′ kwə ti

**A Dangerous Sport**   Racing car drivers are *vulnerable* to dangers that other sportsmen seldom face. Drivers agree that controlling a car at top speeds on a winding course is a singularly* awesome* experience. There is the *bedlam* caused by the roaring motors which move the car from a standing start to 100 miles an hour in eight seconds. One is shaken by the *cacophony* of the brakes, larger than the wheels and producing during the course of a 350 mile race enough heat to warm an eight-room house through a hard winter. The driver needs to be on the alert to *exploit* any mistake by an opponent, and he must be constantly aware of the *propinquity* of sudden death. All of this makes car racing one of the most demanding games of all.

*How was your recall today? Look back for that re-introduced word.*

**Sample Sentences:**   Insert the new words in the sentences.

1. Astronauts are alert to the _____ of sudden accidents.
2. The egotist* is _____ to slights and insults.
3. Electronic music is considered nothing more or less than _____ by many.
4. Advertisers spend large sums to _____ the lucrative* teen-age market.
5. The winning team's dressing room was a scene of _____.

**Definitions:**   Match your new words to their definitions.

6. vulnerable _____  a. discord, harsh sound, dissonance
7. bedlam _____  b. open to attack, susceptible
8. cacophony _____  c. profit by, utilize
9. exploit (v.) _____  d. nearness in time or place
10. propinquity _____  e. confusion, uproar

**Today's Idiom**   *a white elephant*—a costly and useless possession
When he discovered the 30-volume encyclopedia, dated 1895, in his attic, he knew he had *a white elephant* on his hands.

ANSWERS ARE ON PAGE 237

**New Words:**

| disgruntled | infallible | panacea | eradicate | impede |
|---|---|---|---|---|
| dis grun' təld | in fal' ə bəl | pan' ə sē' ə | i rad' i kāt | im pēd' |

**The Mystery of Creativity**

In order to create, it is said that a man must be *disgruntled*. The creative individual is usually one who is dissatisfied with things as they are; he wants to bring something new into the world—to make it a different place. There is no *infallible* way to identify a potentially creative person. The speed-up in the sciences has forced schools and industry to seek a *panacea* for the shortages that they face. The need to discover and develop the creative person has been the source of much study. The paramount* objectives of the studies are to *eradicate* anything which will *impede* the discovery of creative talent and to exploit* this talent to the limit.

**Sample Sentences:** Place the new words in these sentences.

1. It is the prevalent* mood for youngsters to be _____ with the world situation.

2. Many people hoped that the United Nations would be the _____ for the problems of our time.

3. The criminal tried to _____ all of the witnesses to the bizarre* murder.

4. An _____ sign of spring is the blooming of the crocus.

5. Nothing could _____ the bigot* from his vitriolic* verbal attack.

**Definitions:** Match the new words with their definitions.

6. disgruntled _____ a. exempt from error, right

7. infallible _____ b. unhappy, displeased

8. panacea _____ c. wipe out

9. eradicate _____ d. cure-all

10. impede _____ e. interfere, block, hinder

**Today's Idiom**

*lock, stock, and barrel*—entirely, completely
    The company moved its operations to another state *lock, stock, and barrel.*

ANSWERS ARE ON PAGE 237

**New Words:**
| sedate | equanimity | compatible | serenity | revere |
|--------|-----------|------------|----------|--------|
| si dāte′ | ē′ kwə nim′ ə ti | kəm pat′ ə bəl | sə ren′ ə ti | ri vēr′ |

**The Dutch**    The first impression one gets of Holland is that it is a calm, *sedate* and simple land. The slow rhythm of life is even seen in the barges on the canals and the bicycles on the roads. One gradually discovers this *equanimity* of daily existence is not in accord with the intrinsic* nature of the Dutch. These people are moved by strong feelings that are not *compatible* with the *serenity* of the world around them. There is a conflict between the rigid, traditional * social rules and the desire for liberty and independence, both of which the Dutch *revere*.

**Sample Sentences:**    Pay attention to the fine differences in meaning.

1. There is something absurd * about a well-dressed, _____ man throwing snowballs.

2. The _____ of the countryside was shattered by the explosion.

3. The speaker lost his _____ and began to use invective* when the audience started to laugh.

4. The boy and girl discovered they had many _____ interests.

5. There are not many people in this world whom one can _____.

**Definitions:**    Match the new words with their definitions.

6. sedate _____    a. peaceful repose

7. equanimity _____    b. quiet, still, undisturbed, sober

8. compatible _____    c. evenness of mind, composure

9. serenity _____    d. honor, respect, admire

10. revere _____    e. harmonious, well-matched

**Today's Idiom**    *a feather in one's cap*—something to be proud of.
    If she could get the movie star's autograph, she knew it would be *a feather in her cap*.

**ANSWERS ARE ON PAGE 237**

**New Words:**

| irrational | avarice | insatiable | nadir | moribund |
|---|---|---|---|---|
| i rash′ ən əl | av′ ə ris | in sā′ shə bəl | nā′ dər | môr′ ə bund |

**Tulip Fever**

The tulip reached Holland in 1593 and was, at first, looked upon as a curiosity. There soon developed an *irrational* demand for new species. Specimens were sold at awesomely* high prices. In their *avarice*, speculators bought and sold the same tulip ten times in one day. The entire Dutch population suffered from the craze. There was an *insatiable* desire for each new color or shape. At one point a man purchased a house for three bulbs! Before long the inevitable* crash came and the demand for bulbs quickly reached its *nadir*. A $1,500 bulb could be bought for $1.50. With the *moribund* tulip market came financial disaster to thousands of people.

**Sample Sentences:** Fill in the blank spaces with the new words.

1. Who is not vulnerable* to some measure of _____?

2. The American consumer appears to have an _____ need for new products.

3. He looked upon the last-place finish of his team with equanimity;* from this _____ the only place to go was up.

4. We ought to expect some _____ behavior from a senile* person.

5. With the expansion of the supermarket, the small, local grocery store is in a _____ state.

**Definitions:** Match the new words with their definitions.

6. irrational _____    a. lowest point

7. avarice _____    b. dying, at the point of death

8. insatiable _____    c. unreasonable, absurd

9. nadir _____    d. greed, passion for riches

10. moribund _____    e. cannot be satisfied

**Today's Idiom**

*out on a limb*—in a dangerous or exposed position
    He went *out on a limb* and predicted he would win the election by a wide margin.

ANSWERS ARE ON PAGE 237

You have been learning how to use many new words by seeing them in a natural situation. Each day's story is the setting in which you meet the new words. The weekly review enables you to isolate the word and its many meanings. In this way you can reinforce your understanding and word power. At this point you have learned almost 600 words. Keep up the good work.

**REVIEW WORDS**

_____ 1 avarice
_____ 2 bedlam
_____ 3 cacophony
_____ 4 compatible
_____ 5 disgruntled
_____ 6 equanimity
_____ 7 eradicate
_____ 8 exploit
_____ 9 impede
_____ 10 infallible
_____ 11 insatiable
_____ 12 irrational
_____ 13 moribund
_____ 14 nadir
_____ 15 panacea
_____ 16 propinquity
_____ 17 revere
_____ 18 sedate
_____ 19 serenity
_____ 20 vulnerable

**DEFINITIONS**

a. susceptible, open to attack
b. exempt from error, right
c. well-matched, harmonious
d. lowest point
e. at the point of death, dying
f. peaceful repose
g. cure-all
h. uproar, confusion
j. harsh sound, discord, dissonance
k. wipe out
l. sober, still, quiet, undisturbed
m. nearness in time and place
n. displeased, unhappy
o. absurd, unreasonable
p. cannot be satisfied
r. utilize, profit by
s. composure, evenness of mind
t. passion for riches, greed
u. hinder, interfere, block
v. admire, respect, honor

**IDIOMS**

_____ 21 lock, stock, and barrel
_____ 22 out on a limb
_____ 23 a feather in one's cap
_____ 24 a white elephant

w. a costly and useless possession

x. entirely, completely

y. in a dangerous or exposed position

z. something to be proud of

The answers can be found on page 237. Consistent study and use of difficult words will work quickly to bring them into your daily vocabulary.

**WORDS FOR FURTHER STUDY** | **MEANINGS**

1. _____  _____

2. _____  _____

3. _____  _____

**New Words:**

| lithe | obese | adherent | bliss | pathetic |
|-------|-------|----------|-------|----------|
| līth | ō bes' | ad hēr' ənt | blis | pə thet' ik |

**A Sport for Everyone**

Of the many highly popular sports in the United States, football must be rated around the top. This sport allows the speedy and *lithe* athlete to join with the slower and *obese* one in a team effort. The skills and strengths of many men are welded together so that one team may work as a unit to gain mastery over its opponent. The knowledgeable *adherent* of a team can follow action covering many parts of the playing field at the same time. He is in a state of *bliss* when his team executes a movement to perfection. However, there is no one more *pathetic* than the same fan when the opposition functions to equal perfection.

**Sample Sentences:** Use the new words in these sentences.

1. The disgruntled * _____ switched his loyalty to the opposition party.

2. It was a pleasure to watch the _____ body of the ballet dancer as she performed the most difficult steps.

3. There is something _____ about a great athlete who continues to compete long after he has been bereft* of his talents.

4. His insatiable* hunger for sweets soon made him _____.

5. Oh, what _____ could be seen in the eyes of the ardent* couple as they announced their engagement!

**Definitions:** Match the new words with their definitions.

6. lithe _____ a. backer, supporter

7. obese _____ b. very fat

8. adherent _____ c. sad, pitiful, distressing

9. bliss _____ d. graceful

10. pathetic _____ e. happiness, pleasure

**Today's Idiom**

*on the spur of the moment*—on impulse, without thinking
*On the spur of the moment* he turned thumbs down* on the new job.

ANSWERS ARE ON PAGE 238

| New Words: | exhort | apathy | fracas | inebriated | adversary |
|---|---|---|---|---|---|
| | eg zôrt′ | ap′ ə thi | frā kəs | in ē bri ā ted | ad′ vər ser′ i |

**Rah! Rah! Rah!**   The spectators at a football game play more than a superficial * role. A spirited cheer from the stands often gives the player on the field a reason to try even harder. Cheer leaders *exhort* the fans, who may be in a state of *apathy* because their team is losing, to spur on the team. In particularly close games between rivals of long standing, feelings begin to run high, and from time to time a *fracas* may break out in the stands. While the teams compete below, the fan who is a bit *inebriated* may seek out a personal *adversary*. On the whole the enthusiasm of the spectators is usually constricted * to cheering and shouting for their favorite teams.

**Sample Sentences:**   Complete the sentences with the new words.

1. The feeling of _____ was so prevalent* during the election campaign that the candidates hardly bothered to make speeches.

2. Doctors _____ obese* individuals to go on diets.

3. He was usually sedate,* but when _____ he became hostile.*

4. The _____ started when he besmirched * my good name.

5. My _____ became disgruntled * because my arguments were so cogent.*

**Definitions:**   Match the new words with their definitions.

6. exhort   _____   a. opponent, enemy, foe

7. apathy   _____   b. drunk, intoxicated

8. fracas   _____   c. lack of interest, unconcern

9. inebriated   _____   d. urge strongly, advise

10. adversary   _____   e. noisy fight, brawl

**Today's Idiom**   *a fly in the ointment*—some small thing that spoils or lessens the enjoyment

He was offered a lucrative* position with the firm, but *the fly in the ointment* was that he would have to work on Saturday and Sunday.

ANSWERS ARE ON PAGE 238

**New Words:**

| indolent | gusto | garrulous | banal | platitude |
|----------|-------|-----------|-------|-----------|
| in' də lənt | gus' tō | gar' ə les | bā' nəl | plat' ə tüd |

**The 23-Inch Football Field**

The football fan who cannot attend a contest in person may watch any number of games on television. This has the great advantage of permitting an *indolent* fan to sit in the comfort of his living room and watch two teams play in the most inclement* weather. However, some of the spirit, the *gusto*, is missing when one watches a game on a small screen away from the actual scene of the contest. Also, the viewer is constantly exposed to a *garrulous* group of announcers who continue to chatter in an endless way throughout the afternoon. Should the game be a dull one, the announcers discuss the most *banal* bits of information. Even in the poorest game there is constant chatter involving one *platitude* after another about the laudable* performances of each and every player.

**Sample Sentences:** Insert the new words in the sentences.

1. He began to eat the food served at the sumptuous feast with _____.

2. Men believe that women's conversation is filled with _____ comments concerning clothing or food.

3. During the most sultry* days of summer, one hears the _____ asked, "Is it hot enough for you?"

4. The _____ person goes to great lengths to eschew* work.

5. She was usually so _____, we considered anything under a five minute speech as a cryptic* remark.

**Definitions:** Match the new words with their definitions.

6. indolent _____ a. enthusiasm, enjoyment, zest

7. gusto _____ b. commonplace or trite saying

8. garrulous _____ c. lazy

9. banal _____ d. talkative, wordy

10. platitude _____ e. trivial, meaningless from overuse

**Today's Idiom**

*to take French leave*—to go away without permission
   The star player was fined $100 when *he took French leave* from the training camp.

ANSWERS ARE ON PAGE 238

**New Words:**  pique   dilettante   atypical   nondescript   wane
pēk   dil′ ə tan′ ti   ā tip′ ə kəl   non′ də skript   wān

**What's On?**   One day each week is set aside for college football, and another for the professional brand. Most fans enjoy both varieties. Nothing can put an avid * viewer into a *pique* more quickly than missing an important contest. It is the *dilettante* who eschews* the amateur variety and watches only the professional games. The *atypical* fan will watch only his home team play; however, enthusiasts will continue to view the most *nondescript* contests involving teams which have no connection with their own town or school. Some intrepid * fans have been known to watch high school games when that was all that was offered. Public interest in football grows each year, while interest in other sports may be on the *wane*.

**Sample Sentences:**   Complete these sentences with the new words.

1. The _____ will scoff * at those who admit that they know very little about modern art.

2. It is the _____ fisherman who does not embellish* the story about the fish that got away.

3. The detective had little to go on because of the _____ nature of the criminal.

4. Many virulent* diseases or now on the _____.

5. He showed his _____ by slamming the door.

**Definitions:**   Match the new words with their definitions.

6. pique   _____   a. decrease, decline

7. dilettante   _____   b. fit of resentment

8. atypical   _____   c. one who has great interest, but little knowledge

9. nondescript   _____   d. non-conforming

10. wane (n.)   _____   e. undistinguished, difficult to describe

**Today's Idiom**   *in the arms of Morpheus*—asleep
The day's activities were so enervating,* he was soon *in the arms of Morpheus*.

**ANSWERS ARE ON PAGE 238**

144

The regular, consistent study of these daily stories is the salient* clue to your success. Sporadic* study tends to disrupt the learning process. Don't give in to the temptation to put your work aside and then rush to "catch up."

## REVIEW WORDS

_____ 1 adherent
_____ 2 adversary
_____ 3 apathy
_____ 4 atypical
_____ 5 banal
_____ 6 bliss
_____ 7 dilettante
_____ 8 exhort
_____ 9 fracas
_____ 10 garrulous
_____ 11 gusto
_____ 12 indolent
_____ 13 inebriated
_____ 14 lithe
_____ 15 nondescript
_____ 16 obese
_____ 17 pathetic
_____ 18 pique
_____ 19 platitude
_____ 20 wane

## DEFINITIONS

a. urge strongly, advise
b. enemy, foe, opponent
c. graceful
d. pitiful, sad, distressing
e. lazy
f. meaningless from overuse, trivial
g. fit of resentment
h. difficult to describe, undistinguished
j. unconcern, lack of interest
k. intoxicated, drunk
l. very fat
m. pleasure, happiness
n. zest, enjoyment, enthusiasm
o. trite saying
p. one with little knowledge and great interest
r. non-conforming
s. brawl, noisy fight
t. supporter, backer
u. wordy, talkative
v. decline, decrease

## IDIOMS

_____ 21 on the spur of the moment

_____ 22 in the arms of Morpheus

_____ 23 to take French leave

_____ 24 a fly in the ointment

w. asleep

x. something that spoils or lessens the enjoyment

y. to go away without permission

z. without thinking, on impulse

Check your answers on page 238. Quick re-inforcement of words you do not yet know will help you retain them. Right now . . . put down the words and meanings. Then, write a sentence using the word correctly.

## WORDS FOR FURTHER STUDY        MEANINGS

1. _____  _____

2. _____  _____

3. _____  _____

**New Words:**

| extinct | idyllic | galvanize | encumbrance | gaudy |
|---------|---------|-----------|-------------|-------|
| eks tingkt′ | i dil′ ik | gal′ və nīz | en kum′ brəns | gôd′ i |

**In Days Gone By**

The man who best described the now *extinct* life aboard a steamer on the Mississippi River is Mark Twain. Having actually worked aboard the river boats, his writing captures the tranquil * or turbulent* events of those days. In his book about life on the Mississippi, Twain recalls the *idyllic* times when man was not in such a great rush to get from one place to another. One chapter deals with the races conducted between the swiftest of the boats. When a race was set, the excitement would *galvanize* activity along the river. Politics and the weather were forgotten, and people talked with gusto* only of the coming race. The two steamers "stripped" and got ready; every *encumbrance* that might slow the passage was removed. Captains went to extremes to lighten their boats. Twain writes of one captain who scraped the paint from the *gaudy* figure which hung between the chimneys of his steamer.

**Sample Sentences:** Insert the new words in these sentences.

1. Today, the trend * is to more and more _____ dress.

2. It is amazing how lithe* football players can be, despite the _____ of the safety features of their uniforms.

3. The dinosaur is an _____ specie.

4. City dwellers often yearn for the _____ life in the country.

5. A dictator will use any pretext* to _____ his people into aggressive actions.

**Definitions:** Match the new words with their definitions.

6. extinct _____    a. burden, handicap, load

7. idyllic _____    b. showy, flashy

8. galvanize _____    c. simple, peaceful

9. encum-
   brance _____    d. excite or arouse to activity

10. gaudy _____    e. no longer existing

**Today's Idiom**

*forty winks*—a short nap

During the night before the big test, he studied continuously, catching *forty winks* now and then.

ANSWERS ARE ON PAGE 238

**New Words:**

| condescend | candor | mortify | jocose | malign |
|---|---|---|---|---|
| kon' di send' | kan' dər | môr' tə fī | jō kōs' | mə līn' |

**The John J. Roe**   Mark Twain's boat was so slow no other steamer would *condescend* to race with it. With the utmost *candor*, Twain comments that his boat moved at such a pathetic* pace, they used to forget in what year it was they left port. Nothing would *mortify* Twain more than the fact that ferry-boats, waiting to cross the river, would lose valuable trips because their passengers grew senile* and died waiting for his boat, the John J. Roe, to pass. Mark Twain wrote in a *jocose* manner about the races his steamer had with islands and rafts. With quiet humor he continued to *malign* the river-boat, but his book is replete* with love for this sort of life.

**Sample Sentences:**   Insert the new words in these sentences.

1. He had such disdain* for us, he would not _____ to speak before our group.

2. It is most common to _____ the wealthy for their avarice.*

3. It is difficult to be _____ in the presence of so many doleful* people.

4. When we cannot speak with _____, we utilize euphemisms.*

5. Good sportsmanship requires that one not _____ a defeated adversary.*

**Definitions:**   Match the new words with their definitions.

6. condescend _____     a. humorous, merry

7. candor _____     b. abuse, slander

8. mortify _____     c. stoop, lower oneself

9. jocose _____     d. frankness, honesty

10. malign _____     e. embarrass, humiliate

**Today's Idiom**   *from pillar to post*—from one place to another
   The company was so large and spread out, he was sent *from pillar to post* before he found the proper official.

ANSWERS ARE ON PAGE 238

**New Words:**

| omnipotent | zenith | fledgling | peremptory | precedent |
|---|---|---|---|---|
| om nip′ ə tənt | zē′ nith | flej′ ling | pĕr emp′ tĕr i | pres′ ə dənt |

**The River-Boat Pilot**

The river-boat pilot was a man considered *omnipotent* by all. Mark Twain once held that high position. He writes that he felt at the *zenith* of his life at that time. Starting out as a *fledgling* pilot's apprentice, he could not abjure* dreams of the time he would become, "the only unfettered and entirely independent human being that lived in the earth." Kings, parliaments, and newspaper editors, Twain comments, are hampered and restricted. The river pilot issued *peremptory* commands as absolute monarch. The captain was powerless to interfere. Even though the pilot was much younger than the captain, and the steamer seemed to be in imminent* danger, the older man was helpless. The captain had to behave impeccably,* for any criticism of the pilot would establish a pernicious* *precedent* that would have undermined the pilot's limitless authority.

**Sample Sentences:** Insert the new words in these sentences.

1. Under the aegis* of an adroit* master, he reached the _____ of his career.

2. We would scoff * at anyone calling himself _____.

3. There is no _____ for voting when there is no quorum.*

4. The _____ poet lived a frugal * life.

5. No one had the temerity* to disobey the officer's _____ order.

**Definitions:** Match the new words with their definitions.

6. omnipotent _____    a. summit, top, prime

7. zenith _____    b. little known, newly developed

8. fledgling _____    c. absolute, compulsory, binding

9. peremptory _____    d. custom, model

10. precedent _____    e. almighty, unlimited power or authority

**Today's Idiom**

*in the lap of the gods*—out of one's own hands

I handed in my application for the job, and now it is *in the lap of the gods.*

ANSWERS ARE ON PAGE 238

148

**New Words:**

| wheedle | rustic | jubilant | decorum | charlatan |
|---------|--------|----------|---------|-----------|
| hwē′ əl | rus′ tik | jü′ bə lənt | di kō′ rəm | shar′ lə tən |

**The Double-Cross**

Many incidents that took place aboard his ship are re-told by Twain. One has to do with a wealthy cattle man who was approached by three gamblers. The cattle farmer had let it be known that he had a great deal of money, and the gamblers were trying to *wheedle* him into a card game. He protested that he knew nothing about cards. His *rustic* appearance confirmed that fact. On the last night before landing the three gamblers got him drunk. When the first hand was dealt, a *jubilant* expression came over his face. The betting became furious. All of the proper *decorum* was put aside, and ten thousand dollars soon lay on the table. With the last wager one of the gamblers showed a hand of four kings. His partner was to have dealt the sucker a hand of four queens. At this point the victim, the *charlatan,* removed the veneer* of respectability, and showed a hand of four aces! One of the three professional gamblers was a clandestine* confederate of the "rich cattle farmer." They had been planning this duplicity* for many weeks.

**Sample Sentences:** Insert the new words in these sentences.

1. The child tried to _____ from her mother the place where the cookies had been cached.*

2. They could discern* that the faith-healer was a _____.

3. The _____ life is supposed to be a tranquil* one.

4. Repress* your uncouth* manners and act with _____ at the party.

5. We were _____ when our indolent* cousin got a job.

**Definitions:** Match the new words with their definitions.

6. wheedle _____    a. coax, persuade, cajole*

7. rustic _____    b. joyful, in high spirits

8. jubilant _____    c. politeness, correct behavior

9. decorum _____    d. pretender, fraud

10. charlatan _____    e. countrified, unpolished

**Today's Idiom**

*Achilles heel*—weak spot
    He wanted to lead an ascetic* life, but his obsession with liquor was his *Achilles* heel.

ANSWERS ARE ON PAGE 238

Because you are learning these new words in context, they will stay with you. It is the natural method for seeing new words. Your ability to master words as they appear in normal situations should carry over to your learning many other words as you read.

| REVIEW WORDS | DEFINITIONS |
|---|---|
| _____ 1 candor | a. arouse or excite to activity |
| _____ 2 charlatan | b. humiliate, embarrass |
| _____ 3 condescend | c. little known, newly developed |
| _____ 4 decorum | d. in high spirits, joyful |
| _____ 5 encumbrance | e. peaceful, simple |
| _____ 6 extinct | f. honesty, frankness |
| _____ 7 fledgling | g. unpolished, countrified |
| _____ 8 galvanize | h. top, prime, summit |
| _____ 9 gaudy | j. load, handicap, burden |
| _____ 10 idyllic | k. merry, humorous |
| _____ 11 jocose | l. correct behavior, politeness |
| _____ 12 jubilant | m. unlimited power or authority, almighty |
| _____ 13 malign | n. no longer existing |
| _____ 14 mortify | o. lower oneself, stoop |
| _____ 15 omnipotent | p. persuade, coax, cajole* |
| _____ 16 peremptory | r. binding, compulsory, absolute |
| _____ 17 precedent | s. showy, flashy |
| _____ 18 rustic | t. slander, abuse |
| _____ 19 wheedle | u. fraud, pretender |
| _____ 20 zenith | v. custom, model |

**IDIOMS**

| | |
|---|---|
| _____ 21 Achilles heel | w. a short nap |
| _____ 22 forty winks | x. weak spot |
| _____ 23 in the lap of the gods | y. from one place to another |
| _____ 24 from pillar to post | z. out of one's own hands |

Check your answers on page 238. Go right to it. Learn the words you have missed. Make them as much a part of your vocabulary as the other words you knew correctly.

**WORDS FOR FURTHER STUDY** — **MEANINGS**

1. _____ _____
2. _____ _____
3. _____ _____

**New Words:**

| heresy | prudent | ostensible | fervid | spurious |
|--------|---------|------------|--------|----------|
| her′ ə si | prü′ dənt | os ten′ sə bəl | fir′ vid | spyoor′ i əs |

**Choose Sagely***   Today, the paramount* influence in the forming of public opinion is propaganda. It is not a *heresy* to our democratic beliefs to state that pressure groups play an important part in our lives. Propaganda makes one vulnerable* to the influences of others. The *prudent* person will choose between cogent* and specious* propaganda efforts. While propaganda has the *ostensible* purpose of informing the public, the most *fervid* propagandists use methods that must be examined by the thoughtful citizen. The ability to distinguish the *spurious* from the true facts requires more than a perfunctory* examination of prevalent* propaganda efforts.

**Sample Sentences:**   Use care. The words have many meanings.

1. His _____ appeal for action threw his adherents* into a frenzy*.

2. He accused the leader of the opposition of political _____, and the mob was exhorted * to burn his effigy*.

3. In the bedlam* that followed it was not _____ to appear too apathetic*.

4. While the _____ enemy was the opposition leader, the main purpose of this rash* behavior was the eradication* of all opponents.

5. In the conflagration* that followed, no one questioned whether the original charge had been _____.

**Definitions:**   Study the fine differences. Be sure how to use them.

6. heresy _____    a. intense, enthusiastic, passionate

7. prudent _____    b. false, counterfeit, specious*

8. ostensible _____    c. unbelief, dissent, lack of faith

9. fervid _____    d. wise, cautious

10. spurious _____    e. outward, pretended, seeming

**Today's Idiom**   *cold shoulder*—to disregard or ignore

    She was so piqued * at his uncouth* behavior, she gave him the *cold shoulder* for over a week.

**ANSWERS ARE ON PAGE 238**

**New Words:**

| propagate | anomaly | innocuous | surfeit | milieu |
|---|---|---|---|---|
| prop′ ə gāt | ə nom′ ə li | i nok′ ū əs | ser′ fit | mē lyœ′ |

**A Free Society**  In a free society it is intrinsic* that individuals and groups have the inherent* right to *propagate* ideas and try to win converts. We do not look upon an idea different from ours as an *anomaly* which should be precluded*. Nor do we premit only *innocuous* or congenial* beliefs and forbid those that we believe are dubious* or spurious*. In a country of competing pressures we are accosted* by a *surfeit* of propaganda that tends to overwhelm us. Thus, we live in a *milieu* of ubiquitous* bombardment from countless, and often unrecognized, propagandists.

**Sample Sentences:**  Insert the new words in these sentences.

1. I must inveigh* against your attempt to _____ the belief that your political system will result in a panacea* for all problems.

2. It is incongruous* to find an abstemious* person in a _____ of avarice* and affluence*.

3. Siamese twins are considered a birth _____.

4. There appears to be no such thing as an _____ heresy*.

5. When can we expect a respite* from the _____ of TV commercials?

**Definitions:**  Match the new words with their definitions.

6. propagate _____ a. excess, superabundance

7. anomaly _____ b. environment, setting

8. innocuous _____ c. irregularity, abnormality

9. surfeit _____ d. produce, multiply, spread

10. milieu _____ e. harmless, mild, innocent

**Today's Idiom**  *without rhyme or reason*—making no sense
*Without rhyme or reason* the pennant-winning baseball team decided to jettison* its manager.

ANSWERS ARE ON PAGE 238

**New Words:**  strident   concomitant   lassitude   deleterious   efficacy
strī′ dənt   kon kom′ ə tənt   las′ ə tüd   del′ ə tir′ ē əs   ef′ ə ka si

**Who Listens?**   As the quantity of propaganda becomes greater, ideas are presented in more *strident* tones in order to overcome the increased competition. Those who are the targets of the propaganda find it more difficult to discern* between or analyze the new and expanded pressures. The *concomitant* situation which develops with the stepped-up propaganda is one in which the individual retreats into a state of *lassitude*. He has an aversion* to all attempts to influence him. So we can see the intrinsic* weakness inherent* in an increased level of propaganda. It has the *deleterious* result of reducing its *efficacy* upon the individuals or groups who were its objective.

**Sample Sentences:**   Insert the new words in these sentences.

1. There are many _____ dangers to obesity.*

2. Her _____ voice added to the bedlam.*

3. After the frenzy* which accompanied the burning of the effigy,* they were all acutely* aware of a feeling of _____.

4. The gist* of the report was that smoking will have a _____ effect on health.

5. The _____ of new drugs cannot be determined without a plethora* of evidence.

**Definitions:**   Match the new words with their definitions.

6. strident _____   a. power to produce an effect

7. concomitant _____   b. bad, harmful

8. lassitude _____   c. accompanying, attending

9. deleterious _____   d. weariness, fatigue

10. efficacy _____   e. shrill, harsh, rough

**Today's Idiom**   *swan song*—final or last (swans are said to sing before they die)

   The ex-champion said that if he lost this fight it would be his *swan song*.

ANSWERS ARE ON PAGE 238

**New Words:**

| dissent | ferment | attenuated | arbiter | incumbent |
|---------|---------|------------|---------|-----------|
| di sent' | fər ment' | ə ten' ū ā tid | ar' bə tər | in kum' bənt |

**The People Decide**

The place of propaganda in a milieu* which is not free differs from its place in an open society. In a dictatorship there is no competing propaganda. Those who *dissent* from the official line may do so only in a clandestine* manner. Where there is no open *ferment* of ideas, the possibility of discerning* the true from the spurious* is *attenuated*. In a democracy, the inevitable* *arbiter* of what propaganda is to be permitted is the people. It is *incumbent* upon each citizen to choose between competing propagandas while remaining cognizant* of the value for a democracy in the existence of all points of view.

**Sample Sentences:** Insert the new words in these sentences.

1. It is _____ on us to be zealous* in combatting the deleterious* effects of drugs.

2. With each generation it becomes the vogue* for the youth to be in a state of _____.

3. The gist* of his ominous* suggestion was that we _____ from the majority opinion.

4. The strength of his appeal was _____ by the flamboyant* embellishments* for which many had a strong aversion.*

5. The Supreme Court is our ultimate* _____ of legality.

**Definitions:** Always be cognizant* of the fact that words are used in the paragraphs and sentences with only one meaning. They often have many others. Look up the word *incumbent* for a good example.

6. dissent (v.) _____    a. a duty, morally required

7. ferment _____    b. weakened, thinned, decreased

8. attenuated _____    c. differ, disagree, protest

9. arbiter _____    d. uproar, agitation, turmoil

10. incumbent (adj.) _____    e. judge

**Today's Idiom**

*to get the sack*—to be discharged or fired
    Despite the fact that he was so obsequious* toward the boss, *he got the sack* because he was lethargic* about doing his job.

ANSWERS ARE ON PAGE 238

154

Once more it is time to review this week's words. Always keep in mind that the use of the word, its context, determines its meaning. Used as a noun, a word has a different meaning than when it is used as an adjective or a verb. First, master the words as they appear in the daily stories. Next, look up other meanings in your dictionary. Try writing sentences with the additional meanings.

## REVIEW WORDS

| | | |
|---|---|---|
| _____ 1 | anomaly | |
| _____ 2 | arbiter | |
| _____ 3 | attenuated | |
| _____ 4 | concomitant | |
| _____ 5 | deleterious | |
| _____ 6 | dissent | |
| _____ 7 | efficacy | |
| _____ 8 | ferment | |
| _____ 9 | fervid | |
| _____ 10 | heresy | |
| _____ 11 | incumbent | |
| _____ 12 | innocuous | |
| _____ 13 | lassitude | |
| _____ 14 | milieu | |
| _____ 15 | ostensible | |
| _____ 16 | propagate | |
| _____ 17 | prudent | |
| _____ 18 | spurious | |
| _____ 19 | strident | |
| _____ 20 | surfeit | |

## DEFINITIONS

a. agitation, turmoil, uproar
b. attending, accompanying
c. abnormality, irregularity
d. cautious, wise
e. protest, differ, disagree
f. rough, harsh, shrill
g. multiply, spread, produce
h. lack of faith, dissent, unbelief
j. morally required, a duty
k. power to produce an effect
l. setting, environment
m. counterfeit, false, specious*
n. judge
o. harmful, bad
p. superabundance, excess
r. enthusiastic, passionate, intense
s. decreased, weakened, thinned
t. mild, innocent, harmless
u. fatigue, weariness
v. seeming, pretended, outward

## IDIOMS

| | | |
|---|---|---|
| _____ 21 | cold shoulder | |
| _____ 22 | swan song | |
| _____ 23 | to get the sack | |
| _____ 24 | without rhyme or reason | |

w. to be discharged or fired
x. making no sense
y. final or last
z. to disregard or ignore

Check your answers on page 238. Get to work learning the words that gave you trouble.

**WORDS FOR FURTHER STUDY**  **MEANINGS**

1. _____  _____

2. _____  _____

3. _____  _____

**New Words:**  profound    alleviate    prodigious    expedite    celerity
prə found′    ə lē′ vi āt    prə dij′ əs    eks′ pə dīt    sə ler′ ə ti

**The Library Machine**   As automation permeates\* many new ideas of life, its effect upon us becomes concomitantly\* more *profound*. Information processing and communications machines are finding their way into libraries. Here they *alleviate* the burden of storing and bringing out to the reader the accumulation of information which is becoming more *prodigious* in this era of specialization and threating to inundate\* our already encumbered\* library system. As a way to *expedite* the selection of pertinent\* information for the reader, the machine scans 5,000 words per minute. It is the *celerity* of machine reading that makes automation in the library so valuable.

**Sample Sentences:**   Insert your new words below.

1. We hoped that the arbiter\* would _____ the solution to the fracas\* which had been so elusive\* for a long time.

2. He accepted the lucrative\* position with _____.

3. It is easy to construe\* a superficial\* remark to be a _____ one.

4. If we cannot _____ the harmful effects entirely, at least we can attenuate\* them.

5. The enemy made a _____ effort to repress\* the uprising.

**Definitions:**   Match the new words with their definitions.

6. profound   _____   a. carry out promptly
7. alleviate   _____   b. speed, rapidity
8. prodigious   _____   c. make easier, lighten
9. expedite   _____   d. deep thought, intense
10. celerity   _____   e. extraordinary, enormous

**Today's Idiom**   *ivory tower*—isolated from life; not in touch with life's problems
   Many artists have been said to be living in an *ivory tower*.

**ANSWERS ARE ON PAGE 238**

**New Words:**

| usurp | paltry | condone | trivial | bizarre |
|-------|--------|---------|---------|---------|
| ū zirp′ | pôl′ tri | kən dōn′ | triv′ i əl | bə zär′ |

**The Language Machine**

Those who see the spread of automated machines as a nefarious* force out to *usurp* the proper functions of mankind have corroboration* for their belief in the language machine. The *paltry* handful of expert translators with a profound * knowledge of many foreign languages leaves a wide gap in our sources of vital information. With important technological and scientific work being done abroad, it is difficult to *condone* the situation. A machine may be set to treat a foreign language as a coded message which it can analyze and put into English. Perhaps it will not do an impeccable* job, but it will permit the translation of even the most *trivial* foreign reports and writings. As *bizarre* as it might seem, machines are taking over as translators in ever increasing numbers.

*Don't look back at the "new words." Did you spot the re-introduced word?*

**Sample Sentences:** (note the similarity of *trivial* and *paltry*)

1. Most of us scoff * at and belittle* _____ behavior.

2. They exacerbate* a _____ difference of opinion into a prodigious* conflict.

3. It is during a period of ferment* that a dictator can _____ power.

4. Do you expect me to _____ that reprehensible* act with such celerity? *

5. The most _____ defects may have a deleterious* effect upon the efficacy* of that new process.

**Definitions:** Match the new words with their definitions.

6. usurp _____ a. petty, worthless

7. paltry _____ b. excuse, pardon

8. condone _____ c. seize, annex, grab

9. trivial _____ d. of little importance, insignificant

10. bizarre _____ e. fantastic, odd

**Today's Idiom**

*to feather one's nest*—to enrich oneself on the sly or at every opportunity

He played up to his senile* aunt in the hope of *feathering his nest* when she made out her will.

ANSWERS ARE ON PAGE 238

**New Words:**  menial  venerable  extraneous  ambiguous  succinct
mē′ ni əl  ven′ ẽr ə b'l  iks trā ni əs  am big′ ū əs  sək singkt′

**A Predicting Machine**

While a machine may usurp* many *menial* tasks—typing of letters, making out paychecks—it can also work in less mundane* ways. One such example was the use of a computer to predict the results of a football game. All the information about the two teams: speed of the backs, weight of the linemen, past performances of the teams, even the years served by the *venerable* coaches was fed into the machine. *Extraneous* material was avoided. The astute* computer printed the figure "one" for each team. While this may seem *ambiguous* to the average person, it represented in the *succinct* language of the computer the actual score of one touchdown for each side: 7–7.

**Sample Sentences:**  Complete the sentences with the new words.

1. The prodigy* revered * the _____ master.

2. To those who could understand every nuance* of the cryptic* message, there was nothing _____ about it.

3. He could say the most vitriolic* things in a _____ way.

4. Although she did not find it congenial,* we cajoled * our daughter into doing some of the _____ tasks around the house.

5. The astute* voter is not susceptible* to the many _____ shibboleths* that saturate* a politician's speech.

**Definitions:**  Match the new words with their definitions.

6. menial   _____   a. vague, undefined, not specific

7. venerable   _____   b. humble, degrading

8. extraneous   _____   c. respected, worshipped.

9. ambiguous   _____   d. foreign, not belonging

10. succinct   _____   e. brief, concise

**Today's Idiom**

*the writing on the wall*—an incident or event that shows what will happen in the future

In retrospect* he should have seen *the writing on the wall* when his girl friend gave him only a cursory* greeting on his birthday.

**ANSWERS ARE ON PAGE 238**

**New Words:**

| archaic | emulate | facetious | rabid | salubrious |
|---------|---------|-----------|-------|------------|
| är kā′ ik | em′ ū lāt | fa sē′ shəs | rab′ id | sə lü′ bri əs |

**A Painting Machine**

There is even now a computer machine which may make other art forms *archaic*. Using computer methods, this machine can originate paintings and photographs. A machine that can *emulate* an artist is not as *facetious* as it may appear. Automation is inundating,* some say with deleterious* effects, all areas of self-expression—from music to literature. The most *rabid* adherents* of our technological progress look upon these events as singularly* favorable. They see these as harbingers* of a time when machines will do all of the labor, and man will reap the *salubrious* benefits.

**Sample Sentences:** Use the new words in these sentences.

1. Some maintain that the ascetic* leads a _____ life.

2. With all candor,* I cannot wish for a return to the _____ times when a moribund * society provided an opulent* existence for some, but a loathesome* life for the majority.

3. There is something _____ about an egotist* who has the temerity* to begin a speech with, "In all humility*. . . ."

4. It is not prudent* to malign* or castigate,* or be derogatory* in any way toward a _____ political adherent.*

5. The wish to _____ a great man is laudable.*

**Definitions:** Match the new words with their definitions.

6. archaic _____ a. healthful, wholesome

7. emulate _____ b. out of date

8. facetious _____ c. rival, strive to equal

9. rabid _____ d. comical, humorous, witty

10. salubrious _____ e. fanatical, furious, mad

**Today's Idiom**

*on the bandwagon*—joining with the majority; going along with the trend

Most advertisements showing many people using a product hope to convince the viewer to get *on the bandwagon* and buy the item.

ANSWERS ARE ON PAGE 238

When you can analyze a sentence and determine from the context the meaning of a previously unknown word, you are functioning at the best level. These words will become a permanent part of your ever-growing vocabulary.

| REVIEW WORDS | | DEFINITIONS |
|---|---|---|
| _____ 1 | alleviate | a. out of date |
| _____ 2 | ambiguous | b. concise, brief |
| _____ 3 | archaic | c. intense, deep thought |
| _____ 4 | bizarre | d. annex, grab, seize |
| _____ 5 | celerity | e. wholesome, healthful |
| _____ 6 | condone | f. degrading, humble |
| _____ 7 | emulate | g. rapidity, speed |
| _____ 8 | expedite | h. fantastic, odd |
| _____ 9 | extraneous | j. humorous, comical, witty |
| _____ 10 | facetious | k. not belonging, foreign |
| _____ 11 | menial | l. enormous, extraordinary |
| _____ 12 | paltry | m. pardon, excuse |
| _____ 13 | prodigious | n. furious, mad, fanatical |
| _____ 14 | profound | o. undefined, vague, not specific |
| _____ 15 | rabid | p. carry out promptly |
| _____ 16 | salubrious | r. lighten, make easier |
| _____ 17 | succinct | s. respected, worshiped |
| _____ 18 | trivial | t. strive to equal, rival |
| _____ 19 | usurp | u. of little importance |
| _____ 20 | venerable | v. petty, worthless |

**IDIOMS**

| | | |
|---|---|---|
| _____ 21 | to feather one's nest | w. joining with the majority |
| _____ 22 | ivory tower | x. an event that predicts the future |
| _____ 23 | the writing on the wall | y. out of touch with life |
| _____ 24 | on the band-wagon | z. to enrich oneself at every opportunity |

Check your answers on page 238. Take that extra moment *now* to review and study the words you got wrong.

| WORDS FOR FURTHER STUDY | MEANINGS |
|---|---|
| 1. _____ | _____ |
| 2. _____ | _____ |
| 3. _____ | _____ |

# 33rd Week / 1st Day

**New Words:**

| complacent | somber | debilitate | impetuous | occult |
|---|---|---|---|---|
| kəm plā′ sənt | som′ bər | di bil′ ə tāt | im pech′ ü əs | o kult′ |

**At a Loss**

With the trivial * sum of five dollars in his pockets, Robert Lacy was feeling far from *complacent* about the future. In fact, it was his *somber* estimate that no matter how frugal * he was, his money would run out before the next day. He owed $3.50 in debts to friends; with the remainder he would have to eat enough to maintain his strength. Hunger would *debilitate* him to the point where he could not continue his fervid * search for Evelyn. There was no hope of an *impetuous* stranger suddenly thrusting money upon him. There was still less solace* for him in the hope that, after all this time, he might develop the *occult* power that would give him a mental image of where Evelyn could be found.

**Sample Sentences:** Use the new words in these sentences.

1. The guard was so _____ about the danger of escape that he gave the prisoner only a cursory* inspection.

2. We should be prudent* in our play or work during very hot weather, because the sun has the power to enervate* and _____ those that scoff * at its effects.

3. He looked for a propitious* moment to exhibit his _____ abilities.

4. The deleterious* results of his irate* outburst put the previously jocose* audience in a _____ mood.

5. They were so moved by the idyllic* setting, they exchanged surreptitious,* _____ kisses.

**Definitions:** Match the new words with their definitions.

6. complacent _____    a. secret, mysterious, supernatural

7. somber _____    b. impulsive

8. debilitate _____    c. self-satisfied

9. impetuous _____    d. weaken

10. occult (adj.) _____    e. gloomy, sad

**Today's Idiom**

*to hit the nail on the head*—to state or guess something correctly

When Charlie said there were 3,627 beans in that jar, he *hit the nail on the head*.

ANSWERS ARE ON PAGE 239

**New Words:**

| discreet | foment | glean | quarry | slovenly |
|---|---|---|---|---|
| dis krēt′ | fō ment′ | glēn | kwôr′ i | sluv′ ən li |

**Making Plans**

Robert had arrived in New York a week earlier. He had begun by asking *discreet* questions of Evelyn's former landlord. There was no need to *foment* opposition at the very beginning. The landlord was recondite,* and all Robert had been able to *glean* from the cryptic* replies was that Evelyn had moved to a residence that catered to single women. Robert was in a hapless* situation; in this immense city his *quarry* could be hiding in one of dozens of such places. This would obviate* the possibility of his dashing from one place to another in an impetuous* manner. His search, while it had to be concluded with celerity,* could not be carried out in such *slovenly* fashion. He required a succinct* and meticulous* plan.

**Sample Sentences:** Use the news words in these sentences.

1. In order to _____ trouble, they fabricated* a deplorable* and blatant* untruth.

2. She loathed* doing menial* tasks, and she did them in a _____ manner.

3. Although it seemed inane,* they sought their _____ in the midst of rustic* surroundings that were not its natural habitat*.

4. Despite the plethora* of offers to write her life story, the recently divorced movie queen kept a _____ silence.

5. The reporters could not _____ anything from her servants.

**Definitions:** Match the new words with their definitions.

6. discreet _____ a. careful, cautious, prudent*
7. foment _____ b. gather, collect
8. glean _____ c. something hunted or pursued
9. quarry _____ d. disorderly, carelessly
10. slovenly _____ e. stir up, instigate

**Today's Idiom**

*on the dot*—exactly on time
   Despite his having taken forty winks,* he got to his appointment *on the dot*.

**ANSWERS ARE ON PAGE 239**

162

**New Words:**

| abjure | reproach | penitent | evanescent | tantamount |
|--------|----------|----------|------------|------------|
| ab jür′ | ri prōch′ | pen′ ə tənt | ev′ ə nes′ ənt | tan′ tə mount |

*A Newspaper Ad*   On the premise* that Evelyn knew she was being sought, Robert's first step was to *abjure* fruitless* searching and place an ad in the leading morning newspaper. He would importune* in a most careful way for her return. The ad read, "Evelyn. Come out of hiding. I do not *reproach* you for your actions. I expect no *penitent* confession. There is nothing ambiguous* about my offer. Please contact. Robert." He added a box number for a reply. When Robert went to the paper the next morning, he felt sanguine* about the chances of locating her. His *evanescent* concerns disappeared; there was a letter for him, and with tremulous* fingers he tore it open. It contained one sentence, and it was *tantamount* to a challenge; 'If you really care about me, you will find me by midnight, Friday, Evelyn."

**Sample Sentences:**   Insert the new words in these sentences.

1. The inveterate* gambler became _____ and contrite* when faced with the results of his reprehensible* behavior.

2. The optimist knows that the vicissitudes* of life are _____, and he always looks on the sanguine* side of things.

3. You should not condone* his sordid* behavior; rather, _____ him for his fractious* manner.

4. At the zenith* of his career, he was _____ to a final arbiter* on matters of economic policy.

5. In vain, the entire family tried to importune* him to _____ gambling.

**Definitions:**   Match the new words with their definitions.

6. abjure _____ a. equivalent, identical

7. reproach _____ b. rebuke, reprimand

8. penitent _____ c. renounce, abstain from

9. evanescent _____ d. regretful, confessing guilt

10. tantamount _____ e. fleeting, passing, momentary

*Today's Idiom*   *to take under one's wings*—to become responsible for
As the new term began, the senior took the freshman *under his wing*.

**ANSWERS ARE ON PAGE** 239

**New Words:**  propensity  wary  allay  deter  connoisseur
prə pen′ sə ti  wãr′ i  ə lā′  di tėr′  kon′ ə sėr′

**At the Ballet**  Evelyn was an anomaly*: she had a *propensity* for folk music and rock and roll dancing, and, at the same time, she was an avid * fan of classical ballet. At one time she had been a fledgling* ballet dancer. Robert headed for a theater where a venerable* ballet company was performing. He knew he had to be *wary* so that Evelyn might not see him first. It was Tuesday evening; two days gone with so little to show. Only three more remaining before the deadline set by Evelyn. He tried hard to *allay* the sudden fear that came over him that he might not locate her. Nothing would *deter* him from succeeding! And so, although he was far from a *connoisseur* of the dance, he was standing among the throng* in the lobby, hoping it would be a propitious* evening for him.

**Sample Sentences:**  Insert the new words in these sentences.

1. The _____ scoffs* at the dilettante,* who has only a veneer* of knowledge.

2. It is difficult to _____ the concern of parents about how susceptible* their children are and how easily they succumb* to drugs.

3. Some girls have a _____ for swarthy* men who wear gaudy* clothes.

4. Her father warned her to be _____ of adding the encumbrance* of a steady boy friend as this would attenuate* her chances of finishing college.

5. This did not _____ her from getting into a deplorable* situation due to her rash* and perverse* actions.

**Definitions:**  Match the new words with their definitions.

6. propensity  _____  a. hinder, discourage
7. wary  _____  b. expert
8. allay  _____  c. disposition, inclination, bent
9. deter  _____  d. calm, soothe
10. connoisseur  _____  e. watchful, shrewd

**Today's Idiom**  *out of one's depth*—In a situation that is too difficult to handle
   We thought he knew the ropes,* but we found him behind the eight ball * because *he was out of his depth.*

ANSWERS ARE ON PAGE 239

While each day's story has five new words, there are many others that are repeated from previous weeks. These words are placed within the stories so that you might practice your grasp of their meanings. Repetition will help guarantee that these words will be firmly fixed as part of your ever-expanding vocabulary.

**REVIEW WORDS**

| | | |
|---|---|---|
| _____ | 1 | abjure |
| _____ | 2 | allay |
| _____ | 3 | complacent |
| _____ | 4 | connoisseur |
| _____ | 5 | debilitate |
| _____ | 6 | deter |
| _____ | 7 | discreet |
| _____ | 8 | evanescent |
| _____ | 9 | foment |
| _____ | 10 | glean |
| _____ | 11 | impetuous |
| _____ | 12 | occult |
| _____ | 13 | penitent |
| _____ | 14 | propensity |
| _____ | 15 | quarry |
| _____ | 16 | reproach |
| _____ | 17 | slovenly |
| _____ | 18 | somber |
| _____ | 19 | tantamount |
| _____ | 20 | wary |

**DEFINITIONS**

a. stir up, instigate
b. disorderly, carelessly
c. regretful, confessing guilt
d. abstain from, renounce
e. weaken
f. self-satisfied
g. discourage, hinder
h. bent, inclination, disposition
j. sad, gloomy
k. identical, equivalent
l. something hunted or pursued
m. watchful, shrewd
n. supernatural, mysterious, secret
o. impulsive
p. rebuke, reprimand *
r. momentary, passing, fleeting
s. prudent,* careful, cautious
t. collect, gather
u. expert
v. soothe, calm

**IDIOMS**

| | | |
|---|---|---|
| _____ | 21 | out of one's depth |
| _____ | 22 | to hit the nail on the head |
| _____ | 23 | to take under one's wing |
| _____ | 24 | on the dot |

w. exactly on time
x. in a situation that is too difficult to handle
y. to become responsible for
z. to state or guess something correctly

**WORDS FOR FURTHER STUDY**     **MEANINGS**

1. _____   _____

2. _____   _____

3. _____   _____

Check your answers on page 239. The routine for checking and study should be well implanted by now. Some weeks you will have no words wrong. At other times, you may have several. Don't be discouraged by the differences from week to week.

**New Words:**

| site | vigil | cumbersome | interrogate | divulge |
|------|-------|------------|-------------|---------|
| sīt | vij' əl | kum' bər səm | in ter' ə gāt | də vulj' |

**Another Plan**  Robert was far from tranquil * as he waited in the lobby for almost an hour after the performance had begun. Disgruntled,* he quit the *site* of his *vigil*. He had to face the fact that he was making no tangible* progress. Tomorrow he would telephone several women's residences. It was a *cumbersome* way of going about the hunt, but it was all that he could think of at the moment. He would *interrogate* the desk clerks, and perhaps he might uncover a pertinent* clue to Evelyn's whereabouts. If he could only get someone to *divulge* her hiding place! Perhaps tomorrow would culminate* in success.

**Sample Sentences:**  Insert the new words in these sentences.

1. With rancor* he faced the _____ job of transporting the voluminous* records to his new office.

2. Before they began to _____ the criminal, they had to admonish* him that his testimony might be used to incarcerate* him.

3. The hunter maintained a discreet* and wary* _____ as he waited for the propitious* moment to bag his quarry*.

4. Even under duress,* he was adamant* and would not _____ the secret.

5. The newly married couple selected the _____ for their new home with meticulous* care.

**Definitions:**  Match the new words with their definitions.

6. site  _____  a. unwieldy, burdensome

7. vigil  _____  b. question

8. cumbersome  _____  c. wakeful watching

9. interrogate  _____  d. disclose, reveal

10. divulge  _____  e. location

**Today's Idiom**  *to take a leaf out of someone's book*—to imitate or follow the example
    The chip off the old block* *took a leaf from his father's book* and never sowed wild oats*.

ANSWERS ARE ON PAGE 239

**New Words:**

| fluctuate | unmitigated | commodious | antiquated |
|---|---|---|---|
| fluk′ chü āt | un mit′ ə gāt′ id | kə mō′ di əs | an′ ti kwāt id |

disheveled
də shev′ əld

**A Hope Dashed**

The next day, Wednesday, saw Robert become more frustrated.* He would *fluctuate* between high hopes of finding Evelyn and *unmitigated* despair when he was almost ready to desist* in his search. The phone calls had elicited * almost nothing. Robert had rushed to one women's residence when the clerk described a girl who might just be Evelyn. The desk clerk phoned to her room on the pretext* that she had a special delivery letter. Robert waited in the *commodious* lobby, replete* with large, *antiquated* pieces of furniture. He watched from a discreet* distance as she came down the stairs. One look at her wan* face, slovenly* dress, and *disheveled* hair was enough to inform Robert that he needed no further scrutiny.* This could not be his impeccable* Evelyn.

**Sample Sentences:** Insert the new words in these sentences.

1. He wasn't exactly an _____ liar; he merely embellished * the truth a little.

2. In his sumptuous* house he had a _____ den in which he kept an array* of trophies as incontrovertible* evidence of his skill.

3. Is it banal * to say that good manners are _____ in our milieu? *

4. The current trend * in the stock market is for stocks to _____ in a sporadic* fashion.

5. The nondescript,* indolent* beggar was in a _____ condition.

**Definitions:** Match the new words with their definitions.

6. fluctuate _____    a. large, spacious

7. unmitigated _____    b. shift, alternate

8. commodious _____    c. disorderly clothing or hair

9. antiquated _____    d. unrelieved, as bad as can be

10. disheveled _____    e. out-of-date, obsolete

**Today's Idiom**

*brass tacks*—the real problem or situation
    After some moments of congenial * levity,* they got down to *brass tacks.*

ANSWERS ARE ON PAGE 239

**New Words:**  tenacious    facade    asinine    grimace    calumny
ti nā′ shəs    fə säd′    as′ ə nīn    grə mās′    kal′ əm ni

**To the Police**    Thursday was his next-to-last day. He had been *tenacious* in following up every lead. Now he was behind the eight ball.* He could hardly galvanize* himself to do anything else. The *facade* of hope he had worn for almost a week was crumbling; there was nothing left to be sanguine* about. In desperation he turned to the police and placed his problem within their jurisdiction.* They asked many questions, and they requested that he not expurgate* anything. Some of the questions seemed *asinine*. When they inquired about his relationship to the missing girl, he replied, with a *grimace*, "Fiancee." When they suggested she might be hiding in that part of the city where the "hippie" coterie* congregated, he was incredulous* and accused the police of *calumny* against her good name and reputation.

**Sample Sentences:**    Insert the new words in these sentences.

1. He held on to his antiquated * beliefs with a _____ obsession.*
2. The woman was noted for her vituperative* _____ against her innocuous,* although senile,* neighbor.
3. She could not abjure* a _____ when she saw the disheveled figure.
4. How _____ of the boy to fabricate* that bizarre* story!
5. His face wore the most doleful * _____.

**Definitions:**    Match the new words with their definitions.

6. tenacious ____ a. false accusation, slander
7. facade ____ b. silly, stupid
8. asinine ____ c. front, superficial appearance
9. grimace ____ d. tough, stubborn
10. calumny ____ e. facial expression of disgust

**Today's Idiom**    *hook, line, and sinker*—completely, all the way
    The teacher fell for the practical joke *hook, line, and sinker*.

ANSWERS ARE ON PAGE 239

**New Words:**

| pittance | au courant | fastidious | noisome | unkempt |
|---|---|---|---|---|
| pit′ əns | ō′ kü rant′ | fas tid′ i əs | noi′ səm | un kempt′ |

**Evelyn Discovered**

Failure was imminent,* and Robert was bereft* of hope. It was now Friday. Despite his abstemious* and parsimonious* way of living, his money had been reduced to a mere *pittance*. A perverse* impulse brought him to the section where young people in strange clothing and with uncouth* manners made him recoil * in unmitigated * disgust. He had never been *au courant* with the "hippies" and "beats." He was always *fastidious* about proper dress and behavior. A moment later he saw her! Evelyn! She was sitting at a table in a coffee shop, surrounded by a coterie* of the most *noisome* individuals he had ever seen. Evelyn was not incongruous,* for she herself was *unkempt*. So this was her new habitat! * At that instant Robert knew as an incontrovertible* fact that he had lost her. With a grimace,* he turned and walked, a doleful * and melancholy figure, toward the bus depot and home.

**Sample Sentences:** Insert the new words in these sentences.

1. Styles are such transient* things that what is _____ today, is archaic* tomorrow.

2. The tip he had been offered was a mere _____, and the taxi driver threw it on the ground in disdain.*

3. Children think mothers are asinine* to get upset about _____ rooms.

4. It was inevitable* that they discover the hidden body by its _____ aroma.

5. He was so _____ about table manners that he lost his equanimity* when his son reached for the bread.

**Definitions:** Match the new words with their definition.

6. pittance _____    a. untidy, neglected

7. au courant _____    b. foul, unwholesome

8. fastidious _____    c. small amount

9. noisome _____    d. particular, choosy

10. unkempt _____    e. up-to-date

**Today's Idiom**    *lily-livered*—cowardly

The *lily-livered* gangster got cold feet* and spilled the beans. *

**ANSWERS ARE ON PAGE 239**

As an "old hand" at vocabulary-building by the context method, you realize that this is the most natural and effective way. However, you also know that there is work and self-discipline too. You should carry these fine qualities right through life. The words you learn are valuable, the method is equally so.

## REVIEW WORDS

_____ 1 antiquated
_____ 2 asinine
_____ 3 au courant
_____ 4 calumny
_____ 5 commodious
_____ 6 cumbersome
_____ 7 disheveled
_____ 8 divulge
_____ 9 facade
_____ 10 fastidious
_____ 11 fluctuate
_____ 12 grimace
_____ 13 interrogate
_____ 14 noisome
_____ 15 pittance
_____ 16 site
_____ 17 tenacious
_____ 18 unkempt
_____ 19 unmitigated
_____ 20 vigil

## DEFINITIONS

a. stubborn, tough
b. slander, false accusation
c. small amount
d. neglected, untidy
e. location
f. reveal, disclose
g. alternate, shift
h. disorderly clothing or hair
j. superficial appearance, front
k. facial expression of disgust
l. up-to-date
m. unwholesome, foul
n. wakeful watching
o. question
p. as bad as can be, unrelieved
r. out-of-date, obsolete
s. stupid, silly
t. choosy, particular
u. burdensome, unwieldy
v. spacious, large

## IDIOMS

_____ 21 brass tacks
_____ 22 hook, line, and sinker
_____ 23 lily-livered
_____ 24 to take a leaf out of someone's book

w. cowardly
x. completely, all the way
y. to imitate or follow the example
z. the real problem or situation

The answers can be found on page 239. The method of study and learning requires quick review and re-use of difficult words. Start now!

## WORDS FOR FURTHER STUDY     MEANINGS

1. _____     _____

2. _____     _____

3. _____     _____

**New Words:**  parable     whimsical     lampoon     countenance
par′ ə bəl   hwim′ zə kəl   lam pün′   koun′ tə nəns

sanctimonious
sangk′ tə mō′ ni əs

**A Modern Aesop**    The telling of a story in simple terms that has an inherently* important message is a venerable* art form. The *parable* may be found teaching a moral lesson in the bible. Aesop is an incontrovertible* master of the fable. This story form is far from antiquated * as shown by the *whimsical* approach to life taken by the modern Aesop, James Thurber. His stories *lampoon* the strange behavior of his fellow men. Thurber seems unable to *countenance* the ideas that permeate* our society regarding the rules by which we should live. Least of all is he able to accept the *sanctimonious* notion which some people promulgate* that good always wins out against evil. Thurber's stories often take an exactly opposite didactic* point of view.

**Sample Sentences:**    Note that some words do not have a one word definition. Frequently, several words, or an entire sentence, is required.

1. Jonathan Swift was never reticent* to _____ the egotist* in order to bring him down with alacrity.*

2. What one person finds _____, the other may find asinine.*

3. The expression, "Sour grapes,*" is the gist* of a famous _____ about a fox who couldn't get what he wanted.

4. We should eschew* our _____ facade;* away with pretext! *

5. If we want to live in a salubrious* milieu,* we can not _____ the noisome* fumes which are deleterious* to health.

**Definitions:**    Note the distinction between *countenance* as a noun and as a verb.

6. parable _____     a. humorous, witty

7. whimsical _____     b. hypocritically religious

8. lampoon
(v.) _____     c. tolerate,* approve

9. countenance
(v.) _____     d. a moralistic story

10. sanctimoni-
ous _____     e. ridicule

**Today's Idiom**    *to pull up stakes*—to quit a place
He could no longer rule the roost* or get the lion's share,* so he *pulled up stakes* and moved on.

**ANSWERS ARE ON PAGE 239**

**New Words:**

| | | | |
|---|---|---|---|
| equanimity | effrontery | nonentity | flabbergasted |
| ē kuə nim′ ə ti | ə frun′ tər i | non en′ tə ti | flab′ ər gast əd |
| debacle | | | |
| dā bä′ kəl | | | |

**Modernizing a Parable***

Thurber punctures in an incisive* way the platitudes* that come from stories handed down through the generations. These old saws are accepted by everyone. One such tale is about a tortoise who had read in an ancient book that a tortoise had beaten a hare in a race. The sage* old tortoise construed* this story to mean that he could outrun a hare. With *equanimity* he hunted for a hare and soon found one. "Do you have the *effrontery* to challenge me?" asked the incredulous* hare. "You are a *nonentity*," he scoffed* at the tortoise. A course of fifty feet was set out. The other animals gathered around the site*. At the sound of the gun they were off. When the hare crossed the finish line, the *flabbergasted* tortoise had gone approximately eight and three-quarter inches. The moral Thurber draws from this *debacle* for the tortoise: A new broom may sweep clean, but never trust an old saw.

*Which of the five "new words" have you seen before? It should be spotted easily.*

**Sample Sentences:** Insert the new words in these sentences.

1. He was a precocious* youngster, but he soon reached the nadir* of his career, lost all of his prestige*, and became a _____.

2. Do you have the _____ to take that supercilious* and facetious* attitude toward something as sinister* as this?

3. These turbulent* times requires a leader who does not go into a capricious* pique,* but rather one who faces acrimonious* criticism with _____.

4. When the judge exonerated * the charlatan,* we were all _____.

5. The fortuitous* appearance of a relief column permitted an adroit* escape from the imminent* _____.

**Definitions:** Match the new words with their definitions.

6. equanimity _____    a. calmness, self-control

7. effrontery _____    b. astounded

8. nonentity _____    c. boldness

9. flabber-
     gasted _____    d. ruin, collapse

10. debacle _____    e. one of no importance

**Today's Idiom**

*to raise Cain*—to cause trouble, make a fuss.
    When he found he was left holding the bag,* he decided *to raise Cain.*

**New Words:**

| vivacious | gaunt | mien | hirsute | refute |
|-----------|-------|------|---------|--------|
| vī vā′ shəs | gônt | mēn | her′ süt | ri fūt′ |

**Things Have Changed**

Thurber modernizes an old story that everyone has read or heard. It has to do with a nefarious* wolf who kept a vigil* in an ominous* forest until a little girl came along carrying a basket of food for her grandmother. With alacrity,* this *vivacious* youngster told the wolf the address to which she was going. Hungry and *gaunt* the wolf rushed to the house. When the girl arrived and entered, she saw someone in bed wearing a nightcap and a nightgown. While the figure was dressed like her grandmother, the little girl surmised* with only a perfunctory* glance that it didn't have the old lady's *mien*. She approached and became cognizant* of the *hirsute* face of the wolf. She drew a revolver from her purse and shot the interloper* dead. Thurber arrives at a moral for this story that anyone would find difficult to *refute:* It is not so easy to fool little girls nowadays as it used to be.

**Sample Sentences:** Insert the new words in these sentences.

1. She had a _____ of humility,* but it was only a facade.*

2. He did not waste time trying to _____ an irrelevant* and tortuous* argument.

3. You may have discerned* that the latest vogue* among boys is to permit their faces to become more _____ .

4. They were struck by the anomaly* of one twin who was phlegmatic* while the other was _____ .

5. Women strive for the slender and au courant* _____ look.

**Definitions:** Match the new words with their definition.

6. vivacious _____ a. thin, haggard

7. gaunt _____ b. lively, gay

8. mien _____ c. hairy

9. hirsute _____ d. appearance, bearing

10. refute _____ e. prove wrong or false

**Today's Idiom**

*to leave no stone unturned*—to try one's best, to make every effort

Since you're from Missouri,* I'll *leave no stone unturned* to convince you.

**ANSWERS ARE ON PAGE 239**

173

**New Words:**

| pensive | whet | stupor | wince | cliché |
|---------|------|--------|-------|--------|
| pen' siv | hwet | stü' pər | wins | klē shā |

**Another Surprise**

Thurber's stories are written in a jocose* manner, but they contain enough serious matter to make one *pensive*. He tells of some builders who left a pane of glass standing upright in a field near a house they were constructing. A goldfinch flew across the field, struck the glass and was knocked inert.* He rushed back and divulged* to his friends that the air had crystallized. The other birds derided* him, said he had become irrational,* and gave a number of reasons for the accident. The only bird who believed the goldfinch was the swallow. The goldfinch challenged the large birds to follow the same path he had flown. This challenge served to *whet* their interest, and they agreed with gusto.* Only the swallow abjured.* The large birds flew together and struck the glass; they were knocked into a *stupor*. This caused the astute* swallow to *wince* with pain. Thurber drew a moral that is the antithesis* of the *cliché* we all accept: He who hesitates is sometimes saved.

**Sample Sentences:** Insert the new words in these sentences.

1. He was in such a _____ as a result of the accident that this precluded* his hearing my condolence.*

2. If you juxtapose* one _____ with another, you often get completely opposite lessons about life.

3. The hostile* rebuke* made the usually phlegmatic* boy _____.

4. You cannot _____ his desire for the theater with dubious* histrionics.*

5. The fervid* marriage proposal made the shy girl _____.

**Definitions:** Match the new words with their definitions.

6. pensive _____ a. thoughtful, reflective

7. whet _____ b. stimulate, stir up

8. stupor _____ c. a commonplace phrase

9. wince _____ d. draw back, flinch

10. cliché _____ e. daze, insensible condition

**Today's Idiom**

*tongue in one's cheek*—not to be sincere

John's father surely had *his tongue in his cheek* when he told his son to go sow wild oats* and to kick over the traces* at his kindergarten party.

**ANSWERS ARE ON PAGE 239**

To strengthen your word power, keep adding words from all the sources you use during the day. The words learned while reading this book give you a firm basis. School texts, newspapers, magazines, etc. should all give you the opportunity to corroborate* the fact that your vocabulary is growing, and they should also be the source for new words.

| REVIEW WORDS | | DEFINITIONS | |
|---|---|---|---|
| _____ | 1 cliché | a. | astounded |
| _____ | 2 countenance | b. | one of no importance |
| _____ | 3 debacle | c. | witty, humorous |
| _____ | 4 effrontery | d. | ridicule |
| _____ | 5 equanimity | e. | hairy |
| _____ | 6 flabbergasted | f. | prove wrong, disprove |
| _____ | 7 gaunt | g. | flinch, draw back |
| _____ | 8 hirsute | h. | self-control |
| _____ | 9 lampoon | j. | collapse, ruin |
| _____ | 10 mien | k. | hypocritically religious |
| _____ | 11 nonentity | l. | a moralistic story |
| _____ | 12 parable | m. | gay, lively |
| _____ | 13 pensive | n. | bearing, appearance |
| _____ | 14 refute | o. | stir up, stimulate |
| _____ | 15 sanctimonious | p. | boldness |
| _____ | 16 stupor | r. | approve, tolerate* |
| _____ | 17 vivacious | s. | haggard, thin |
| _____ | 18 whet | t. | reflective, thoughtful |
| _____ | 19 whimsical | u. | a commonplace phrase |
| _____ | 20 wince | v. | insensible condition, daze |

**IDIOMS**

| | | | |
|---|---|---|---|
| _____ | 21 tongue in one's cheek | w. | make a fuss, cause trouble |
| _____ | 22 to leave no stone unturned | x. | to make every effort, to try one's best |
| _____ | 23 to pull up stakes | y. | not to be sincere |
| _____ | 24 to raise Cain | z. | to quit a place |

Check your answers on page 239. Look back at the story to check the use of each word in its context. This will help fix it in your mind.

**WORDS FOR FURTHER STUDY**       **MEANINGS**

1. _____  _____

2. _____  _____

3. _____  _____

**New Words:**

| genre | candid | unsavory | degrade | venial |
|-------|--------|----------|---------|--------|
| zhän′ rə | kan′ did | un sā′ vər i | di grād′ | vē′ ni əl |

**A Lady Novelist**     The nineteenth century saw the woman novelist attain the same prestige* as men. England was prolific* in producing women writers. One of the foremost in this *genre* was Charlotte Brontë. In JANE EYRE she presented a *candid* portrait of a woman caught up in a clandestine* affair with a married man. Miss Bronte's readers were engrossed* in this story. She took this *unsavory* subject and presented it in a way that did not *degrade* the relationship. She showed that true passion can be healthy. Miss Brontë did not disparage* Jane's feelings or besmirch* her character. The author was generous in her verdict. The affair was considered merely a *venial* sin because Jane was never false in her feelings or her actions.

**Sample Sentences:**     Insert the new words in these sentences.

1. Harry held the fallacious* belief that the menial * job would_____ him in the eyes of his friends.

2. Betty's childish fabrications* were judged _____ sins, although they mortified * her mother.

3. Modern abstract painting is a highly lucrative* _____.

4. It is reprehensible,* but it doesn't require much gossip to give a person a(n) _____ reputation.

5. In my _____ opinion he is a sanctimonious* fool.

**Definitions:**     Match the new words with their definitions.

6. genre _____     a. make contemptible, lower

7. candid _____     b. disagreeable, offensive, morally bad

8. unsavory _____     c. a certain form or style in painting or literature

9. degrade _____     d. pardonable, forgivable

10. venial _____     e. frank, open, honest

**Today's Idiom**     *keep a stiff upper lip*—keep up courage, stand up to trouble
    When he heard through the grapevine* that the fat was in the fire,* he knew he had *to keep a stiff upper lip* so as not to spill the beans.*

**ANSWERS ARE ON PAGE 239**

**New Words:**   epitome   dexterity   grotesque   compassion   repugnant
i pit′ ə mi   dek ster′ ə ti   grō tesk′   kəm pash′ ən   ri pug′ nənt

**Victor Hugo**   The *epitome* of French romantic writers in the nineteenth century was Victor Hugo. With the utmost *dexterity* he wrote poetry, novels and drama. His highly popular novels, NOTRE DAME DE PARIS and LES MISERABLES, are replete* with melodramatic situations and *grotesque* characters. He had a profound * sense of social justice and a *compassion* for the poor, hapless* and downtrodden. He could not work under the aegis* of Napolean II and fled into exile. When the *repugnant* rule came to an end, the expatriate* returned from exile. He was received with adulation* and acclaim as the idol of the Third Republic.

**Sample Sentences:**   Insert the new words in these sentences.

1. He was made up in the most _____ way for his role as a man from outer space.

2. We all felt deep _____ for the innocent progeny,* who were bereft* of their parents who had succumbed * during the conflagration.*

3. The Taj Mahal in India is said to be the _____ of grace as an edifice.*

4. The sight of the corpse was _____ to the squeamish* onlookers.

5. With _____ he thwarted * the pugnacious* and belligerent* adversary.*

**Definitions:**   Match the new words with their definitions.

6. epitome _____   a. strange, bizarre,* fantastic

7. dexterity _____   b. person or thing that embodies or represents

8. grotesque _____   c. distasteful, repulsive

9. compassion _____   d. sympathetic feeling, kindness

10. repugnant _____   e. mental or physical skill

**Today's Idiom**   *to throw the book at someone*—to give the maximum punishment
   The judge got his back up* and *threw the book* at the criminal.

**ANSWERS ARE ON PAGE 239**

**New Words:**

| acme | copious | vehemently | depict | naive |
|------|---------|------------|--------|-------|
| ak′ mi | kō′ pi əs | vē′ ə ment li | di pikt′ | nä ēv′ |

**An English Realist**

The movement towards realism in the English novel of the nineteenth century reached its *acme* with the works of Charles Dickens and William Makepeace Thackeray. Charles Dickens was a prolific* writer. Among his *copious* works are OLIVER TWIST, a candid * exposure of the repugnant* poor laws; NICHOLAS NICKLEBY, in which the life of boys in a boarding school is *vehemently* attacked; HARD TIMES, in which the author wanted to *depict* the infamous* life in a factory during an early period of the industrial revolution; THE PICKWICK PAPERS, about a *naive* gentleman who has numerous misadventures. The novels, aimed at exposing the sordid * and pernicious* elements of English life, were said to have helped galvanize* people into action leading to improvement in these conditions.

**Sample Sentences:** Insert the new words in these sentences.

1. At the _____ of his power, the dictator was obsessed * with the belief that those who dissented * were trying to usurp* his position.

2. As a perspicacious* newspaper reporter, he felt it incumbent* upon him to _____ the abortive* coup as a reprehensible* act.

3. The urbane* gentleman was flabbergasted * by the fervid * interest in wrestling shown by the _____ young girl.

4. She lost her decorum* and wept _____ tears at the poignant* story.

5. He objected _____ to a vote taking place in the absence of a quorum.*

**Definitions:** Match the new words with their definitions.

6. acme       _____   a. unworldly, unsophisticated

7. copious    _____   b. violently, eagerly, passionately

8. vehemently _____   c. peak, pinnacle,* zenith*

9. depict     _____   d. ample, abundant, plentiful

10. naive     _____   e. describe clearly, picture, portray

**Today's Idiom**   *terra firma*—solid, firm land

The rough ocean crossing took the wind out of his sails* and he was happy to be on *terra firma* again.

**ANSWERS ARE ON PAGE 239**

**New Words:** perfidious covet ingratiate penury ignominious
pər fid′ i əs kuv′ it in grā′ shi āt pen′ ū ri ig′ nə min′ i əs

**A Scheming Heroine**

William Makepeace Thackeray was known for his moralistic study of upper and middle class English life. His best known work, VANITY FAIR, has as its central character Becky Sharp. She is a *perfidious* woman who has an insatiable* desire to get ahead in the world. She *covets* the wealth of one man, but when marriage is not feasible* she succeeds in a plan to *ingratiate* herself into the heart of her employer's son. Their marriage is not a salubrious* one and Becky, who lives ostentatiously,* forms a surreptitious* liaison with another man. The affair culminates* in a debacle.* She is exposed, her husband leaves her, and she must live in *penury* in Europe. This is the *ignominious* end for a clever, but misguided woman.

**Sample Sentences:** Insert the new words in these sentences.

1. Under the aegis* of a zealous* campaign manager, the candidate was able to _____ himself into the hearts of the public.

2. A favorite parable* has to do with teaching the lesson that one should not _____ that which belongs to someone else.

3. His fortune fluctuated * between _____ and wealth.

4. They made an effigy of their _____ enemy.

5. There was bedlam* as the favored team went down to _____ defeat at the hands of the underdog.

**Definitions:** Match the new words with their definitions.

6. perfidious _____    a. treacherous, false

7. covet _____    b. want, envy, wish

8. ingratiate _____    c. humiliating, disgraceful

9. penury _____    d. poverty

10. ignominious _____    e. win confidence, charm

**Today's Idiom**

*in seventh heaven*—the highest happiness or delight
The oldest child was *in seventh heaven* when her mother let her rule the roost* for a day.

ANSWERS ARE ON PAGE 239

Whether you read a classic novel or a modern one, the one thing they have in common is their use of a rather extensive vocabulary. Don't be handicapped in your reading—increase your vocabulary by constant study and review.

**REVIEW WORDS**          **DEFINITIONS**

_____ 1  acme            a.  open, honest, frank
_____ 2  candid          b.  kindness, sympathetic feeling
_____ 3  compassion      c.  zenith,* pinnacle,* peak
_____ 4  copious         d.  wish, envy, want
_____ 5  covet           e.  false, treacherous
_____ 6  degrade         f.  unsophisticated, unworldly
_____ 7  depict          g.  fantastic, strange, bizarre*
_____ 8  dexterity       h.  lower, make contemptible
_____ 9  epitome         j.  a certain form or style in painting or literature
_____ 10 genre           k.  repulsive, distasteful
_____ 11 grotesque       l.  plentiful, abundant, ample
_____ 12 ignominious     m.  poverty
_____ 13 ingratiate      n.  portray, picture, describe clearly
_____ 14 naive           o.  person or thing that embodies or represents
_____ 15 penury          p.  morally bad, disagreeable, offensive
_____ 16 perfidious      r.  physical or mental skill
_____ 17 repugnant       s.  passionately, violently, eagerly
_____ 18 unsavory        t.  charm, win confidence
_____ 19 vehemently      u.  forgivable, pardonable
_____ 20 venial          v.  disgraceful, humiliating

**IDIOMS**

_____ 21 to throw the    w.  keep up courage, stand up to trouble
           book at some-
           one
_____ 22 in seventh      x.  to give maximum punishment
           heaven
_____ 23 terra firma     y.  solid, firm land
_____ 24 keep a stiff upper   z.  the highest happiness or delight
           lip

**WORDS FOR**
**FURTHER STUDY**        **MEANINGS**

Check your answers on page     1. _____  _____
239. Review incorrect words.

                               2. _____  _____

                               3. _____  _____

**New Words:**

| | | | | |
|---|---|---|---|---|
| confront | antipathy | servile | volition | sojourn |
| kən frunt′ | an tip′ ə thi | ser vəl | vō lish′ ən | sō jėrn′ |

**A Man of Nature**

Henry Thoreau attempted to *confront* the problem and solve the enigma* of how one might earn a living and yet not become an ignominious* slave to the task. He viewed the industrial revolution with *antipathy*. Man in a *servile* role to extraneous* possessions was a main target of his writings. He believed that one could attain genuine wealth not by accumulating objects or money, but through enjoyment and perusal* of nature. By his own *volition* he gave up friends and comforts for a two year *sojourn* by himself at Walden Pond. What others might judge as penury,* was seen by Thoreau as the epitome* of wealth.

**Sample Sentences:** Insert the new words in these sentences.

1. He found his _____ position a degrading* one and could not accept it with equanimity.*

2. The expatriate* decided to make his _____ in France a permanent one in order to give up his nomadic* way of life.

3. Why do we refuse to _____ the unsavory* problems of our times in a candid* and incisive* way?

4. He was a tenacious* competitor, and at his own _____ he placed his title in jeopardy* on many occasions.

5. Her _____ towards men was based on rather nebulous* events which she construed* to prove that they were all perfidious.*

**Definitions:** Match the new words with their definitions.

6. confront _____    a. temporary stay

7. antipathy _____    b. will-power, choice

8. servile _____    c. dislike, distaste, hate

9. volition _____    d. come face to face with

10. sojourn (n.) _____    e. slavish, submissive

**Today's Idiom**

*to tighten one's belt*—to get set for bad times or poverty
   He knew he would have to draw in his horns* and *tighten his belt* or he would wind up on skid row*.

ANSWERS ARE ON PAGE 240

**New Words:**

| austere | felicitous | halcyon | tenable | superfluous |
|---------|-----------|---------|---------|-------------|
| ôs tēr′ | fə lis′ ə təs | hal′ si ən | ten′ ə bəl | su̇ pėr′ flü əs |

**The Good Life**

Thoreau's book about the *austere* but happy life at Walden Pond propagated * his fame around the world. He built a small hut and began living an ascetic* existence. He found it to be a *felicitous* experience. In this idyllic* setting he was able to spend his time reading, studying nature, writing and thinking. Far from being indolent,* he kept busy in many ways. At the end of the experiment he recalled the *halcyon* days with pleasure. He believed he had learned the secret of the truly happy life. The only *tenable* way of life is one in harmony with nature; material possessions are *superfluous*.

**Sample Sentences:**   Insert the new words in these sentences.

1. When he found his sinecure* was no longer _____, he felt it a propitious* time to resign.

2. Far from being ostentatious,* she was considered the acme* of fashion because of her _____ manner of dress.

3. Because he was an itinerant* worker, he had to disdain* carrying _____ equipment.

4. On that _____ occasion the amount of money he spent was irrelevant.*

5. During the turbulent* days of the war, they wished for the _____ days of earlier times.

**Definitions:**   Match the new words with their definitions.

6. austere _____  a. supportable, defendable
7. felicitous _____  b. simple, unadorned, hard
8. halcyon _____  c. peaceful, calm
9. tenable _____  d. happy
10. superfluous _____  e. excessive, surplus

**Today's Idiom**   *off the beaten track*—not usual, out of the ordinary
Because his ideas were always *off the beaten track*, he lived under a sword of Damocles* on his job.

ANSWERS ARE ON PAGE 240

**New Words:**

| motivate | rationalize | therapy | nascent | iconoclast |
|---|---|---|---|---|
| mō′ tə vāt | rash′ ən əl īz | ther′ ə pi | nas′ ənt | ī kon′ ə klast |

**The Mind's Secrets**

The study of the human mind and behavior has had many prominent practitioners, but no one is more revered * than Sigmund Freud. An Austrian physician, he is said to be the father of psychoanalysis. He taught that man has a subconscious mind in which he keeps repugnant* memories which come to the surface surreptitiously* and *motivate* behavior. Man often tries to *rationalize* his actions, when, in reality, they are really the result of suppressed memories coming to the surface. Freud's approach to the disturbed person was to attempt *therapy* by examining the dreams which make cognizant* what the cause of the illness might be. Only with the airing of deleterious, buried emotions can the person move from the *nascent* stage to that of full health. Freud was considered an *iconoclast* in the field of psychology when his ideas first appeared at the beginning of this century.

**Sample Sentences:** Insert the new words in these sentences.

1. The _____ was in favor of jettisoning* one of the traditions that had become an intrinsic* part of his life.

2. In order to complete the _____, the doctor said a trip to a warm, dry climate was mandatory.*

3. Complacent* people are difficult to _____ to altruistic* actions.

4. It is pathetic* the way some citizens _____ their apathy* during election years.

5. His beard was in its _____ state; it would soon be a hirsute* masterpiece.

**Definitions:** Match the new words with their definitions.

6. motivate _____    a. beginning to exist or develop

7. rationalize _____    b. use or give a reason other than the real one

8. therapy _____    c. inspire, stimulate, provoke

9. nascent _____    d. image-breaker, attacker of beliefs

10. iconoclast _____    e. healing or curing process

**Today's Idiom**

A *square peg in a round hole*—an able man in the wrong job
   It was a bitter pill to swallow* when they had to fire him because he was *a square peg in a round hole.*

ANSWERS ARE ON PAGE 240

**New Words:**

| erudite | phobia | germane | vertigo | conducive |
|---------|--------|---------|---------|-----------|
| er′ u dīt | fō′ bi ə | jer mān′ | ver′ tə gō | kən dü′ siv |

**Amateur Psychologists**

The ideas of Freudian psychology have become part of our everyday life. Our language is replete* with clichés* that have their origin in Freud's writings. There is a surfeit* of amateur psychologists who, with celerity,* analyze an individual's problems from the slightest evidence. Despite their dubious* education and training in this field, they discuss symptoms and cures in a most *erudite* fashion. Should a person express a fear of height, this *phobia* is examined; events from childhood are considered *germane* to the problem. Is it possible he or she was dropped as an infant? Perhaps something in a dream is pertinent* to explain the feelings of *vertigo* that accompany height. For some reason, non-trained people find the Freudian approach to the workings of the human mind most *conducive* to their practicing as amateur psychologists.

**Sample Sentences:** Insert the new words in these sentences.

1. She could not countenance* the sight of a lethal * weapon; it was tantamount* to a _____ with her.

2. The _____ man was more than merely bilingual;* he spoke five languages.

3. I would never have the temerity* to walk across the steel girders high up on a new building; an onset of _____ would surely follow.

4. The bedlam* in the study hall was not _____ to good work habits.

5. Epithets* are not _____ when motivating* a child to a task.

**Definitions:** Match the new words with their definitions.

6. erudite _____ a. very scholarly

7. phobia _____ b. dizziness

8. germane _____ c. persistent fear, strong dislike

9. vertigo _____ d. leading, helpful

10. conducive _____ e. appropriate, in close relationship to

**Today's Idiom**

*to upset the apple cart*—to overturn or disturb a plan or intention

It was a bitter pill to swallow* when *they upset the apple cart* and elected a dark horse.*

ANSWERS ARE ON PAGE 240

184

The writings of Thoreau and Freud are replete* with ideas that require deep thought. In order to tackle their ideas, one must understand their vocabulary. Therefore, word mastery is the key to unlocking ideas of some of our greatest thinkers.

## REVIEW WORDS

| | | DEFINITIONS |
|---|---|---|
| _____ | 1 austere | a. supportable, defendable |
| _____ | 2 antipathy | b. choice, will-power |
| _____ | 3 conducive | c. provoke, stimulate, inspire |
| _____ | 4 confront | d. leading, helpful |
| _____ | 5 erudite | e. unadorned, simple, hard |
| _____ | 6 felicitous | f. hate, distaste, dislike |
| _____ | 7 germane | g. attacker of beliefs, image-breaker |
| _____ | 8 halcyon | h. in close relationship to, appropriate |
| _____ | 9 iconoclast | j. calm, peaceful |
| _____ | 10 motivate | k. come face to face with |
| _____ | 11 nascent | l. curing or healing process |
| _____ | 12 phobia | m. very scholarly |
| _____ | 13 rationalize | n. happy |
| _____ | 14 servile | o. submissive, slavish |
| _____ | 15 sojourn | p. beginning to develop or exist |
| _____ | 16 superfluous | r. dizziness |
| _____ | 17 tenable | s. surplus, excessive |
| _____ | 18 therapy | t. temporary stay |
| _____ | 19 vertigo | u. use or give a reason other than the real one |
| _____ | 20 volition | v. strong dislike, persistent fear |

## IDIOMS

| | | |
|---|---|---|
| _____ | 21 to upset the apple cart | w. not usual, out of the ordinary |
| _____ | 22 to tighten one's belt | x. an able man in the wrong job |
| _____ | 23 off the beaten track | y. to get set for bad times or poverty |
| _____ | 24 a square peg in a round hole | z. to overturn or disturb a plan or intention |

Check your answers on page 240.

**WORDS FOR FURTHER STUDY**     **MEANINGS**

1. _____    _____

2. _____    _____

3. _____    _____

New Words:
| glib | homogenous | malleable | legerdemain | trend |
|------|------------|-----------|-------------|-------|
| glib | hō moj' ə nəs | mal' i ə bəl | lej' ər də mān | trend |

**The Enigma\* of Fashion**

Of all the pressures young people face, the most pernicious\* is that of fashion. By this is meant the current vogue\* in dress. The teen-agers, who are so *glib* when they speak of "individuality," are turned into a *homogenous* mass by the latest craze in fashion. How can youngsters who vehemently\* resist advice from the older generation become so *malleable* in the hands of those who "make" fashion? Perhaps the sudden shifts in fashion occur fortuitously\*. Or is there some group who, through *legerdemain,* switch styles and customs on us right before our eyes? Today's teen-agers seem to be quite gullible\* when it comes to embracing the latest *trend* in fashions. But then, they have their elders as sage\* examples to follow.

**Sample Sentences:** Insert the new words in these sentences.

1. The charlatan\* was able to wheedle\* money out of the naive\* audience with a _____ talk on the medicine that would expunge\* pain.

2. They could not follow the _____ of his ideas, but his verbal dexterity\* galvanized \* the gullible\* listeners.

3. They were engrossed \* as an ill man was "cured" before their eyes; some of the more urbane\* said it was _____.

4. He ingratiated \* himself into their confidence, and the _____ crowd was shaped into a subjugated \* mass.

5. While they started out as individuals, they became an _____ group whom he could motivate as he willed.

**Definitions:** Match the new words with their definitions.

6. glib _____    a. capable of being shaped or formed

7. homogenous _____    b. sleight of hand, deceptive adroitness\*

8. malleable _____    c. smooth of speech

9. legerdemain _____    d. same or uniform

10. trend _____    e. general direction

**Today's Idiom**    *by hook or by crook*—any way at all, at any cost

He had bought the white elephant\* without rhyme or reason\*; now he had to get rid of it *by hook or by crook.*

ANSWERS ARE ON PAGE 240

**New Words:**

| stagnant | fatal | passé | procrastinate | facet |
|----------|-------|-------|---------------|-------|
| stag′ nənt | fā′ təl | pa sā | prō kras′ tə nāt | fas′ it |

**The Economics of Fashion**

In dress, the fashion appears to be "set" by a few foreign designers and a handful of affluent* individuals who purchase these designs. The fashion industry is cognizant* of the fact that fashions must change rapidly and often or their economy would become *stagnant*. For this industry it would prove *fatal* if it were not vigilant* and prepared well in advance for a new fashion trend.* As the old fashion becomes *passé* and a new fashion seems to be in the making, the garment manufacturers cannot afford to *procrastinate*. They rush large sums of money into production for a mass market. Having invested heavily, the manufacturers do everything possible to influence and motivate* the purchasers. Through every *facet* of publicity and advertising the industry exploits* the natural desire for people to be au courant* with the latest fashions.

**Sample Sentences:** Insert the new words in these sentences.

1. To the consternation* of the distraught* parents they learned their son was accused of using the lethal * weapon on that _____ occasion.

2. We wish for halcyon* days when the warlike solutions will have become _____.

3. He recalled with nostalgia* many _____ of his school days.

4. We all tend to _____ when faced with an unsavory* task.

5. The iconoclast* has the propensity* for reproaching* those who feel complacent* with leading a _____ existence.

**Definitions:** Match the new words with their definitions.

6. stagnant _____ a. delay, put off

7. fatal _____ b. motionless, dull, inactive

8. passé _____ c. deadly, disastrous

9. procrastinate _____ d. one side or view of person or situation

10. facet _____ e. outmoded, old-fashioned

**Today's Idiom**

*to get up on the wrong side of the bed*—to be in a bad mood
   When his mother raised Cain* about his slovenly* room, he accused her of *getting up on the wrong side of the bed*.

ANSWERS ARE ON PAGE 240

**New Words:**

| foist | stigmatize | capitulate | audacity | tantalize |
|-------|-----------|------------|----------|-----------|
| foist | stig' mə tīz | kə pich' u lāt | ô das' ə ti | tan' tə līz |

**What Next?**

Once the fashion industry has been able to *foist* a new style on the teen-ager, the older generation tends to *stigmatize* it as some form of rebellion. What is often ignored is that the young consumers *capitulate* to what is originated * by someone outside of their group. The feelings of individuality and *audacity* that the teen-ager gets from a new style of dress result from the propensity* of their elders to disparage* them. The actual situation is that the clothing fashions soon become accepted by all; there is nothing upsetting or revolutionary about them. While people are becoming complacent* about the "new," the clothing industry is busy planning how to *tantalize* the teen-ager with next year's "fashion." This arbitrary* decision is guaranteed to foment* consternation* among adults once again in the following year.

**Sample Sentences:** Insert the new words in these sentences.

1. Despite tenacious* resistance, they were ousted * from the strong-point and had to _____ to the enemy.

2. It was an asinine* thing to do—to _____ his opponent as a bigot* and thus exacerbate* an already bitter campaign.

3. It is common to hear people disparage* those who paint in the modern genre*; they speak about the _____ of the artist who submits a high white canvas with a black border as a serious work.

4. They are dubious* of such an artist and accuse him of trying to _____ as a work of art a rudimentary* exercise.

5. It is reprehensible* to _____ a young child with the promise of a reward for being good when you have no intention of giving it.

**Definitions:** Match the new words with their definitions.

6. foist _____ a. surrender, make terms

7. stigmatize _____ b. to mark with a disgrace

8. capitulate _____ c. boldness, daring

9. audacity _____ d. pass off slyly, pass as genuine

10. tantalize _____ e. tease or torment by offering something good, but not deliver

**Today's Idiom**  *castles in the air*—a dream about some wonderful future
People on Skid Row* often build *castles in the air.*

**ANSWERS ARE ON PAGE 240**

**New Words:**

| retort | reticent | tacit | chicanery | docile |
|--------|----------|-------|-----------|--------|
| ri tôrt′ | ret′ ə sənt | tas′ it | shi kān′ ər i | dos′ əl |

**Something for Everyone**

To the derogatory* comments from the older generation the teen-agers might *retort* that new fashions and styles are adopted by the elders with alacrity.* Though they complain, women emulate* their daughters by shortening or lengthening their hems. They may appear *reticent* about the bother and expense of altering their wardrobe, but they give *tacit* approval to the change by rushing to the department stores where they jostle* each other to buy copies of the more expensive dresses. The conclusion one might reach after observing how women countenance* the arbitrary* changes year after year is that they are naive* or victims of some *chicanery* practiced by the clothing industry. Women may appear hapless* before the intimidation* of "style," but the real truth may lie in the fact that they are so *docile* because they secretly enjoy the yearly excitement around the latest fashions.

*There's another familiar word re-introduced today. Did you recognize it?*

**Sample Sentences:** Insert the new words in these sentences.

1. The reporter divulged* the blatant _____ involved in the awarding of the contract.

2. Even the most _____ person may become fractious* when he gets only a pittance* for his hard labor.

3. His egregious* behavior brought a _____ reproach to his mother's eyes.

4. Most politicians are _____ when asked to divulge* their ambitions.

5. He refused to _____ to the rash* question about his propensity* for imbibing.*

**Definitions:** Match the new words with their definitions.

6. retort (v.) _____    a. understood, implied, not stated

7. reticent _____    b. easy to manage

8. tacit _____    c. to answer, reply

9. chicanery _____    d. silent or reserved

10. docile _____    e. trickery, underhandedness

**Today's Idiom**    *to maintain the status quo*—to keep things as they are

You hit the nail on the head * when you said we ought *to maintain the status quo* and not change horses in midstream.*

**ANSWERS ARE ON PAGE 240**

No matter what the fashion in dress, the fashion in education is an extensive vocabulary. Keep up with the fashion; build your vocabulary wardrobe.

**REVIEW WORDS**

| | | |
|---|---|---|
| _____ | 1 | audacity |
| _____ | 2 | capitulate |
| _____ | 3 | chicanery |
| _____ | 4 | docile |
| _____ | 5 | facet |
| _____ | 6 | fatal |
| _____ | 7 | foist |
| _____ | 8 | glib |
| _____ | 9 | homogenous |
| _____ | 10 | legerdemain |
| _____ | 11 | malleable |
| _____ | 12 | passé |
| _____ | 13 | procrastinate |
| _____ | 14 | reticent |
| _____ | 15 | retort |
| _____ | 16 | stagnant |
| _____ | 17 | stigmatize |
| _____ | 18 | tacit |
| _____ | 19 | tantalize |
| _____ | 20 | trend |

**DEFINITIONS**

a. reserved, silent
b. pass as genuine, pass off slyly
c. disastrous, deadly
d. smooth of speech
e. one side or view of person or situation
f. daring, boldness
g. reply, answer
h. uniform, same
j. capable of being formed or shaped
k. put off, delay
l. make terms, surrender
m. underhandedness, trickery
n. not stated, understood, implied
o. to mark with a disgrace
p. inactive, dull, motionless
r. general direction
s. old-fashioned, outmoded
t. easy to manage
u. deceptive adroitness,* sleight of hand
v. tease or torment by offering something good, but fail to deliver

**IDIOMS**

| | | |
|---|---|---|
| _____ | 21 | castles in the air |
| _____ | 22 | to get up on the wrong side of the bed |
| _____ | 23 | by hook or by crook |
| _____ | 24 | to maintain the status quo |

w. to be in a bad mood
x. dream about a wonderful future

y. at any cost, any way at all

z. to keep things as they are

Answers on page 240. Take that extra few minutes now to master the few words you made errors with.

**WORDS FOR FURTHER STUDY**          **MEANINGS**

1. _____   _____

2. _____   _____

3. _____   _____

**New Words:**  saga     belated     decrepit     imperturbable     vacillate
                    sä′ ga     bi lāt′ tid     di krep′ it     im′ pər tėr′ bə bəl     vas′ ə lāt

**Rule, Brittania**     An unforgettable *saga* of World War II has to do with the small French coastal town of Dunkirk. There, in 1940, thousands of British troops made a *belated* escape from the awesome* power of the German army and air force. They were removed by an array* of private boats, from huge yachts to *decrepit* fishing boats. At their own volition,* the skippers came close to the shore, while German planes bombed implacably.* They remained *imperturbable* under heavy fire. When their vessels were loaded, they dashed back to England. Once unloaded, they did not *vacillate*, but returned with equanimity* to their vigil* in the danger zone. The British proved once again that they are paragons* of comradeship in times of jeopardy.*

**Sample Sentences:**     Insert the new words in these sentences.

1. The _____ of a lone man confronting* the turbulent* oceans in a small boat is an exploit* we find laudable.*

2. The speaker remained _____ while his audience shouted caustic* comments about his mendacious* activities.

3. The ingrate* refused to accept his _____ gift.

4. When released from incarceration,* he was gaunt* and _____.

5. We are all familiar with the cliché* that he who _____ is lost.

**Definitions:**     Match the new words with their definitions.

6. saga     _____     a. hesitate, fluctuate

7. belated     _____     b. heroic story

8. decrepit     _____     c. broken down, worn out

9. imperturbable     _____     d. late, delayed

10. vacillate     _____     e. calm, steady, serene

**Today's Idiom**     *a sacred cow*—a person who cannot be criticized (From India, where cows may not be harmed because of religious rules.)

    I decided to throw down the gauntlet* by exposing the boss's son who had been ruling the roost* as *the sacred cow* of the business.

**ANSWERS ARE ON PAGE 240**

**New Words:**

| | | | |
|---|---|---|---|
| staunch | opprobrium | Machiavellian | unconscionable |
| stônch | ə prō′ bri əm | Mak′ ē ə vel′ ē ən | un kon′ shən ə bəl |
| pandemonium | | | |
| pan′ də mō′ ni əm | | | |

**The Good Guys vs. The Bad Guys**

The international adventure stories prevalent* on television follow meticulously* a plot that is inexorable* in its development. Those on the side of law and justice face perfidious* men and organizations. These are anathema* to those values the *staunch* heroes would defend. These infamous* men have no capacity for compassion,* and they treat the lovely women with *opprobrium.* The intrepid * heroes are placed in deleterious* situations as a result of the *Machiavellian* maneuvers of their opponents. One *unconscionable* act of duplicity* follows another until the total destruction of the "good guys" seems at hand. At the last moment, usually amidst the *pandemonium* of a battle, the cause for which the heroes strive triumphs. However, evil is ubiquitous,* and next week another fracas* will erupt.

**Sample Sentences:** Insert the new words in these sentences.

1. The coach heaped _____ upon the fledgling* ball player.

2. We are ready to rationalize* _____ activities on the part of our side if they are to the detriment* of our adversary.*

3. It was _____ for Abraham Lincoln to keep a book he had borrowed without making tenacious* efforts to return it.

4. There was _____ as the presidential nominee entered the convention site.*

5. He is such a _____ friend, my reprehensible* actions do not cause a schism* between us.

**Definitions:** Match the new words with their definitions.

6. staunch _____    a. scorn, insult

7. opprobrium _____    b. strong, trusty, firm

8. Machiavellian _____    c. without conscience, unreasonable

9. unconscionable _____    d. governed by opportunity, not principled

10. pandemonium _____    e. disorder, uproar

**Today's Idiom**

*through thick and thin*—in spite of all sorts of difficulties
    He decided to stick with his fairweather friends* *through thick and thin.*

ANSWERS ARE ON PAGE 240

**New Words:**

| flay | demeanor | delineation | vindicate | heinous |
|------|----------|-------------|-----------|---------|
| flā | di mēn′ ər | di lin′ i ā′ shən | vin′ də kāt | hā′ nəs |

**A Famous Mutiny**

One of the most repugnant* names in popular legend is that of Captain William Bligh. He was the captain of the H.M.S. Bounty in 1789, and the mutiny that erupted* aboard that ship was the basis for a film in which Charles Laughton portrayed Bligh as an awesome* bully and an unmitigated* villain. He would *flay* both the body and the spirit of anyone who crossed him. The crew developed such an aversion* to Bligh's mortifying actions and *demeanor* that, led by Fletcher Christian, they set the captain and 17 shipmates off in a lifeboat in the South Pacific. The ship continued to The Pitcairn Islands where the crew remained to live with the islanders. Laughton's *delineation* of Bligh remains as the image we have of him. Only recently has any attempt been made to *vindicate* Captain Bligh and to remove the *heinous* reputation that permeates* history.

**Sample Sentences:** Insert the new words in these sentences.

1. The Mayor tried to _____ his actions which had been called capricious* and irrational* by critics.

2. He castigated* his opponents and went to great lengths to _____ them with accusations of megalomania*.

3. His _____ was atypical*; usually phlegmatic*, he was belligerent* and garrulous* during the broadcast.

4. "The most _____ thing I have done," he said in a stentorian* voice, "is eradicate* the untruth that my party is not compatible* with progress."

5. Then he gave an incisive* _____ of his fulsome* opponents as an antiquated* group, complacent* about the noisome* conditions in a moribund* city.

**Definitions:** Match the new words with their definitions.

6. flay _____ a. hatefully evil

7. demeanor _____ b. absolve, justify

8. delineation _____ c. sketch, description in words

9. vindicate _____ d. conduct, bearing

10. heinous _____ e. strip off skin, scold harshly

**Today's Idiom**

*to take by storm*—to make a fast impression
   The new opera star *took the critics by storm* and carried the day.*

ANSWERS ARE ON PAGE 240

**New Words:**

| turpitude | infraction | callous | redress |
|---|---|---|---|
| tėr′ pə tüd | in frak′ shən | kal′ əs | ri dres′ |

vituperation
vī tü′ pər ā′ shən

**Fair Play!** Recently, there has been an attempt to improve Captain Bligh's tainted * image. Historians maintain that there was no *turpitude* in Bligh's actions aboard the H.M.S. Bounty. Perhaps he was imprudent* in failing to keep his temper under control. While an *infraction* aboard ship was quickly criticized, Bligh never carried out those *callous* actions the movie dramatized in order to depict* an evil man, say his defenders. After the mutiny, Captain Bligh astutely* navigated the lifeboat with the other 17 men for over 3,000 miles to safety. This prodigious* feat alone, say those who would restore Bligh's good name, should be enough to allow for a full *redress* of the wrongs that have been blamed on him for over 150 years. While the coterie* defending Captain Bligh do not ask the public to praise him, they do request a more benevolent* attitude towards this traditionally* reprehensible* figure, and an end to the *vituperation* heaped upon him for these many years.

**Sample Sentences:** Insert the new words in these sentences.

1. We do not condone* or tolerate* an _____ of even the most trivial * kind.

2. It takes a _____ person to watch with equanimity* as a gullible,* naive* girl falls for the line of a loathesome* boy.

3. How easy it is to heap _____ upon someone at the nadir* of his career.

4. There seems to be no way to _____ a grievance against an omnipotent* ruler.

5. From any facet* of his life, the acme* of moral _____ was reached by Adolph Hitler.

**Definitions:** Match the new words with their definitions.

6. turpitude _____    a. unfeeling

7. infraction _____    b. vileness, evil wickedness

8. callous _____    c. to right a wrong, remedy

9. redress _____    d. violation

10. vituperation _____    e. blame, abuse

**Today's Idiom** *to be in fine fettle*—to be in high spirits, or feeling well

     He did a lot of woolgathering* and *was in fine fettle* during the whole of the Indian summer.*

ANSWERS ARE ON PAGE 240

Our British cousins have a vocabulary that differs from ours in many ways. Isn't it fortunate that we have to be responsible for the American version of this language only?

**REVIEW WORDS**

|  |  |
|---|---|
| _____ 1 | belated |
| _____ 2 | callous |
| _____ 3 | decrepit |
| _____ 4 | delineation |
| _____ 5 | demeanor |
| _____ 6 | flay |
| _____ 7 | heinous |
| _____ 8 | imperturbable |
| _____ 9 | infraction |
| _____ 10 | Machiavellian |
| _____ 11 | opprobrium |
| _____ 12 | pandemonium |
| _____ 13 | redress |
| _____ 14 | saga |
| _____ 15 | staunch |
| _____ 16 | turpitude |
| _____ 17 | unconscionable |
| _____ 18 | vacillate |
| _____ 19 | vindicate |
| _____ 20 | vituperation |

**DEFINITIONS**

a. description in words, sketch
b. firm, trusty, strong
c. fluctuate, hesitate
d. violation
e. abuse, blame
f. serene, steady, calm
g. uproar, disorder
h. hatefully evil
j. scold harshly, strip off the skin
k. bearing, conduct
l. not principled, governed by opportunity
m. heroic story
n. delayed, late
o. unfeeling
p. evil, wickedness, vileness
r. worn out, broken down
s. unreasonable, without conscience
t. to right a wrong
u. justify, absolve
v. insult, scorn

**IDIOMS**

| _____ 21 | through thick and thin |
| _____ 22 | to take by storm |
| _____ 23 | a sacred cow |
| _____ 24 | to be in fine fettle |

w. to make a fast impression
x. in spite of all sorts of difficulties
y. to be in high spirits, feeling well
z. a person who cannot be criticized

The answers can be found on page 240.

**WORDS FOR FURTHER STUDY**     **MEANINGS**

1. _____   _____

2. _____   _____

3. _____   _____

195

**New Words:**

| rhetoric | clique | extol | mentor | facile |
|----------|--------|-------|--------|--------|
| ret′ ə rik | klēk | eks tōl′ | men′ tər | fas′ əl |

**A Political Show**

There are few forms of entertainment more enjoyable than a glib* politician running for office. Most politicians have prepared speeches dealing with the prevalent* topics of the day. They can maintain a fervid* flow of *rhetoric* for hours at a time. In each locality where he is to appear, the advance work is prepared by a *clique* of trustworthy aides. In preparation for the show, they have dispersed* leaflets, put up posters, and sent out cars and trucks with loudspeakers to *extol* the erudite* qualities of their candidate. Soon, the crowd gathers. Loyal party workers come forward to shake the hand of their *mentor*. Now, with the *facile* solutions to complex problems carefully memorized, the show is ready to begin. One moment facetious,* the next moment profound,* the candidate works to convince the incredulous* among the voters.

**Sample Sentences:** Insert the new words in these sentences.

1. It is not long before a young star has a _____ around him who sporadically* get their names into the newspapers.

2. At a time that requires tangible* proposals, all he offers is unconscionable* _____.

3. The detective interrogated* the adamant* prisoner in such a _____ way that he confessed after giving incontrovertible* evidence.

4. Youngsters scoff* when their elders _____ the halcyon* days of long ago.

5. Amidst the adulation* of the throng,* the film star, in all humility,* credited her _____ as the one most responsible.

**Definitions:** Match the new words with their definitions.

6. rhetoric   _____    a. counselor, coach, tutor

7. clique   _____    b. use (sometimes exaggerated) of language

8. extol   _____    c. easily accomplished or attained

9. mentor   _____    d. praise highly

10. facile   _____    e. small, exclusive group of people

**Today's Idiom**

to live in a fool's paradise—to be happy without a real basis
    He *lived in a fool's paradise* while he sowed wild oats*, but he soon had to pay the piper.*

ANSWERS ARE ON PAGE 240

**New Words:**

| cant | umbrage | magnanimous | vilify | elucidate |
|------|---------|-------------|--------|-----------|
| kant | um′ brij | mag nan′ ə məs | vil′ ə fī | i lü′ sə dāt |

**Getting a Good Look**

The television press interview is conducive* to close scrutiny* of a candidate. His public speeches may contain many *cant* phrases, but a sharp question by an astute* reporter can destroy a cliché* filled statement. The politician now will procrastinate* in his answer; a new facet* of his personality may be revealed by his demeanor.* Perhaps he will take *umbrage* at a suggestion that he favors the affluent.* His record is searched for evidence that he has been equally *magnanimous* to the indigent.* He accuses the reporter of attempting to *vilify* him. Is he being accused of turpitude* in office? It is time to discreetly* go on to another topic. The candidate wishes to extol * the virtues of his program and record. The press wants to allude* to things that keep him in the midst of controversy. They insist that he *elucidate* positions that the politician would rather leave in a nebulous* state.

**Sample Sentences:** Insert the new words in these sentences.

1. We feel so sanctimonious* when we _____ the character of a felon*.

2. The diplomat was astute* enough to see through the _____ of the Machiavellian ambassador.

3. A somber* examination of those indigent* families, bereft* of hope, sunken in apathy,* should motivate* us to be more _____ in our attempts to improve their lot.

4. I was flabbergasted * when he took _____ at my whimsical * remarks.

5. The judge ordered the censor to _____ his reasons for removing passages from the book in such a capricious* manner.

**Definitions:** Match the new words with their definitions.

6. cant _____    a. insincere or almost meaningless talk

7. umbrage _____    b. to make clear

8. magnani-
   mous _____    c. resentment, offense

9. vilify _____    d. malign,* slander

10. elucidate _____    e. generous, noble

**Today's Idiom**

*the sum and substance*—the heart or substantial part
    The *sum and substance* of our pyrrhic victory* was that our hopes for a stable future had gone up in smoke.*

ANSWERS ARE ON PAGE 240

**New Words:**

| vapid | unwieldy | proximity | lassitude | vitiate |
|-------|----------|-----------|-----------|---------|
| vap′ id | un wēl′ di | proks im′ ə ti | las′ ə tōōd | vish′·i āt |

**Seeing Is Learning**

While we are all cognizant* of the importance of words to create certain impressions, gesture is relegated* to a much lesser role. Gestures are an important concomitant* to even the most *vapid* speech, enhancing it and giving the hearer something to look at while he listens. The value of seeing at the same time as listening was shown when a class at a university, *unwieldy* because of its large size, was split up. One group was put into a room in close *proximity* to good loudspeakers. Every nuance* of the lecturer's voice could be heard clearly. Because they had no person on whom to place their attention, they soon took on the appearance of extreme *lassitude;* most students became lethargic* and rested their heads on their desks. The separation of visual and aural communication tended to *vitiate* the learning process. The listening group received grades lower than those received by those who could look at as well as hear the instructor.

*Once more your keen eye and memory were being tested by a re-introduced "new" word.*

**Sample Sentences:** Insert the new words in these sentences.

1. As the scion* of an affluent* family, he was often in _____ to opulence.*

2. After playing with his progeny* in the enervating* sun, he staggered back to his room where he was overcome with _____.

3. As a concomitant* to his belligerent* and vituperative* antipathy* toward his government, he became an expatriate,* but he found it a _____ life.

4. He was so disgruntled* about having to move the _____ piano, he procrastinated* for days.

5. The irrelevant* evidence seemed to _____ the prosecutor's case and precluded* a conviction.

**Definitions:** Match the new words with their definitions.

6. vapid _____    a. bulky, difficult to handle

7. unwieldy _____    b. destroy the use or value

8. proximity _____    c. uninteresting, dull

9. lassitude _____    d. nearness

10. vitiate _____    e. weariness, weakness

**Today's Idiom**

*on pins and needles*—to be on edge, jumpy

He was *on pins and needles* while he cooled his heels* in the principal's office.

ANSWERS ARE ON PAGE 240

**New Words:**

| augment | fatuous | contort | repertoire |
| ôg ment′ | fach′ ü es | kən tôrt′ | rep′ ər twär |

imperceptible
im′ pər sep′ tə bəl

**The Hammy Old Days**

Actors depend upon their ability to gesticulate* almost as much as upon speech to obtain their desired histrionic* effects. With them, gesture serves much more than merely to *augment* speech. When their communication is by gesture alone, it is called pantomime. In the early silent motion picture period, gestures were flamboyant.* To show that he was distraught* about the danger in which the heroine had been placed, the hero would go through the most *fatuous* actions. He would stagger, beat his breast, tear his hair, and *contort* his face into the most doleful* appearance. There weren't many simple or restrained gestures in his *repertoire*. The heroine, to indicate her love, would fling her arms wide and ardently* jump into her sweetheart's arms. It was only much later that actors became skilled enough to communicate with the audience through discreet* gestures and almost *imperceptible* changes in facial expression which could transmit nuances* of emotion.

**Sample Sentences:** Insert the new words in these sentences.

1. The new employee wanted to gain favor with his boss, and his obsequious* desires led to the most _____ behavior.

2. His virtuosity* was demonstrated by the works he performed from his _____.

3. He had always appeared virile,* so that the _____ decline towards senility* went unnoticed until he succumbed * and began to use a cane.

4. The paroxysm* of coughing served to _____ her body until she could gain a respite.*

5. The parsimonious* octogenarian* sought to _____ his wealth by removing it from its cache* and placing it in a bank.

**Definitions:** Match the new words with their definitions.

6. augment _____   a. extremely slight or gradual

7. fatuous _____   b. enlarge, increase

8. contort _____   c. foolish, silly, inane*

9. repertoire _____   d. twist violently

10. imperceptible _____   e. works that an artist is ready to perform

**Today's Idiom**

*to have at one's finger-tips*—to have thorough knowledge, to have ready

    *He had at his finger-tips an extensive repertoire.**

If there's one thing a politician must know how to do, it is to use words effectively. He must weigh carefully each and every utterance. He must also select the proper word for the audience he is addressing. You may never run for office, but it would be comforting to know you were ready for it—vocabulary-wise!

**REVIEW WORDS**

_____ 1 augment
_____ 2 cant
_____ 3 clique
_____ 4 contort
_____ 5 elucidate
_____ 6 extol
_____ 7 facile
_____ 8 fatuous
_____ 9 imperceptible
_____ 10 lassitude
_____ 11 magnanimous
_____ 12 mentor
_____ 13 proximity
_____ 14 repertoire
_____ 15 rhetoric
_____ 16 umbrage
_____ 17 unwieldy
_____ 18 vapid
_____ 19 vilify
_____ 20 vitiate

**DEFINITIONS**

a. twist violently
b. increase, enlarge
c. nearness
d. destroy the use or value
e. praise highly
f. use (sometimes exaggerated) of language
g. to make clear
h. slander, malign*
j. difficult to handle, bulky
k. works that an artist is ready to perform
l. tutor, counselor, coach
m. noble, generous
n. insincere or almost meaningless talk
o. small, exclusive group of people
p. extremely slight or gradual
r. dull, uninteresting
s. weakness, weariness
t. inane,* foolish, silly
u. easily accomplished or attained
v. offense, resentment

**IDIOMS**

_____ 21 to live in a fool's paradise
_____ 22 the sum and substance
_____ 23 on pins and needles
_____ 24 to have at one's finger-tips

w. the heart or substantial part

x. to be on edge, jumpy

y. to have ready, to have a thorough knowledge

z. to be happy without a real basis

Check your answers on page 240. Get to work learning the words that gave you trouble.

**WORDS FOR FURTHER STUDY**      **MEANINGS**

1. _____    _____

2. _____    _____

3. _____    _____

**New Words:**

| curry | pall | succulent | satiety | intrinsic |
|---|---|---|---|---|
| ker′ i | pôl | suk′ ū lənt | sə tī′ ə ti | in trin′ sik |

**Queen of the Supermarket**

The American housewife is queen of all she surveys in the supermarket. She decides what items shall be purchased. Grocery manufacturers are well aware of her power to make one product a success and another a failure. They spend huge sums developing new products with which to *curry* her favor. Fearful that a successful product will soon begin to *pall*, the manufacturers, without cessation,* come out with "new and improved" versions to whet* her appetite. Sometimes it is only a box or package that has been changed— perhaps a colorful photo of a *succulent* meal on a T.V. dinner box. In the larger supermarkets the housewife is faced with a *satiety* of merchandise, particularly in the copiously* stocked laundry detergent section. While there may be almost no *intrinsic* difference among the many brands, advertising and packaging serves to importune* her to buy one rather than another.

*Did you spot it? The "new word" you've seen before? Look again.*

**Sample Sentences:** Insert the new words in these sentences

1. The connoisseur* of fine foods declared the restaurant the ultimate* in the preparation of _____ meat dishes.

2. She coveted* the antiquated* locket even though it had only an _____ value.

3. He discreetly* tried to _____ favor with his employer.

4. Robert was squeamish* about going to the dance because there would be a _____ of boys that might preclude* his getting to know any girl.

5. Those conditions were not conducive* to a felicitous* evening as the dance would soon _____ for the lack of feminine companionship.

**Definitions:** Match the new words with their definitions.

6. curry _____    a. excess, overly full, surfeit*

7. pall _____    b. within itself, inherent*

8. succulent _____    c. to seek favor by flattery

9. satiety _____    d. juicy

10. intrinsic _____    e. cease to please, become dull

**Today's Idiom**   *a pretty kettle of fish*—a mess, troubles.
He thought it was an innocent white lie,* but it got him into *a pretty kettle of fish.*

ANSWERS ARE ON PAGE 241

201

**New Words:**

| potpourri | sanction | denote | allude | insidious |
|---|---|---|---|---|
| pō′ pü rē′ | sangk′ shən | di nōt′ | ə lüd′ | in sid′ i əs |

**It's What's Outside That Counts**

Packaging of grocery items is a facet* of advertising that is too little appreciated by consumers. Walking up and down the aisles of a supermarket, one seldom stops to analyze the individual package in the *potpourri* of items on the shelves. The manufacturer had to glean* and test many different designs before he accepted the one you see in the array* before you. Before he will *sanction* the use of a particular can, box, or bottle, he must know many things about its efficacy.* He wants to know if the colors attract: a white box may *denote* cleanliness, a red one, strength. There may be a photo or a drawing which will *allude* to the product's use or special qualities. A lackluster* package may be fatal.* Next, the size and shape are important elements. The housewife may want a small package for easy storing, but a larger package may suggest economy. A round bottle may look attractive, but a square one is easier to stack. These are some of the *insidious* aspects of packaging, the main purpose of which is to attract your attention as you peruse* the crowded supermarket shelves.

**Sample Sentences:** Insert the new words in these sentences.

1. I cannot _____ your lax* attitude towards the imminent* threat of a conflagration.*

2. In some _____ way the glib* salesman played upon my repressed * desires and sold me a gaudy* sports car.

3. You can be sure the candidate will _____ to the moribund * state of our economy and offer his panacea.*

4. A _____ of today's musical hits sounds more like cacophony* than harmony.

5. His levity* at such a serious moment _____ a lack of feeling.

**Definitions:** Match the new words with their definitions.

6. potpourri _____ a. sly, seductive, treacherous
7. sanction _____ b. hint, suggest
8. denote _____ c. endorse, certify
9. allude _____ d. medley, mixture
10. insidious _____ e. indicate, show, mean

**Today's Idiom** *the acid test*—a severe test

The new job was an *acid test* of his ability to bring home the bacon.*

ANSWERS ARE ON PAGE 241

**New Words:**

| propriety | advent | impious | proffer | spate |
|-----------|--------|---------|---------|-------|
| prə prī ə ti | ad′ vent | im′ pi əs | prof′ ər | spāt |

**"Tried and True"**    Few question the *propriety* of the current haste on the part of manufacturers to bring out "new and improved" products at the prevalent* rate. At one time, in the dim, distant past before the *advent* of television, it was the vogue* for products to be advertised on the merits of their "tried and true" qualities. Few advertisers were *impious* enough to jettison* any part of a product that had been accepted by the public. Year after year, the local grocery-store owner would *proffer* the same box of cereal, the same house cleanser. The acceptance was of the time-tested product, and it appeared almost unconscionable* for the manufacturer to change his merchandise. Today's *spate* of transient* products would have been considered an anomaly* in those days.

**Sample Sentences:**    Insert the new words in these sentences.

1. A few years ago there was a _____ of science-fiction films about awesome* monsters causing pandemonium* on our planet, but after a surfeit* of that genre*, their popularity began to wane.*

2. With the _____ of mandatory* safety inspections, some of the more decrepit* automobiles have been eradicated .*

3. We question the _____ of making fun of obese* people.

4. I'd like to _____ my belated * congratulations on your 25 years of married serenity.*

5. In the milieu* of city street life it is not atypical * to hear _____ comments about authority.

**Definitions:**    Match the new words with their definitions.

6. propriety _____ a. suitability, correctness

7. advent _____ b. offer for acceptance

8. impious _____ c. the coming of an important event

9. proffer _____ d. lacking respect, irreverent

10. spate _____ e. rush, flood

**Today's Idiom**    *a blind alley*—a direction which leads nowhere
    The modus operandi* was leading up *a blind alley* and they were barking up the wrong tree.*

ANSWERS ARE ON PAGE 241

**New Words:**

| shibboleth | bogus | substantiate | nutritive | raucous |
|---|---|---|---|---|
| shib′ ə lith | bō′ gəs | səb stan′ shi āt | nü′ trə tiv | rô′ kəs |

**What's in a Name?**

Supermarkets now carry their own products to compete with the national brands. These "house" brands are not in a felicitous* position because they cannot be advertised widely. Supermarkets overcome this encumbrance* by making these brands less expensive. Many people believe the *shibboleth,* "You get what you pay for," and they purchase items on the premise* that quality varies as the price does. Are the claims made by nationally advertised brands *bogus?* How can one bread company *substantiate* its *nutritive* superiority over another? As there is no incontrovertible* evidence, the more expensive bread (or coffee, etc.) must compensate* by increased advertising. They make inordinate* claims, using those *raucous* techniques proven so successful in convincing the frugal * consumer to switch to a more costly brand.

**Sample Sentences:** Insert the new words in these sentences.

1. Mothers should be vigilant* that their children's food has the proper _____ value.

2. There were _____ complaints about the inordinate* number of fatal * accidents caused by inebriated * drivers.

3. People often try to compensate* for their deplorable* lack of culture by repeating the _____, "I know what I like."

4. He had the audacity* to try to foist* a _____ dollar on me.

5. The reporter wanted to elicit* the pertinent* facts from the reticent* witness so he could _____ the charge of moral turpitude* against the high city official.

**Definitions:** Match the new words with their definitions.

6. shibboleth  _____    a.  pet phrase, slogan

7. bogus  _____    b.  harsh, shrill

8. substantiate  _____    c.  counterfeit, fake

9. nutritive  _____    d.  having nourishing properties

10. raucous  _____    e.  confirm, ratify

**Today's Idiom**  *to twist around one's finger*—to control completely
   He winked at* the little girl's bad behavior; she had him *twisted around her finger.*

ANSWERS ARE ON PAGE 241

You can be sure of a balanced language if you are well acquainted with all the products (words) available in your supermarket (vocabulary).

## REVIEW WORDS

| | | DEFINITIONS |
|---|---|---|
| _____ | 1 advent | a. suggest, hint |
| _____ | 2 allude | b. surfeit,* excess, overly full |
| _____ | 3 bogus | c. coming of an important event |
| _____ | 4 curry | d. having nourishing properties |
| _____ | 5 denote | e. slogan, pet phrase |
| _____ | 6 impious | f. correctness, suitability |
| _____ | 7 insidious | g. juicy |
| _____ | 8 intrinsic | h. mixture, medley |
| _____ | 9 nutritive | j. mean, show, indicate |
| _____ | 10 pall | k. to seek favor by flattery |
| _____ | 11 potpourri | l. irreverent, lacking respect |
| _____ | 12 proffer | m. fake, counterfeit |
| _____ | 13 propriety | n. ratify, confirm |
| _____ | 14 raucous | o. rush, flood |
| _____ | 15 sanction | p. become dull, cease to please |
| _____ | 16 satiety | r. treacherous, sly, seductive |
| _____ | 17 shibboleth | s. certify, endorse |
| _____ | 18 spate | t. inherent,* within itself |
| _____ | 19 substantiate | u. offer for acceptance |
| _____ | 20 succulent | v. shrill, harsh |

## IDIOMS

| | | |
|---|---|---|
| _____ | 21 to twist around one's finger | w. a severe test |
| _____ | 22 the acid test | x. a direction which leads nowhere |
| _____ | 23 a pretty kettle of fish | y. a mess, trouble |
| _____ | 24 a blind alley | z. to control completely |

Now check your answers on page 241. Make a record of those words you missed.

**WORDS FOR FURTHER STUDY**     **MEANINGS**

1. _____  _____

2. _____  _____

3. _____  _____

**ANSWERS ARE ON PAGE**

**New Words:**

| quandary | callous | expedient | negligible | blasé |
|----------|---------|-----------|------------|-------|
| kwon′ də ri | kal′ əs | ik spē′ di ənt | neg′ lə jə bəl | blä zā′ |

**You Can't Help But Watch**

The housewife is in a quandary about making a felicitous* selection among the array* of products. The advertisers must influence the malleable* consumer, and often they do it in the most *callous* ways. Television offers many tangible* advantages for reaching the consumer. As a result, the consumer is inundated * by commercials. The advertiser knows that a television commercial is the most *expedient* way to reach large numbers of people. The cost for each commercial film is prodigious,* but because the audience is so large, the cost per viewer is *negligible*. Each commercial is prepared in the most meticulous* way in order to catch the attention of even the most *blasé* viewer and hold it until the message is through.

*The re-introduced "new word" should have stood out immediately. Did it?*

**Sample Sentences:** Insert the new words in these sentences.

1. It was fortuitous* that the accident occurred when there were _____ numbers of children in the buses.

2. He was in a _____ about which selection from his extensive repertoire* it would be feasible* to perform for the children.

3. Because she had committed only a venial * offense, he thought it _____ to abjure* a severe punishment.

4. Who can be _____ about the presence of many indigent* families in close proximity* to affluence?*

5. People have become so _____ about the once thrilling, now mundane* transatlantic flights.

**Definitions:** Match the new words with their definitions.

6. quandary   ____    a. indifferent, not responsive to excitement

7. callous   ____    b. hardened, unfeeling

8. expedient (adj.)   ____    c. doubt, dilemma

9. negligible   ____    d. advisable, fit

10. blasé   ____    e. trifling, inconsiderable

**Today's Idiom**

*to do one's heart good*—to make one feel happy or better
    It *did my heart good* to see that inveterate* egotist* eat humble pie.*

ANSWERS ARE ON PAGE 241

New Words:  ennui      comely     frenetic     artifice     diversity
            än′ wē      kum′ li    frə net′ ik  är′ tə fis   də ver′ sə ti

**Tricks of the Trade**   Some television commercials, trying to break through the *ennui* built up in the viewer by the plethora* of competition, employ humor. Others feature a *comely* girl as a pretext* for getting the viewer to stay tuned in. At times raucous* music, accompanied by some frenetic activities, is designed to preclude* the viewer's loss of attention. The advertiser will employ every bit of *artifice* at the film maker's command to make a trenchant* commercial. The *diversity* of appeals made to the viewer is a concomitant* of the many ways people react to commercials. A great deal of time and money has gone into placing the consumer's psychological make-up under scrutiny*.

**Sample Sentences:**   Insert the new words in these sentences.

1. The omnipotent* dictator employed all of his rhetoric* to vilify* those who would be brash* enough to suggest that a _____ of opinions should be expressed.

2. The fledgling* pianist knew that his mentor* would take umbrage* at his yawning during the lesson, but the feeling of _____ was overwhelming.

3. He was reticent* about revealing his clandestine* meetings with a _____ young girl counselor at this camp.

4. They furtively* employed every kind of _____ to be able to meet.

5. They were vigilant* in order that their surreptitious* meetings would not be discovered, and it often required _____ changes of plans to preclude exposure.

**Definitions:**   Match the new words with their definitions.

6. ennui       _____    a. frantic, frenzied
7. comely      _____    b. boredom
8. frenetic    _____    c. beautiful, handsome
9. artifice    _____    d. strategy, trickery
10. diversity  _____    e. variety, change

**Today's Idiom**   *worth one's weight in gold*—extremely valuable, very useful
The coach said the new star center was *worth his weight in gold*.

ANSWERS ARE ON PAGE 241

New Words:
qualm    expurgate    begrudge    artless    gratuity
kwäm    eks′ pər gāt    bi gruj′    ärt′ lis    grə tü′ ə ti

**Going to the Source**

The wide diversity* of reasons people have for buying one product rather than another are investigated by the advertising people in order to prepare efficacious* commercials. They do not have the slightest *qualm* about questioning the consumer about personal things in her own domicile.* The consumer is requested not to *expurgate* her answers. Generally, people are not reticent* and do not *begrudge* giving the time and effort. The questions delve rather deeply, and what the *artless* responses divulge* will help the advertiser decide what to put into his next commercial. After a large number of interviews, the copious* results make it feasible* to prognosticate* how well the commercial will do. The interviewer usually offers no *gratuity* to the person who has helped, but often a sample of the product is proffered * as thanks.

**Sample Sentences:** Insert the new words in these sentences.

1. A successful television program was built around the _____ comments of very young children.

2. At times, the producer must _____ some of the things said by these children because they are too candid.*

3. He had a serious _____ about hunting for the nearly extinct* quarry.*

4. He took umbrage* when I offered a _____ to augment* his small salary.

5. She did not _____ paying the pittance* extra for a better coat.

**Definitions:** Match the new words with their definitions.

6. qualm    _____    a. remove objectionable parts or passages

7. expurgate    _____    b. to be resentful or reluctant

8. begrudge    _____    c. innocent, naive

9. artless    _____    d. tip

10. gratuity    _____    e. twinge of conscience

**Today's Idiom**

*to make the best of a bad bargain*—to change or go along with a poor situation

After he bought the white elephant,* *he made the best of a bad bargain* and let sleeping dogs lie.*

ANSWERS ARE ON PAGE 241

**New Words:**
| | | | | |
|---|---|---|---|---|
| manifest | delve | capricious | requisite | replenish |
| man′ ə fest | delv | ke prish′ əs | rek′ wə zit | ri plen′ ish |

**It Seems to Work**

Despite the antipathy* towards commercials expressed by the viewers, the remarkable success of television commercials in selling products makes it *manifest* that the advertiser has gleaned* what the viewer wants to see and hear from his research interview. This has helped the advertiser *delve* deeply into what motivates* people when they go into the supermarket to purchase products. The advertising agency is never *capricious* and can vindicate* spending large sums of money on research. Having uncovered what the public wants, the advertiser expedites* putting the *requisite* words, music, and photographs of the product on film. He will thus *replenish* the never-ending, ubiquitous* television commercial supply in the hope that the housewife will remember some facet* of the film and buy the product.

**Sample Sentences:**   Insert the new words in these sentences.

1. If we _____ below and behind the rhetoric* and invective,* we may discover the profound * reasons for the ferment* in our land.

2. He was reticent* about emulating* those who, after eating almost to satiety,* rushed to _____ the food on their plates.

3. It was _____ that an arbiter* would be needed because neither side would capitulate* to a plan foisted * on them by the other side.

4. When the acrimonious* discussion about his _____ actions had attenuated,* he was able to vindicate* his conduct.

5. One mortifying* _____ for the position was that he would have to work for one year under the aegis* of a fatuous* egotist.*

**Definitions:**   Match the new words with their definitions.

6. manifest _____    a. requirement
7. delve _____    b. evident, obvious
8. capricious _____    c. fanciful, whimsical *
9. requisite _____    d. to fill again, to restock
10. replenish _____    e. dig, do research

**Today's Idiom**   *to make ends meet*—to manage on a given income

He turned thumbs down* on a new car; he was having enough trouble *making ends meet,* as it was.

ANSWERS ARE ON PAGE 241

As you watch your next television commercial try to imagine what questions were asked by the research people as they interviewed the possible consumers. Advertisers have to select their words carefully. You can select words only when you have large numbers at your command.

| REVIEW WORDS | DEFINITIONS |
|---|---|
| _____ 1 artifice | a. remove objectionable parts or passages |
| _____ 2 artless | b. twinge of conscience |
| _____ 3 begrudge | c. handsome, beautiful |
| _____ 4 blasé | d. strategy, trickery |
| _____ 5 callous | e. fit, advisable |
| _____ 6 capricious | f. indifferent, not responsive to excitement |
| _____ 7 comely | g. fanciful, whimsical * |
| _____ 8 delve | h. do research, dig |
| _____ 9 diversity | j. to be resentful or reluctant |
| _____ 10 ennui | k. inconsiderable, trifling |
| _____ 11 expedient | l. boredom |
| _____ 12 expurgate | m. obvious, evident |
| _____ 13 frenetic | n. to restock, fill again |
| _____ 14 gratuity | o. change, variety |
| _____ 15 manifest | p. dilemma, doubt |
| _____ 16 negligible | r. unfeeling, hardened |
| _____ 17 qualm | s. frenzied, frantic |
| _____ 18 quandary | t. requirement |
| _____ 19 replenish | u. tip |
| _____ 20 requisite | v. naive, innocent |

## IDIOMS

| | |
|---|---|
| _____ 21 to make the best of a bad bargain | w. extremely valuable, very useful |
| _____ 22 to do one's heart good | x. to make one feel happy or better |
| _____ 23 worth one's weight in gold | y. to manage on a given income |
| _____ 24 to make ends meet | z. to change or go along with a poor situation |

Check your answers on page 241. Take that extra moment *now* to review and study the words you got wrong.

WORDS FOR
FURTHER STUDY       MEANINGS

1. _____   _____

2. _____   _____

3. _____   _____

ANSWERS ARE ON PAGE

**New Words:**

| roster | stunted | atrophy | maim | ameliorate |
|---|---|---|---|---|
| ros′ tər | stunt′ id | at′ rə fi | mām | ə mēl′ ye rāt |

**It Takes More Than Medicine**

If one were to look at the *roster* of physical handicaps, one would reach the somber* conclusion that the list is a long one. Included would be *stunted* development of an arm or leg due to a birth anomaly.* Others would be the result of a crippling disease which has caused muscles to *atrophy*. The list would go on with illnesses and injuries which *maim* and debilitate.* Modern medicine has done much to *ameliorate* the physical problems. However, there are an inordinate* number of problems of the handicapped which have still to be alleviated.* People are not naturally callous,* but in some perverse* way they have the propensity* to repress* any concern with the physically handicapped. The social problems seem to be inherent* in our own attitudes.

**Sample Sentences:** Insert the new words in these sentences.

1. If you heap opprobrium* on an impious* child, it probably will not _____ the conditions which led to the rebelliousness.

2. The coach knew he would have to add experienced players to the _____ to compensate* for the spate* of freshmen on the team.

3. There seems to be voluminous* evidence that smoking will _____ the individual in many ways.

4. The prodigy* allowed his musical talent to _____ in order to become a boxing champion.

5. His friends, with a constricted * outlook on life, soon _____ his curiosity about many things.

**Definitions:** Match the new words with their definitions.

6. roster _____ a. checked the natural growth, held back growth
7. stunted _____ b. waste away
8. atrophy _____ c. a list of names
9. maim _____ d. improve, relieve
10. ameliorate _____ e. disable, cripple

**Today's Idiom**

*to burn the midnight oil*—to study or work until very late

The Jerry-built* radio was such an enigma* that he had *to burn the midnight oil* * for several nights in order to get it working.

ANSWERS ARE ON PAGE 241

**New Words:**

| cynic | unctuous | benevolent | subservient | iniquity |
|-------|----------|------------|-------------|----------|
| sin′ ik | ungk′ chü əs | bə nev′ ə lənt | səb sėr′ vi ənt | in ik′ wə ti |

**Doing the Right Thing**

The obstacles which frustrate* the physically handicapped person who is seeking employment may turn him into a *cynic*. Too often a prospective employer, with a rather *unctuous* manner, actually tends to degrade* the handicapped by proffering* employment that is really beneath him and his abilities. The employer appears to be acting in a *benevolent* manner, but this attitude shows no compassion,* for he really expects the man seeking the job to remain *subservient*. This *iniquity* cannot but give the handicapped a feeling that he is being discriminated against. He does not expect a sinecure,* but he has an aversion* to the prevalent* belief that he should consider himself lucky to find any employment.

**Sample Sentences:** Insert the new words in these sentences.

1. We had to wince* as we watched the newcomer try to wheedle* and ingratiate* himself into the teacher's favor in the most _____ manner.

2. It is easy to become a _____ when the same adults who inveigh* most vehemently* against the uncouth* actions that they say permeate* our youth drink to satiety* and behave fatuously.*

3. We all have moments when we vacillate* between selfish and _____ desires.

4. While his demeanor* remained imperturbable,* there was latent* anger at the ignominious* and _____ role he had to play.

5. Those who are complacent* about any _____ in our society should be wary* of the unsavory* consequences for all.

**Definitions:** Match the new words with their definitions.

6. cynic _____ a. servile, obsequious*

7. unctuous _____ b. pessimist, skeptic

8. benevolent _____ c. affectedly emotional

9. subservient _____ d. kindly, charitable

10. iniquity _____ e. injustice, wickedness

**Today's Idiom**

*to lay one's cards on the table*—to talk frankly.
   He knew he was out of his depth* so *he laid his cards on the table* and asked for assistance.

**ANSWERS ARE ON PAGE 241**

New Words:
| largess | criterion | repent | mollify | mercenary |
| lär′ jis | krī tēr′ i ən | ri pent′ | mol′ ə fī | mėr′ sə ner′ ē |

**A Better Way**    Why is there any question about the propriety* of hiring the physically handicapped? No one who understands their needs can condone* this attitude. The offering of employment should not be considered a *largess*. There should be no need to vindicate* the hiring of a handicapped person. The only *criterion* should be what he is capable of doing. If this is the approach, the handicapped worker will not feel he is an encumbrance* to his boss. The employer, on the other hand, will find it conducive* to good work and will not *repent* his having tried something new just to *mollify* his conscience. Even for the most *mercenary* employer, there should be no reticence* in eliciting* the best that is possible from the handicapped worker.

**Sample Sentences:**    Insert the new words in these sentences.

1. He felt it would be ignominious* for him to accept any _____ from the charlatan* whose Machiavellian* schemes had made him affluent.*

2. Behind the facade* of ostensible* benevolence* there was a _____ streak.

3. The platitude, "I know what I like," is often used to rationalize* our lack of a _____ for things about which we are dubious.*

4. When Mother is in a pique* about some infraction* of a rule, it takes all of our dexterity* to _____ her.

5. After every election we _____, in a belated * criticism, the apathy* and complacency* of so many people who failed to vote.

**Definitions:**    Match the new words with their definitions.

6. largess        _____    a. gift, gratuity*, liberality

7. criterion      _____    b. model, standard, test

8. repent         _____    c. motivated * by desire for gain, greedy

9. mollify        _____    d. pacify, appease

10. mercenary
    (adj.)        _____    e. regret, desire to make amends

**Today's Idiom**    *a bolt from the blue*—a great surprise
    The windfall * from his distant cousin came like *a bolt from the blue*.

ANSWERS ARE ON PAGE 241

**New Words:**

| pariah | aloof | pragmatic | vestige | guise |
|--------|-------|-----------|---------|-------|
| pə rī ə | ə lüf′ | prag mat′ ik | ves′ tij | gīz |

**Just Be Yourself**

Socially, the handicapped person is often treated as a *pariah*. Most people hold themselves *aloof* from normal contact with those who are "different." This social separation propagates* additional feelings of antipathy*. If the "normal" individual would socialize with the handicapped individual, he would learn in a *pragmatic* way that these are people who happen to have a physical handicap; the handicap does not make them any less human. The iniquity* of assuming that physical superiority equals moral superiority prevents all of us from direct human relationships. As long as there is a *vestige* of feeling that handicapped people are inferior then we are all handicapped in one way or another. Under the *guise* of physical superiority we demonstrate a moral turpitude* that is harmful to all.

**Sample Sentences:** Insert the new words in these sentences.

1. After therapy*, there remained hardly a _____ of his phobia*.

2. He was stigmatized * as a _____ when he had the audacity* to boast of his nefarious* and sordid * career printing bogus* money.

3. Although many people say this is a propitious* time to invest in the stock market, there is a tenable argument for remaining _____.

4. In the _____ of maintaining national unity under military rule, there was a paucity* of even innocuous* dissent*.

5. "You can't argue with success," was his _____ reply to derogatory* remarks about a movie star who had only superficial * talent as an actor.

**Definitions:** Match the new words with their definitions.

6. pariah _____ a. manner, appearance, mien*

7. aloof _____ b. social outcast

8. pragmatic _____ c. distant, apart, reserved

9. vestige _____ d. trace, evidence

10. guise _____ e. practical, based on experience

**Today's Idiom**

*to tell tales out of school*—to reveal harmful secrets

The fat was in the fire* for the politician when his private secretary started *telling tales out of school* about his secret sources of income.

ANSWERS ARE ON PAGE 241

There are various kinds of handicaps. One which we can do something about, and *you* are now doing it, is the language handicap. Our fullest potential can be realized only when there is no barrier between what we want to say or write and our ability to express ourselves.

| REVIEW WORDS | | DEFINITIONS |
|---|---|---|
| _____ 1 | aloof | a. based on experience, practical |
| _____ 2 | ameliorate | b. mien,* appearance, manner |
| _____ 3 | atrophy | c. a list of names |
| _____ 4 | benevolent | d. skeptic, pessimist |
| _____ 5 | criterion | e. test, model, standard |
| _____ 6 | cynic | f. desire to make amends, regret |
| _____ 7 | guise | g. obsequious,* servile |
| _____ 8 | iniquity | h. held back or checked the natural growth |
| _____ 9 | largess | j. social outcast |
| _____ 10 | maim | k. evidence, trace |
| _____ 11 | mercenary | l. waste away |
| _____ 12 | mollify | m. charitable, kindly |
| _____ 13 | pariah | n. appease, pacify |
| _____ 14 | pragmatic | o. wickedness, injustice |
| _____ 15 | repent | p. cripple, disable |
| _____ 16 | roster | r. reserved, apart, distant |
| _____ 17 | stunted | s. greedy, motivated * by desire for gain |
| _____ 18 | subservient | t. liberality, gift, gratuity* |
| _____ 19 | unctuous | u. affectedly emotional |
| _____ 20 | vestige | v. relieve, improve |

**IDIOMS**

| | | |
|---|---|---|
| _____ 21 | to burn the midnight oil | w. to reveal harmful secrets |
| _____ 22 | to lay one's cards on the table | x. a great surprise |
| _____ 23 | a bolt from the blue | y. to talk frankly |
| _____ 24 | to tell tales out of school | z. to study or work until very late |

**ANSWERS ARE ON PAGE 241**

| WORDS FOR FURTHER STUDY | MEANINGS |
|---|---|
| 1. _____ | _____ |
| 2. _____ | _____ |
| 3. _____ | _____ |

New Words:
| nullify | deluge | futility | carnage | technology |
|---|---|---|---|---|
| nul′ ə fī | del′ ūj | fū til′ ə ti | kär′ nij | tek nol′ ə ji |

**Have We Mastered Our Environment?**

Natural disasters tend to *nullify* the best efforts of mankind. It is as though there are forces at work that are contemptuous* of our proud achievements. Who has not read of or seen the waters which *deluge* our towns and cities, jeopardizing* lives and culminating* in the destruction of the results of endless work in the space of a few moments? We are all vulnerable* to feelings of *futility* as we view the *carnage* caused to cattle from the sudden inundation.* Despite the laudable* advances made in *technology*, it can be seen that we cannot yet say we have mastered our environment. Disasters of this type, leaving only pathetic* vestiges* of homes and shops, are accepted as inevitable,* and all we can do is to attempt to ameliorate* the conditions that result.

*Haven't you met one of these "new words" before? Sure you have.*

**Sample Sentences:** Insert the new words in these sentences.

1. In spite of his efforts to cajole* the girl, she remained aloof,* and the _____ of his efforts made him lugubrious.*

2. To our consternation,* modern _____ has made feasible* a spate* of lethal* devices which could lead to the inadvertent* destruction of the world.

3. In order to _____ the height advantage of his adversary,* he abjured* smoking and did an inordinate amount of exercise until he was the acme of litheness* and dexterity.*

4. We found it impossible to mollify* the irate* owner of three prize cats as he viewed the _____ caused by our large dog.

5. The office was _____ with requests for his autograph as the girls became cognizant of his identity.

**Definitions:** Match the new words with their definitions.

6. nullify _____ a. slaughter

7. deluge (v.) _____ b. to flood

8. futility _____ c. abolish, cancel

9. carnage _____ d. applied science

10. technology _____ e. uselessness

**Today's Idiom**

*to build upon sand*—to have a poor base, or not sufficient preparation

Because they were amateurs and without money, the political campaign was *built upon sand* and the candidate was a flash in the pan.*

ANSWERS ARE ON PAGE 241

**New Words:** libel    defamatory    plaintiff    canard    deprecate
              lī′ bəl    di fam′ ə tô′ ri    plān′ tif    kə närd′    dep′ rə kāt

### Good News— and Bad

One of the latent* dangers indigenous* to our constitutional guarantee of freedom of the press has to do with the protection of the individual against the detriment* that might come from news reports involving him. There are *libel* laws which protect against false charges. If an individual believes his character or livelihood have been damaged by a *defamatory* article, he can sue. As the *plaintiff* he must refute* the story and show how the defendant caused him harm by printing a *canard*. The defendant attempts to substantiate* the truth of the article. The printing of news may besmirch* an individual's character, but there is no way to alleviate* this problem without changes in the constitution. This would be tantamount* to destroying the efficacy* of our coveted * right to learn the truth from the press. We all *deprecate* a situation in which someone suffers because of exposure in the newspapers. Only when the harm is caused by someone with a desire to malign* under the guise* of printing the news can the individual expect to win compensation* through the courts.

**Sample Sentences:** Insert the new words in these sentences.

1. The mayor vehemently* denied there was any antipathy* between the governor and himself and blamed this _____ on their political opponents.

2. I resent your _____ remark which depicts* me as a culprit.*

3. The egregious* calumny* of the defendant worked to the advantage of the _____.

4. Publishers of newspapers and magazines augment* their staff with lawyers to represent them when they are sued for _____.

5. The cynic* will _____ the motives of anyone who tries to ameliorate* the iniquities* in our society.

**Definitions:** *Study these carefully for the fine differences in meaning.*

6. libel (n.)  _____     a. express disapproval

7. defamatory  _____     b. the complaining party, in law

8. plaintiff  _____     c. to degrade by writing or publishing

9. canard  _____     d. damaging character by false reports

10. deprecate  _____     e. a made-up sensational story

### Today's Idiom

*a pretty kettle of fish*—a messy situation, a problem
He knew that when he attacked the sacred cow* he would be in *a pretty kettle of fish.*

ANSWERS ARE ON PAGE 241

New Words:

| reputed | frail | potent | excoriate | devout |
|---------|-------|--------|-----------|--------|
| ri pūt′ id | frāl | pō′ tənt | eks kô′ ri āt | di vout′ |

**A Philosopher for Our Time**

Soren Kierkegaard was a Danish philosopher who is *reputed* to be the forerunner of the current vogue* of existentialism. In appearance he was a *frail* and ungainly man. An extremely erudite* thinker and writer, he was a *potent* force in propagating* the new approach to life. His philosophy would *excoriate* those who believed that man could stand aside from life. In his philosophy it is a heresy* to take a detached point of view; it is incumbent* upon the individual to get involved. What is germane* is not that we exist, but that our existence is determined by our acts. He was a religiously *devout* man who fervidly* believed that the individual is always paramount.*

**Sample Sentences:**  Insert the new words in these sentences.

1. Even though she was piqued * at his indolent* manner, it was pathetic* to listen to her _____ him in public.

2. His awesome* mental dexterity* compensated * for his _____ physical condition.

3. When his muscles began to atrophy,* the doctor initiated * therapy* with a _____ new drug.

4. The drug is _____ to have a salubrious* effect on nascent* conditions of this type.

5. Although he was a _____ adherent* of the party, he remained aloof* during the vitriolic* primary campaign.

**Definitions:**  Match the new words with their definitions.

6. reputed    _____    a. thought, supposed, believed

7. frail    _____    b. religious, sincere

8. potent    _____    c. delicate, weak

9. excoriate    _____    d. criticize severely

10. devout    _____    e. powerful, strong, intense

**Today's Idiom**

*to toe the mark*—to obey or stick to a rule or policy

He wanted to kick over the traces,* but his parents made him *toe the mark.*

ANSWERS ARE ON PAGE 241

**New Words:**

| diminutive | profuse | dulcet | impromptu | malevolent |
|---|---|---|---|---|
| də min′ ū tiv | prə fūs′ | dul′ sit | im promp′ tü | mə lev′ ə lənt |

**The Island of Wild Dogs**

The saga* of the introduction of that *diminutive* song bird, the canary, into the homes of the world as tame pets is an interesting one. In the sixteenth century a trading ship going to Italy stopped at an island named "Canis," from the Latin word for wild dog, which could be found there in *profuse* numbers, off the coast of Africa. The *dulcet* song of the wild birds whetted* the interest of the captain. In *impromptu* cages hundreds were taken aboard to be traded. The sailors called these gray-green birds, spotted with yellow, "canaries." As they approached the island of Elba, near Italy, a *malevolent* storm put the boat in jeopardy* of sinking. A member of the crew released the birds, and the intrepid* canaries instinctively flew towards land. The peasants on Elba took the wild canaries in as pets. Eventually, the birds found their way into homes throughout Europe where they were domesticated and bred for variety of song and shades of colors. The canaries prevalent* today differ greatly from the ones discovered over four hundred years ago.

**Sample Sentences:**   Insert the new words in these sentences.

1. As the music reached a frenetic* tempo, the audience lost all decorum* and broke into _____ dancing.

2. He had no qualms* about opposing the clique* who insidiously* exerted a _____ influence on the president.

3. The connoisseur* was able to glean* a worthwhile painting from the _____ variety of poor ones at the exhibit.

4. Europeans drive _____ cars because their narrow roads and high prices for gasoline are not conducive* to or compatible* with our large ones.

5. The blasé* devotee* of the opera was awakened from his ennui* by the _____ tones of the new soprano.

**Definitions:**   Match the new words with their definitions.

6. diminutive  _____    a. ill-disposed, ill-intentioned

7. profuse  _____    b. tiny, small

8. dulcet  _____    c. spur of the moment, offhand

9. impromptu  _____    d. sweet or melodious to the ear

10. malevolent  _____    e. overflowing, abundant

**Today's Idiom**   *to be under a cloud*—to be in temporary disgrace or trouble
  Until they discovered the real thief, he *was under a cloud*.

ANSWERS ARE ON PAGE 241

The history, or derivation, of words is called "etymology." This is a fascinating study, and it gives insight to the background of words such as "canary," and thousands of others. Knowing the history of a word helps you remember it.

## REVIEW WORDS

_____ 1 canard
_____ 2 carnage
_____ 3 defamatory
_____ 4 deluge
_____ 5 deprecate
_____ 6 devout
_____ 7 diminutive
_____ 8 dulcet
_____ 9 excoriate
_____ 10 frail
_____ 11 futility
_____ 12 impromptu
_____ 13 libel
_____ 14 malevolent
_____ 15 nullify
_____ 16 plaintiff
_____ 17 potent
_____ 18 profuse
_____ 19 reputed
_____ 20 technology

## DEFINITIONS

a. flood
b. express disapproval
c. intense, strong, powerful
d. sincere, religious
e. sweet or melodious to the ear
f. abundant, overflowing
g. slaughter
h. uselessness
j. criticize severely
k. damaging character by false reports
l. a made-up sensational story
m. small, tiny
n. cancel, abolish
o. ill-disposed, ill-intentioned
r. the complaining party, in law
s. applied science
t. believed, thought, supposed
u. offhand, spur of the moment
v. to degrade by writing or publishing

## IDIOMS

_____ 21 a pretty kettle of fish
_____ 22 to be under a cloud
_____ 23 to toe the mark
_____ 24 to build upon sand

w. to be in temporary disgrace or trouble

x. to obey or stick to a rule or policy

y. a messy situation, a problem

z. to have a poor base, or not sufficient preparation

**ANSWERS ARE ON PAGE 241**

### WORDS FOR FURTHER STUDY        MEANINGS

1. _____  _____

2. _____  _____

3. _____  _____

**New Words:**

| wistful | raiment | brigand | corpulent | rail |
|---------|---------|---------|-----------|------|
| wist′ fəl | rā′ mənt | brig′ ənd | kôr′ pū lənt | rāl |

**In Days of Yore**   Current novels are replete* with lurid* crimes, carnage* and death. Do you get *wistful* when you recall the romantic tales which begin with an innocent maiden travelling through the rustic* countryside? She is dressed in glittering *raiment*. The scene is idyllic.* Without warning, the group is set upon by a virile* *brigand*, who, in the most perfunctory* and callous* fashion, carries her off. Pandemonium* results! Her entourage* is in a state of bedlam.* Her *corpulent* escort is irate*, but unable to do anything to thwart* this debacle.* All he can do is *rail* against the catastrophe. What to do? What to do?

**Sample Sentences:**   Insert the new words in these sentences.

1. The potpourri* of au courant* fashionable _____ includes the fatuous* and the discreet.*
2. While all disgruntled* men may _____ against malevolent* or Machiavellian leaders, democracy offers a way to ameliorate* iniquities* through the ballot.
3. Is there any veracity* in the platitude* that _____ men are jocose?*
4. To be candid,* there is little to be _____ about in the "good old days."
5. They captured the _____, and he was incarcerated* for a mandatory* period.

**Definitions:**   Match the new words with their definitions.

6. wistful    _____    a. dress, clothing
7. raiment    _____    b. scold, use abusive language
8. brigand    _____    c. longing, pensive,* wishful
9. corpulent    _____    d. robber, bandit
10. rail (v.)    _____    e. fleshy, obese,* excess of fat

**Today's Idiom**   *to flog a dead horse*—to continue to make an issue of something that is over

     He thought he could keep the pot boiling* about his opponent's winking at* crime, but *he was flogging a dead horse.*

ANSWERS ARE ON PAGE 242

**New Words:**

| raconteur | sullen | rift | emissary | ruminate |
|---|---|---|---|---|
| rak′ on tėr′ | sul′ ən | rift | em′ ə ser′ i | rü′ mə nāt |

**Woe Is Me!**

The *raconteur* of our story about idyllic* times gone by goes on to elucidate* how the comely* heroine is taken to the bandits' hide-out. There, a *sullen* crew of cutthroats is gathered. They don't wish to procrastinate;* she must be taken immediately to a foreign land where much treasure will be paid for her. Their cupidity* knows no bounds. The leader wants to hold her for ransom from her wealthy parents. The gang demurs;* they are reticent.* There is a *rift* among the criminals. Their leader remains truculent,* and they agree to wait for just two days for the ransom money. An *emissary* from the grief-stricken parents is expected at any moment. The wan* maiden, her spirits at their nadir,* has time to *ruminate* about her lugubrious* fate.

**Sample Sentences:** Insert the new words in these sentences.

1. He alluded * to the _____ caused in the school by the plethora* of hirsute* boys who ignored the criterion* for appearance.

2. Well known as a(n) _____, he was never chagrined * when asked to tell a story from his large repertoire.*

3. Despite all attempts to mollify* her, she remained _____ about the levity* caused by her slovenly* raiment.*

4. The obscure* country, an aspirant* for membership in the United Nations, sent a(n) _____.

5. An anomaly* of our modern technology* is that the more we need to know, the less time we have to _____.

**Definitions:** Match the new words with their definitions.

6. raconteur _____ a. ill-humored, grim
7. sullen _____ b. ponder, reflect upon
8. rift _____ c. a skilled story-teller
9. emissary _____ d. a split, an opening
10. ruminate _____ e. an agent

**Today's Idiom**

*the die is cast*—an unchangeable decision has been made
The fat was in the fire* and *the die was cast* when he decided to tell the white lie* about how he had found the money.

ANSWERS ARE ON PAGE 242

**New Words:**

| | | | | |
|---|---|---|---|---|
| taut | livid | martinet | yen | bagatelle |
| tôt | liv′ id | mär′ tə net′ | yen | bag′ ə tel′ |

**To the Rescue**

Back at the castle, the situation is *taut* with emotion. The fair maiden's mother is *livid* with fear and anxiety; she has attacks of vertigo.* She talks about her daughter's audacity* in riding out into the ominous* forests despite many similar kidnappings. The girl's father, a *martinet* who rules his family with an iron hand, staunchly* refuses to pay the ransom. Iniquity* shall not be rewarded! At this moment of crisis a heroic knight volunteers to rescue our heroine; he has had a secret *yen* for the young beauty. Avoiding rhetoric,* he pledges his all to castigate* those responsible for this ignominious* deed. He holds his life as a mere *bagatelle* against the duty he owes his beloved mistress. At the propitious* moment, he rides off to do or die for her.

**Sample Sentences:** Insert the new words in these sentences.

1. The rabid * baseball fan lost his equanimity* and became _____ when the star pitcher became pugnacious* and was removed from the game.

2. There was a _____ international situation caused by the proximity* of unidentified submarines to our coasts.

3. When one enlists in the army, one expects to be under the aegis* of a _____.

4. His _____ for imbibing* and romping* with girls worked to his detriment*

5. The little boy tried to wheedle* a larger allowance from his father by the caustic* observations that it was a mere _____ when compared to the allowances of his friends.

**Definitions:** Match the new words with their definitions.

6. taut _____ a. strict disciplinarian
7. livid _____ b. tense, keyed up, on edge
8. martinet _____ c. pale
9. yen _____ d. a trifle
10. bagatelle _____ e. strong desire, strong longing

**Today's Idiom**

*a cat's paw*—a person used as a tool or dupe*
   The spy used the innocent girl as *a cat's paw* to get military information from the grapevine.*

ANSWERS ARE ON PAGE 242

| New Words: | callow | appalled | penchant | decapitate | termagant |
|---|---|---|---|---|---|
| | kal′ ō | ə pôld′ | pen′ chənt | di kap′ ə tāt | ter′ mə gənt |

**Well Done, Sir Knight!**

Seeking his adversaries,* the knight rides to their hide-out. Despite his *callow* appearance, he is reputed * to disdain* danger and to be a prodigious* horseman. The kidnappers lose their equanimity* at his approach. They are *appalled* at the prospect, and they are in a quandary* as to which one will meet him on the field of combat. The leader, under duress,* rides out. "Do you have a *penchant* to die?" derides* the knight. More vituperative* remarks follow. They spur their horses towards each other. It takes but one blow for our hero to *decapitate* the villain. The others flee to avoid their imminent* destruction. The knight takes the maiden on his horse, and they ride back to the castle. Their wedding soon follows. Little does the knight realize that the fair maiden is a garrulous* *termagant* who will make his life miserable with caustic* remarks. Still, the cliché, "And they lived happily ever after," must conclude our fabricated * tale.

**Sample Sentences:** Insert the new words in these sentences.

1. We do not _____ criminals because of our aversion* to such repugnant* punishments.

2. I do not wish to deprecate* your _____ for cowboy music, but I find it banal.*

3. Why do you remain docile* while that _____ besmirches, maligns* and belittles* you?

4. Each long holiday week-end we are _____ at the carnage* on our highways.

5. It was deplorable* the way the capricious* girl led the _____ youth on a merry chase.

**Definitions:** Match the new words with their definitions.

6. callow ____ a. youthful, inexperienced

7. appalled ____ b. behead

8. penchant ____ c. a strong leaning in favor

9. decapitate ____ d. a scolding woman, a shrew

10. termagant ____ e. dismayed, shocked

**Today's Idiom** *coup de grâce*—the finishing stroke

When my girl friend left me, it was a bitter pill to swallow,* but the *coup de grâce* was that she kept my engagement ring.

ANSWERS ARE ON PAGE 242

Language grows and changes. In "days of yore" there were not nearly as many words in our language as we have today. Within the next 50 years hundreds of new words will be added. The educated and alert individual makes new words part of his vocabulary as quickly as they come into accepted use.

**REVIEW WORDS**

| | | | **DEFINITIONS** |
|---|---|---|---|
| _____ | 1 | appalled | a. behead |
| _____ | 2 | bagatelle | b. shocked, dismayed |
| _____ | 3 | brigand | c. pale |
| _____ | 4 | callow | d. a trifle |
| _____ | 5 | corpulent | e. bandit, robber |
| _____ | 6 | decapitate | f. an agent |
| _____ | 7 | emissary | g. grim, ill-humored |
| _____ | 8 | livid | h. clothing, dress |
| _____ | 9 | martinet | j. on edge, keyed up, tense |
| _____ | 10 | penchant | k. strict disciplinarian |
| _____ | 11 | raconteur | l. wishful, pensive,* longing |
| _____ | 12 | rail | m. a strong leaning in favor |
| _____ | 13 | raiment | n. an opening, a split |
| _____ | 14 | rift | o. a skilled story-teller |
| _____ | 15 | ruminate | p. inexperienced, youthful |
| _____ | 16 | sullen | r. excess of fat, fleshy, obese* |
| _____ | 17 | taut | s. reflect upon, ponder |
| _____ | 18 | termagant | t. a shrew, a scolding woman |
| _____ | 19 | wistful | u. use abusive language, scold |
| _____ | 20 | yen | v. strong desire, strong longing |

**IDIOMS**

| | | | |
|---|---|---|---|
| _____ | 21 | a cat's paw | w. the finishing stroke |
| _____ | 22 | the die is cast | x. an unchangeable decision has been made |
| _____ | 23 | coup de grâce | y. to continue to make an issue of something that is over |
| _____ | 24 | to flog a dead horse | z. a person used as a tool or dupe.* |

**ANSWERS ARE ON PAGE 242**

**WORDS FOR FURTHER STUDY**     **MEANINGS**

1. _____  _____

2. _____  _____

3. _____  _____

**New Words:**

| ascertain | dormant | burgeoned | potentate | disseminate |
|---|---|---|---|---|
| as′ ər tān′ | dôr′ mənt | bėr′ jənd | pō′ tən tāt | di sem′ ə nāt |

**A Mighty Empire**

One of the anomalies* of our approach to history is the propensity* to study the venerable* empires of Europe, but we do not feel it incumbent* upon us to *ascertain* anything about the civilizations in our own hemisphere. We deprecate* the history of this part of the world as though progress lay *dormant* and that other peoples were irrelevant* until the settlers of North America arrived at Plymouth Rock. In South America, from 2,000 B.C. until their empire reached its acme* at the beginning of the 16th century, lived the Incas. The site* of the capital city of the Inca empire, Cusco, lay at a height of 11,000 feet. This civilization is reputed * to have *burgeoned* until it covered more than 2,500 miles of the western part of the continent. Its population fluctuated * between 4 and 7 million. This empire had a highly efficacious* political and social system. Its *potentate* ruled with absolute power. As the empire conquered new lands, it would *disseminate* its language, religion and social customs.

**Sample Sentences:** Insert the new words in these sentences.

1. While some moribund * economies atrophied * after World War II, others _____ under the salubrious* affects of loans from the U.S.

2. In order to _____ the relationship between his girl friend and his brother, he kept a wary* and discreet* vigil .*

3. We are quick to _____ calumny,* but reticent* about things that may be construed * as compliments.

4. He was appalled * at the apathy* concerning the important issue that had remained _____ for so long a time.

5. The callous* _____ kept an imperturbable* mien* when requested to alleviate* the unconscionable* conditions existing in his land.

**Definitions:** Match the new words with their definitions.

6. ascertain _____    a. spread, scatter

7. dormant _____    b. discover, find out about

8. burgeoned _____    c. resting, asleep

9. potentate _____    d. flourished, grew

10. disseminate _____    e. ruler

**Today's Idiom**

*straight from the shoulder*—in a direct, open way

I took the wind out of his sails* by telling him *straight from the shoulder* that I was not going to wink at* his apple polishing.*

ANSWERS ARE ON PAGE 242

**New Words:**

| derived | prerogative | nepotism | dearth | internecine |
|---------|-------------|----------|--------|-------------|
| di rīvd' | pri rog' ə tiv | nep' ə tiz əm | dėrth | in' tər nē' sən |

**A Battle for Power**

The Inca emperor *derived* his prodigious* power and authority from the gods. The paramount* god was the sun god. It was from him the ruler passed on his *prerogative* to rule to his most astute* son. This *nepotism* had worked with great efficacy* for centuries. The land holdings were immense;* there were rich farmlands and llamas and alpacas for wool. Precious metals were plentiful: silver, copper, bronze, and the most sacred of all, gold. This metal resembled the sun god whom they extolled.* There was no *dearth* of idols and ornaments hammered from this gleaming metal. There was always more gold coming from the mines to replenish* the supply. At the acme* of his power, the Inca ruler died without naming the requisite* successor. In 1493 two sons began an *internecine* struggle for control. For the next 40 years the empire sank into the lassitude* caused by civil war.

**Sample Sentences:** Insert the new words in these sentences.

1. The emissary* from the president tried to allay* the fears that a deleterious* _____ feud was inevitable within the party.

2. A pragmatic* philosopher _____ the theory that we have noses in order to hold up our eyeglasses.

3. Your efforts to ingratiate* yourself into your boss's favor are nullified * by the unmitigated * _____ manifest* in this firm.

4. He gave his adversary* the dubious* _____ of choosing the weapon by which he was to meet his inevitable* end.

5. In the potpourri* of restaurants there is no _____ of succulent* dishes.

**Definitions:** Match the new words with their definitions.

6. derived _____ a. scarcity, lack

7. prerogative _____ b. conflict within a group, mutually destructive

8. nepotism _____ c. an exclusive right or power

9. dearth _____ d. descended from, received from a source

10. internecine _____ e. favoritism towards relatives

**Today's Idiom**

*to rub a person the wrong way*—to do something that irritates or annoys

The quickest way *to rub a person the wrong way* is to give him the cold shoulder.*

ANSWERS ARE ON PAGE 242

**New Words:**

| tyro | sophistry | factitious | encomium | obloquy |
|------|-----------|------------|----------|---------|
| tī′ rō | sof′ is tri | fak tish′ əs | en kō′ mi əm | ob′ lə kwi |

**A Perfidious\* Conqueror**

The feuding between the rival sons reached its pinnacle\* in 1532; at that moment Francisco Pizarro came onto the scene. A native of Spain, he was sojourning\* in Panama when he heard of the riches to be found in that far off land. Overwhelmed with cupidity,\* but still a *tyro* when it came to wresting\* power and wealth from hapless\* people, he joined with an inveterate\* adventurer. They gathered a small band of mercenaries.\* The first two attempts failed, and Pizarro returned to Spain to request authority and money in order to conquer the West Coast of South America. Whether by *sophistry* or cajolery,\* he was given the requisite\* aid. With a force of 180 men, the dregs\* of society, he invaded Inca territory. He reached the city where the current ruler, Atahualpa, was holding court. The Incas welcomed Pizarro who, in a *factitious* display of friendship, heaped *encomiums* upon Atahualpa. Unknown to the Incas, Pizarro had brought guns which were still beyond the technology\* of these people. The *obloquy* of his next act, ambushing the Incas and taking Atahualpa prisoner, will live in the history books which are replete\* with tales of conquest.

**Sample Sentences:** Insert the new words in these sentences.

1. Although he was erudite\* about a prolific\* number of things, he was a naive,\* callow\* _____ when it came to relating to girls.
2. John Wilkes Booth's egregious\* act remains an infamous\* _____.
3. His _____ made use of every glib\* artifice.\*
4. In the office he played the _____ role of a martinet,\* while at home he was filled with compassion\*.
5. The modest prodigy\* treated the fervid\* _____ that followed his performance as though they were a mere bagatelle.\*

**Definitions:** Match the new words with their definitions.

6. tyro _____ a. high praise
7. sophistry _____ b. beginner, novice
8. factitious _____ c. false reasoning or argument
9. encomium _____ d. sham, artificial
10. obloquy _____ e. disgrace, shame, dishonor

**Today's Idiom** *to draw in one's horns*—to become cautious

He knew he was out of his depth,\* so he *drew in his horns* and quit the poker game.

ANSWERS ARE ON PAGE 242

**New Words:**

| hyperbole | munificent | prevarication | charisma |
|---|---|---|---|
| hī pŭr′ bə li | mū nif′ ə sənt | pri var′ ə kā′ shen | ker iz′ ma |
| genocide | | | |
| jen′ ə sīd | | | |

**The End of an Empire**

The Machiavellian* Pizarro held the captured Atahualpa for ransom. He was adamant* about receiving a room filled with gold to the height of a man's shoulder. This was taken as an *hyperbole* at first, but Pizarro knew the gullible* Incas would be *munificent* when it came to rescuing their sacred ruler. They did not procrastinate,* and a frenetic* collection of gold took place. Pizarro, to whom *prevarication** was natural in dealing with the Incas, had no qualms* about executing their ruler as soon as he had the gold. The Inca empire was moribund,* but the *charisma* that surrounded Atahualpa was such that, after his death, the Incas fought on tenaciously* in his name for several years. Eventually, superior weapons quelled* all opposition. A policy of *genocide* was adopted by the Spanish conquerors, and almost two million of these proud people died in the carnage* which followed. The saga* of an ancient civilization thus came to an end.

**Sample Sentences:** Insert the new words in these sentences.

1. Even those who were not adherents* of the late President Kennedy candidly* admit the _____ which surrounded him.

2. The United Nations has outlawed _____ as the ultimate* crime, which must be eradicated .*

3. Her constant _____ made her a pariah* to her friends.

4. The rhetoric* soared into flagrant* _____.

5. He was surprised by the _____ gratuity* given by the usually parsimonious* termagant.*

**Definitions:** Match the new words with their definitions.

6. hyperbole _____    a. quality of leadership inspiring enthusiasm

7. munificent _____   b. planned destruction of an entire people

8. prevarication

_____   c. deviating from the truth, lying

9. charisma _____     d. generous

10. genocide _____    e. exaggerated figure of speech

**Today's Idiom**

*to throw cold water*—to discourage a plan or idea

    I was going to pull up stakes* and move out lock, stock and barrel ,* but my wife *threw cold water* on the whole thing.

ANSWERS ARE ON PAGE 242

This is your *last* week. At this point you have worked with over 1100 of the most useful words and idioms in our language. The final review test will give you some idea of how well you have mastered them. From time to time you should re-read sections of this book to refresh your memory. Remember, keep learning new words at every opportunity!

**REVIEW WORDS**

| | | |
|---|---|---|
| _____ | 1 | ascertain |
| _____ | 2 | burgeoned |
| _____ | 3 | charisma |
| _____ | 4 | dearth |
| _____ | 5 | derived |
| _____ | 6 | disseminate |
| _____ | 7 | dormant |
| _____ | 8 | encomium |
| _____ | 9 | factitious |
| _____ | 10 | genocide |
| _____ | 11 | hyperbole |
| _____ | 12 | internecine |
| _____ | 13 | munificent |
| _____ | 14 | nepotism |
| _____ | 15 | obloquy |
| _____ | 16 | potentate |
| _____ | 17 | prerogative |
| _____ | 18 | prevarication |
| _____ | 19 | sophistry |
| _____ | 20 | tyro |

**DEFINITIONS**

a. lack, scarcity
b. favoritism towards relatives
c. novice, beginner
d. artificial, sham
e. lying, deviating from the truth
f. ruler
g. scatter, spread
h. an exclusive power or right
j. dishonor, disgrace, shame
k. high praise
l. quality of leadership inspiring enthusiasm
m. asleep, resting
n. grew, flourished
o. planned destruction of an entire people
p. false reasoning or argument
r. mutually destructive, conflict within a group
s. received from a source, descended from
t. generous
u. exaggerated figure of speech
v. find out about, discover

**IDIOMS**

| | | |
|---|---|---|
| _____ | 21 | to draw in one's horns |
| _____ | 22 | straight from the shoulder |
| _____ | 23 | to throw cold water |
| _____ | 24 | to rub a person the wrong way |

w. in a direct, open way

x. to discourage a plan or idea

y. to become cautious

z. to do something to irritate or annoy

ANSWERS ARE ON PAGE 242

**WORDS FOR FURTHER STUDY**     **MEANINGS**

1. _____    _____

2. _____    _____

3. _____    _____

---

With your expanded vocabulary, you are now ready to deal with a more advanced word book. The next publication in this series is WORDS WITH A FLAIR by Murray Bromberg and Julius Liebb.

WORDS WITH A FLAIR is organized around unified themes, and presents difficult but useful words that regularly appear in print. As with all Barron's texts, the material is offered in a lively, practical format to enable you to master 600 important words. Remember, words are the tools of educated and cultured people.

(If you found 1100 WORDS too difficult or you wish to recommend an easier vocabulary book to a friend, you might try 504 ABSOLUTELY ESSENTIAL WORDS — the first in this series of vocabulary builders.)

# Answers

*1st Week / 1st Day:* 1. replete  2. eminent  3. steeped  4. voracious  5. indiscriminate  6. d  7. c  8. a  9. e  10. b

*1st Week / 2nd Day:* 1. prognosticate  2. automatons  3. matron  4. abound  5. technology  6. d  7. b  8. e  9. c  10. a

*1st Week / 3rd Day:* 1. compounded  2. annals  3. paradoxes  4. tinge  5. realm  6. b  7. e  8. d  9. c  10. a

*1st Week / 4th Day:* 1. drudgery  2. badgers *or* badgered  3. perceives *or* perceived  4. implored  5. interminable  6. e  7. c  8. a  9. b  10. d

*1st Week / 5th Day:* REVIEW

| 1. o | 4. d | 7. j | 10. v | 13. r | 16. s | 19. l | 22. w |
| 2. p | 5. g | 8. h | 11. k | 14. b | 17. a | 20. n | 23. y |
| 3. t | 6. m | 9. e | 12. u | 15. c | 18. f | 21. x | 24. z |

---

*2nd Week / 1st Day:* 1. laconic  2. accosted  3. reticent  4. throng  5. intrepid  6. a  7. d  8. b  9. c  10. e

*2nd Week / 2nd Day:* 1. hapless  2. irate  3. furtive  4. plethora  5. felon  6. e  7. b  8. d  9. c  10. a

*2nd Week / 3rd Day:* 1. vigilant  2. adroit  3. fabricate  4. pretext  5. gesticulate  6. c  7. a  8. b  9. e  10. d

*2nd Week / 4th Day:* 1. rudimentary  2. cajoled  3. enhance  4. nuance  5. avid  6. a  7. c  8. e  9. d  10. b

*2nd Week / 5th Day:* REVIEW

| 1. f | 4. u | 7. k | 10. h | 13. p | 16. g | 19. o | 22. w |
| 2. m | 5. v | 8. t | 11. e | 14. s | 17. a | 20. c | 23. x |
| 3. b | 6. n | 9. r | 12. j | 15. d | 18. l | 21. z | 24. y |

---

*3rd Week / 1st Day:* 1. wrest  2. lackluster  3. caustic  4. loathe  5. reprimand  6. b  7. e  8. a  9. c  10. d

*3rd Week / 2nd Day:* 1. incipient  2. infamous  3. dupe  4. jostle  5. inadvertent  6. a  7. c  8. d  9. b  10. e

*3rd Week / 3rd Day:* 1 ominous  2. repudiate  3. bristle  4. tremulous  5. cessation  6. d  7. e  8. b  9. a  10. c

*3rd Week / 4th Day:* 1. stipulate  2. euphemism  3. condolence  4. mundane  5. incongruous  6. b  7. a  8. d  9. e  10. c

*3rd Week / 5th Day:* REVIEW

| 1. g | 4. o | 7. k | 10. c | 13. a | 16. p | 19. f | 22. y |
| 2. h | 5. n | 8. e | 11. m | 14. j | 17. t | 20. r | 23. w |
| 3. d | 6. v | 9. s | 12. u | 15. b | 18. l | 21. x | 24. z |

---

*4th Week / 1st Day:* 1. intimidate  2. feint  3. alacrity  4. belligerent  5. disdain  6. e  7. a  8. c  9. d  10. b

*4th Week / 2nd Day:* 1. promulgate  2. brash  3. scoff  4. pugnacious  5. belittle  6. a  7. e  8. d  9. c  10. b

*4th Week / 3rd Day:* 1. laceration  2. tangible  3. castigate  4. octogenarian  5. sordid  6. a  7. c  8. b  9. d  10. e

*4th Week / 4th Day:* 1. scurrilous  2. aspirant  3. frenzy  4. dregs  5. solace  6. c  7. e  8. a  9. d  10. b

*4th Week / 5th Day:* REVIEW

| 1. v | 4. l | 7. a | 10. c | 13. d | 16. e | 19. u | 22. x |
| 2. j | 5. n | 8. r | 11. b | 14. f | 17. m | 20. s | 23. z |
| 3. k | 6. o | 9. g | 12. t | 15. h | 18. p | 21. y | 24. w |

# ANSWERS

**5th Week / 1st Day:**  1. rampant  2. clandestine  3. ethics  4. inane  5. concur  6. e  7. c  8. b  9. d  10. a

**5th Week / 2nd Day:**  1. culprit  2. inexorable  3. duress  4. admonish  5. flagrant  6. c  7. e  8. b  9. d  10. a

**5th Week / 3rd Day:**  1. egregious  2. acrimonious  3. duplicity  4. paucity  5. distraught  6. d  7. c  8. b  9. e  10. a

**5th Week / 4th Day:**  1. impunity  2. elicit  3. tolerate  4. construe  5. pernicious  6. d  7. e  8. c  9. b  10. a

**5th Week / 5th Day:**  REVIEW

| | | | | | | |
|---|---|---|---|---|---|---|
| 1. v | 4. p | 7. f | 10. k | 13. l | 16. b | 19. d | 22. x |
| 2. e | 5. s | 8. a | 11. h | 14. n | 17. u | 20. g | 23. z |
| 3. r | 6. t | 9. m | 12. o | 15. c | 18. j | 21. y | 24. w |

---

**6th Week / 1st Day:**  1 sally  2. affluent  3. consternation  4. feasible  5. discern  6. d  7. b  8. e  9. a  10. c

**6th Week / 2nd Day:**  1. precocious  2. perfunctory  3. deride  4. perverse  5. chagrin  6. b  7. a  8. c  9. d  10. e

**6th Week / 3rd Day:**  1. laudable  2. disparaged  3. masticate  4. fiasco  5. eschews  6. a  7. d  8. e  9. c  10. b

**6th Week / 4th Day:**  1. dubious  2. quell  3. confidant  4. obsolescence  5. voluble  6. d  7. b  8. a  9. c  10. e

**6th Week / 5th Day:**  REVIEW

| | | | | | | |
|---|---|---|---|---|---|---|
| 1. k | 4. b | 7. o | 10. g | 13. c | 16. j | 19. m | 22. w |
| 2. r | 5. h | 8. s | 11. d | 14. v | 17. e | 20. f | 23. y |
| 3. p | 6. m | 9. l | 12. t | 15. a | 18. n | 21. x | 24. z |

---

**7th Week / 1st Day:**  1. implacable  2. jurisdiction  3. paroxysm  4. skirmish  5. reprehensible  6. b  7. a  8. d  9. e  10. c

**7th Week / 2nd Day:**  1. fray  2. indigent  3. arbitrary  4. monolithic  5. harass  6. e  7. c  8. b  9. a  10. d

**7th Week / 3rd Day:**  1. effigy  2. stymie  3. cognizant  4. flout  5. turbulent  6. b  7. e  8. c  9. d  10. a

**7th Week / 4th Day:**  1. terminate  2. forthwith  3. oust  4. revert  5. exacerbate  6. c  7. d  8. e  9. b  10. a

**7th Week / 5th Day:**  REVIEW

| | | | | | | |
|---|---|---|---|---|---|---|
| 1. v | 4. k | 7. c | 10. j | 13. s | 16. o | 19. m | 22. y |
| 2. u | 5. h | 8. p | 11. g | 14. l | 17. t | 20. r | 23. x |
| 3. n | 6. e | 9. d | 12. a | 15. f | 18. b | 21. z | 24. w |

---

**8th Week / 1st Day:**  1. emaciated  2. tranquil  3. sanctuary  4. surge  5. ascend  6. d  7. a  8. c  9. b  10. e

**8th Week / 2nd Day:**  1. sinister  2. besieged  3. afflicted  4. malnutrition  5. privation  6. b  7. e  8. d  9. a  10. c

**8th Week / 3rd Day:**  1. ubiquitous  2. remote  3. harbinger  4. thwart  5. malignant  6. b  7. a  8. d  9. e  10. c

**8th Week / 4th Day:**  1. excruciating  2. reverberating  3. fretful  4. respite  5. succumb  6. d  7. a  8. c  9. b  10. e

**8th Week / 5th Day:**  REVIEW

| | | | | | | |
|---|---|---|---|---|---|---|
| 1. d | 4. f | 7. l | 10. a | 13. t | 16. o | 19. v | 22. y |
| 2. m | 5. e | 8. s | 11. g | 14. k | 17. j | 20. c | 23. x |
| 3. r | 6. u | 9. b | 12. p | 15. h | 18. n | 21. z | 24. w |

*9th Week / 1st Day:* 1. extortion  2. impresario  3. bigot  4. assets  5. adverse
6. c  7. e  8. b  9. d  10. a

*9th Week / 2nd Day:* 1. entourage  2. virulent  3. spew  4. venom  5. blatant
6. b  7. a  8. e  9. c  10. d

*9th Week / 3rd Day:* 1. loath  2. solicit  3. astute  4. advocate  5. ineffectual
6. d  7. e  8. a  9. b  10. c

*9th Week / 4th Day:* 1. vexatious  2. amicable  3. malady  4. nefarious
5. scrutinize  6. c  7. b  8. e  9. a  10. d

*9th Week / 5th Day:* REVIEW

| | | | | | | | |
|---|---|---|---|---|---|---|---|
| 1. p | 4. c | 7. j | 10. f | 13. u | 16. e | 19. g | 22. y |
| 2. a | 5. b | 8. h | 11. n | 14. d | 17. t | 20. m | 23. x |
| 3. r | 6. o | 9. v | 12. s | 15. k | 18. l | 21. z | 24. w |

---

*10th Week / 1st Day:* 1. peruse  2. premonition  3. desist  4. recoiled  5. inclement  6. a  7. b  8. d  9. c  10. e

*10th Week / 2nd Day:* 1. obsessed  2. mastiff  3. doleful  4. pertinent  5. wan
6. b  7. e  8. d  9. a  10. c

*10th Week / 3rd Day:* 1. frustrated  2. interjected  3. histrionics  4. elusive
5. symptomatic  6. d  7. b  8. e  9. a  10. c

*10th Week / 4th Day:* 1. imminent  2. squeamish  3. engrossed  4. salient
5. inert  6. b  7. a  8. c  9. e  10. d

*10th Week / 5th Day:* REVIEW

| | | | | | | | |
|---|---|---|---|---|---|---|---|
| 1. d | 4. u | 7. r | 10. e | 13. h | 16. b | 19. g | 22. x |
| 2. a | 5. c | 8. f | 11. k | 14. m | 17. l | 20. t | 23. w |
| 3. s | 6. v | 9. j | 12. n | 15. p | 18. o | 21. z | 24. y |

---

*11th Week / 1st Day:* 1. poignant  2. garbled  3. fruitless  4. inundated  5. sanguine  6. d  7. a  8. e  9. b  10. c

*11th Week / 2nd Day:* 1. phlegmatic  2. zealous  3. comprehensive  4. coerced
5. corroborate  6. b  7. c  8. d  9. a  10. e

*11th Week / 3rd Day:* 1. elapse  2. sporadic  3. domicile  4. lax  5. meticulous
6 b  7. e  8. d  9. a  10. c

*11th Week / 4th Day:* 1. conjecture  2. lurid  3. rash  4. obviated  5. quip
6. e  7. c  8. a  9. d  10. b

*11th Week / 5th Day:* REVIEW

| | | | | | | | |
|---|---|---|---|---|---|---|---|
| 1. t | 4. f | 7. d | 10. o | 13. k | 16. v | 19. p | 22. y |
| 2. r | 5. b | 8. l | 11. h | 14. g | 17. e | 20. u | 23. w |
| 3. m | 6. n | 9. a | 12. s | 15. c | 18. j | 21. z | 24. x |

---

*12th Week / 1st Day:* 1. diatribe  2. ilk  3. incoherent  4. fortuitous  5. inhibitions  6. d  7. e  8. c  9. b  10. a

*12th Week / 2nd Day:* 1. placard  2. prestigious  3. remuneration  4. nominal
5. integral  6. e  7. b  8. a  9. d  10. c

*12th Week / 3rd Day:* 1. utopia  2. schism  3. anathema  4. flamboyant  5. expunge  6. d  7. e  8. b  9. a  10. c

*12th Week / 4th Day:* 1. truncated  2. jaunty  3. ostentatious  4. timorous  5. fractious  6. a  7. b  8. c  9. e  10. d

*12th Week / 5th Day:* REVIEW

| | | | | | | | |
|---|---|---|---|---|---|---|---|
| 1. l | 4. o | 7. c | 10. r | 13. t | 16. k | 19. p | 22. z |
| 2. m | 5. g | 8. e | 11. f | 14. d | 17. u | 20. v | 23. y |
| 3. n | 6. b | 9. j | 12. h | 15. a | 18. s | 21. w | 24. x |

*13th Week / 1st Day:* 1. importune 2. haven 3. subjugate 4. surreptitious 5. incontrovertible 6. b 7. a 8. e 9. d 10. c

*13th Week / 2nd Day:* 1. eventuated 2. subterranean 3. emit 4. ultimate 5. viable 6. b 7. e 8. d 9. a 10. c

*13th Week / 3rd Day:* 1. premise 2. incredulous 3. jeopardize 4. permeated 5. propitious 6. e 7. b 8. d 9. c 10. a

*13th Week / 4th Day:* 1. curtailed 2. cryptic 3. repress 4. surmised 5. inchoate 6. b 7. d 8. c 9. a 10. e

*13th Week / 5th Day:* REVIEW

| | | | | | | | |
|---|---|---|---|---|---|---|---|
| 1. u | 4. l | 7. t | 10. p | 13. f | 16. j | 19. k | 22. y |
| 2. g | 5. o | 8. b | 11. m | 14. e | 17. c | 20. h | 23. x |
| 3. v | 6. a | 9. s | 12. r | 15. n | 18. d | 21. z | 24. w |

---

*14th Week / 1st Day:* 1. nettle 2. aspire 3. inveigh 4. overt 5. relegate 6. d 7. e 8. a 9. b 10. c

*14th Week / 2nd Day:* 1. supine 2. razed 3. repulse 4. mammoth 5. havoc 6. d 7. c 8. b 9. a 10. e

*14th Week / 3rd Day:* 1. incisive 2. scurry 3. lethal 4. precipitated 5. stereotype 6. d 7. b 8. a 9. e 10. c

*14th Week / 4th Day:* 1. sinecure 2. stentorian 3. valor 4. singular 5. bias 6. e 7. d 8. c 9. a 10. b

*14th Week / 5th Day:* REVIEW

| | | | | | | | |
|---|---|---|---|---|---|---|---|
| 1. d | 4. j | 7. a | 10. l | 13. o | 16. m | 19. p | 22. x |
| 2. h | 5. n | 8. t | 11. r | 14. k | 17. v | 20. c | 23. w |
| 3. u | 6. f | 9. b | 12. e | 15. g | 18. s | 21. z | 24. y |

---

*15th Week / 1st Day:* 1. complicity 2. liquidation 3. culpable 4. recant 5. accomplice 6. b 7. d 8. c 9. e 10. a

*15th Week / 2nd Day:* 1. preclude 2. alleged 3. abrogate 4. invalidate 5. access 6. e 7. b 8. a 9. c 10. d

*15th Week / 3rd Day:* 1. extrinsic 2. persevere 3. landmark 4. declaim 5. fetter 6. d 7. e 8. b 9. c 10. a

*15th Week / 4th Day:* 1. nomadic 2. paragon 3. controversial 4. asperity 5. epithets 6. b 7. c 8. a 9. e 10. d

*15th Week / 5th Day:* REVIEW

| | | | | | | | |
|---|---|---|---|---|---|---|---|
| 1. k | 4. c | 7. v | 10. a | 13. o | 16. t | 19. l | 22. y |
| 2. s | 5. h | 8. d | 11. b | 14. u | 17. g | 20. p | 23. z |
| 3. f | 6. n | 9. m | 12. r | 15. e | 18. j | 21. x | 24. w |

---

*16th Week / 1st Day:* 1. cursory 2. indigenous 3. interloper 4. habitat 5. gregarious 6. b 7. d 8. c 9. a 10. e

*16th Week / 2nd Day:* 1. prolific 2. antithesis 3. sedentary 4. frugal 5. bulwark 6. a 7. c 8. e 9. b 10. d

*16th Week / 3rd Day:* 1. cache 2. cupidity 3. altruistic 4. coterie 5. embellish 6. b 7. d 8. a 9. c 10. e

*16th Week / 4th Day:* 1. amorous 2. virtuosity 3. progeny 4. temerity 5. saturate 6. e 7. d 8. b 9. a 10. c

*16th Week / 5th Day:* REVIEW

| | | | | | | | |
|---|---|---|---|---|---|---|---|
| 1. f | 4. s | 7. h | 10. b | 13. m | 16. v | 19. p | 22. z |
| 2. t | 5. a | 8. j | 11. c | 14. l | 17. r | 20. u | 23. y |
| 3. d | 6. g | 9. e | 12. o | 15. k | 18. n | 21. w | 24. x |

*17th Week / 1st Day:* 1. fallacious 2. consummate 3. concoct 4. perpetrate 5. subterfuge 6. c 7. b 8. d 9. a 10. e

*17th Week / 2nd Day:* 1. manifold 2. fraught 3. impeccable 4. resourceful 5. assiduous 6. c 7. d 8. b 9. e 10. a

*17th Week / 3rd Day:* 1. hoax 2. components 3. labyrinth 4. evaluate 5. murky 6. a 7. b 8. c 9. d 10. e

*17th Week / 4th Day:* 1. gullible 2. deploy 3. attest 4. exult 5. enigma 6. e 7. a 8. b 9. c 10. d

*17th Week / 5th Day:* REVIEW

| | | | | | | | |
|---|---|---|---|---|---|---|---|
| 1. c | 4. e | 7. f | 10. l | 13. b *or* t | 16. s | 19. h | 22. y |
| 2. d | 5. j | 8. r | 11. k | 14. n | 17. v | 20. b *or* t | 23. x |
| 3. g | 6. a | 9. m | 12. o | 15. p | 18. u | 21. w | 24. z |

---

*18th Week / 1st Day:* 1. innate 2. abortive 3. modify 4. spontaneous 5. accommodate 6. a 7. e 8. b 9. d 10. c

*18th Week / 2nd Day:* 1. crave 2. myriad 3. irrelevant 4. urbane 5. veneer 6. d 7. b 8. c 9. a 10. e

*18th Week / 3rd Day:* 1. deem 2 buff 3. romp 4. latent 5. inherent 6. e 7. c 8. d 9. b 10. a

*18th Week / 4th Day:* 1. tortuous 2. conjugal 3. peregrination 4. itinerant 5. barometer 6. b 7. a 8. c 9. d 10. e

*18th Week / 5th Day:* REVIEW

| | | | | | | | |
|---|---|---|---|---|---|---|---|
| 1. c | 4. p | 7. n | 10. a | 13. u | 16. h | 19. e | 22. z |
| 2. f | 5. s | 8. m *or* d | 11. o | 14. t | 17. g | 20. b | 23. y |
| 3. k | 6. j | 9. d *or* m | 12. v | 15. r | 18. l | 21. x | 24. w |

---

*19th Week / 1st Day:* 1. profligate 2. strife 3. legion 4. coup 5. megalomania 6. e 7. c 8. a 9. d 10. b

*19th Week / 2nd Day:* 1. mendacious 2. exonerate 3. expatriate 4. fiat 5. amnesty 6. c 7. a 8. d 9. e 10. b

*19th Week / 3rd Day:* 1. dismantle 2. sumptuous 3. parsimonious 4. pecuniary 5. underwrite 6. d 7. b 8. c 9. e 10. a

*19th Week / 4th Day:* 1. restrictive 2. blunt 3. nostalgia 4. rife 5. balk 6. e 7. c 8. b 9. d 10. a

*19th Week / 5th Day:* REVIEW

| | | | | | | | |
|---|---|---|---|---|---|---|---|
| 1. t | 4. a | 7. h | 10. g | 13. u | 16. l | 19. d | 22. w |
| 2. m | 5. c | 8. o | 11. j | 14. s | 17. p | 20. f | 23. x |
| 3. k | 6. e | 9. r | 12. v | 15. n | 18. b | 21. z | 24. y |

---

*20th Week / 1st Day:* 1. nebulous 2. reviled 3. indict 4. pesky 5. derogatory 6. d 7. b 8. e 9. c 10. a

*20th Week / 2nd Day:* 1. repose 2. abstemious 3. redolent 4. omnivorous 5. disparate 6. b 7. e 8. d 9. a 10. c

*20th Week / 3rd Day:* 1. extant 2. vicissitudes 3. edifice 4. sultry 5. trenchant 6. d 7. b 8. e 9. c 10. a

*20th Week / 4th Day:* 1. lugubrious 2. puissant 3. unabated 4. maudlin 5. levity 6. e 7. d 8. a 9. c 10. b

*20th Week / 5th Day:* REVIEW

| | | | | | | | |
|---|---|---|---|---|---|---|---|
| 1. p | 4. c | 7. e | 10. f | 13. m | 16. v | 19. u | 22. y |
| 2. g | 5. l | 8. d | 11. h | 14. o | 17. s | 20. t | 23. w |
| 3. a | 6. j | 9. b | 12. n | 15. k | 18. r | 21. x | 24. z |

21st Week / 1st Day:  1. opulence  2. scion  3. obsequious  4. indoctrinate  5. fulsome  6. b  7. e  8. c  9. a  10. d

21st Week / 2nd Day:  1. lush  2. ponder  3. destitution  4. supplication  5. decadence  6. e  7. b  8. c  9. d  10. a

21st Week / 3rd Day:  1. disciple  2. metamorphosis  3. penance  4. ascetic  5. desultory  6. b  7. d  8. c  9. e  10. a

21st Week / 4th Day:  1. nurture  2. bona fide  3. salvation  4. nirvana  5. materialism  6. d  7. e  8. b  9. a  10. c

21st Week / 5th Day:  REVIEW

| | | | | | | | |
|---|---|---|---|---|---|---|---|
| 1. a | 4. h | 7. k | 10. c | 13. l | 16. s | 19. n | 22. w |
| 2. v | 5. f | 8. j | 11. u | 14. t | 17. p | 20. o | 23. z |
| 3. e | 6. r | 9. d | 12. m | 15. b | 18. g | 21. x | 24. y |

22nd Week / 1st Day:  1. juxtapose  2. incompatibility  3. cope  4. plight  5. covert  6. b  7. c  8. d  9. e  10. a

22nd Week / 2nd Day:  1. fabricate  2. connubial  3. demur  4. appellation  5. incapacitated  6. e  7. c  8. d  9. a  10. b

22nd Week / 3rd Day:  1. escalation  2. indifference  3. potential  4. cumulative  5. recondite  6. d  7. e  8. a  9. b  10. c

22nd Week / 4th Day:  1. acknowledge  2. delude  3. palliate  4. prelude  5. chimerical  6. b  7. d  8. c  9. a  10. e

22nd Week / 5th Day:  REVIEW

| | | | | | | | |
|---|---|---|---|---|---|---|---|
| 1. b | 4. n | 7. a | 10. j | 13. u | 16. c | 19. s | 22. z |
| 2. f | 5. k | 8. e | 11. d | 14. t | 17. g | 20. l | 23. w |
| 3. m | 6. h | 9. r | 12. v | 15. p | 18. o | 21. y | 24. x |

23rd Week / 1st Day:  1. maladjusted  2. heterogeneous  3. perspicacious  4. analogous  5. gamut  6. e  7. a  8. b  9. d  10. c

23rd Week / 2nd Day:  1. neurotic  2. decade  3. mortality  4. susceptible  5. phenomenon  6. d  7. a  8. c  9. e  10. b

23rd Week / 3rd Day:  1. enunciate  2. irascible  3. introspective  4. pedagogue  5. inordinate  6. e  7. c  8. b  9. a  10. d

23rd Week / 4th Day:  1. perpetuate  2. catastrophic  3. neutralize  4. mandate  5. compensatory  6. d  7. b  8. a  9. c  10. e

23rd Week / 5th Day:  REVIEW

| | | | | | | | |
|---|---|---|---|---|---|---|---|
| 1. f | 4. u | 7. j | 10. b | 13. r | 16. c | 19. p | 22. x |
| 2. a | 5. v | 8. n | 11. d | 14. m | 17. e | 20. s | 23. y |
| 3. t | 6. k | 9. o | 12. h | 15. l | 18. g | 21. w | 24. z |

24th Week / 1st Day:  1. inanimate  2. artifact  3. fetish  4. anthropologist  5. bizarre  6. d  7. a  8. e  9. c  10. b

24th Week / 2nd Day:  1. tainted  2. prohibition  3. imprudent  4. taboo  5. imperative  6. c  7. e  8. b  9. d  10. a

24th Week / 3rd Day:  1. contemptuous  2. absurd  3. bigot  4. abhor  5. universal  6. e  7. a  8. d  9. c  10. b

24th Week / 4th Day:  1. originate  2. entreaty  3. inviolable  4. vulnerable  5. tradition  6. b  7. d  8. c  9. a  10. e

24th Week / 5th Day:  REVIEW

| | | | | | | | |
|---|---|---|---|---|---|---|---|
| 1. o | 4. a | 7. n | 10. s | 13. d | 16. j | 19. f | 22. w |
| 2. t | 5. c | 8. u | 11. b | 14. g | 17. v | 20. m | 23. z |
| 3. h | 6. l | 9. e | 12. p | 15. r | 18. k | 21. y | 24. x |

*25th Week / 1st Day:* 1. eruption   2. puny   3. debris   4. awesome   5. dispersed   6. c   7. d   8. a   9. e   10. b

*25th Week / 2nd Day:* 1. conflagration   2. obliterate   3. rue   4. initiate   5. deplorable   6. c   7. b   8. d   9. e   10. a

*25th Week / 3rd Day:* 1. hoard   2. sage   3. congenial   4. aegis   5. detriment   6. b   7. d   8. e   9. c   10. a

*25th Week / 4th Day:* 1. senile   2. longevity   3. doddering   4. imbibe   5. virile   6. a   7. c   8. b   9. d   10. e

*25th Week / 5th Day:* REVIEW

| | | | | | | |
|---|---|---|---|---|---|---|
| 1. h | 4. j | 7. m | 10. c | 13. s | 16. g | 19. d | 22. y |
| 2. r | 5. f | 8. k | 11. t | 14. u | 17. b | 20. p | 23. w |
| 3. o | 6. l | 9. a | 12. n | 15. v | 18. e | 21. x | 24. z |

---

*26th Week / 1st Day:* 1. hostile   2. prevalent   3. lethargic   4. paramount   5. remiss   6. b   7. a   8. d   9. e   10. c

*26th Week / 2nd Day:* 1. aversion   2. superficial   3. rebuke   4. evince   5. vogue   6. b   7. c   8. e   9. d   10. a

*26th Week / 3rd Day:* 1. tussle   2. intrinsic   3. jettison   4. inevitable   5. lucrative   6. e   7. a   8. d   9. c   10. b

*26th Week / 4th Day:* 1. acute   2. transient   3. gist   4. terse   5. cogent   6. e   7. c   8. d   9. b   10. a

*26th Week / 5th Day:* REVIEW

| | | | | | | |
|---|---|---|---|---|---|---|
| 1. m | 4. a | 7. p | 10. v | 13. h | 16. n | 19. f | 22. z |
| 2. r | 5. l | 8. j | 11. s | 14. o | 17. g | 20. k | 23. x |
| 3. d | 6. u | 9. c | 12. t | 15. e | 18. b | 21. y | 24. w |

---

*27th Week / 1st Day:* 1. array   2. culminate   3. pinnacle   4. ardent   5. obscure   6. b   7. c   8. d   9. a   10. e

*27th Week / 2nd Day:* 1. bereft   2. exultation   3. constrict   4. prodigy   5. falter   6. d   7. e   8. c   9. b   10. a

*27th Week / 3rd Day:* 1. invective   2. voluminous   3. besmirch   4. retrospect   5. vitriolic   6. d   7. a   8. c   9. b   10. e

*27th Week / 4th Day:* 1. inveterate   2. pungent   3. adamant   4. humility   5. egotist   6. b   7. a   8. d   9. e   10. c

*27th Week / 5th Day:* REVIEW

| | | | | | | |
|---|---|---|---|---|---|---|
| 1. b | 4. p | 7. a | 10. s | 13. u | 16. m | 19. h | 22. z |
| 2. t | 5. n | 8. f | 11. l | 14. v | 17. o | 20. r | 23. x |
| 3. k | 6. g | 9. c | 12. j | 15. e | 18. d | 21. y | 24. w |

---

*28th Week / 1st Day:* 1. propinquity   2. vulnerable   3. cacophony   4. exploit   5. bedlam   6. b   7. e   8. a   9. c   10. d

*28th Week / 2nd Day:* 1. disgruntled   2. panacea   3. eradicate   4. infallible   5. impede   6. b   7. a   8. d   9. c   10. e

*28th Week / 3rd Day:* 1. sedate   2. serenity   3. equanimity   4. compatible   5. revere   6. b   7. c   8. e   9. a   10. d

*28th Week / 4th Day:* 1. avarice   2. insatiable   3. nadir   4. irrational   5. moribund   6. c   7. d   8. e   9. a   10. b

*28th Week / 5th Day:* REVIEW

| | | | | | | |
|---|---|---|---|---|---|---|
| 1. t | 4. c | 7. k | 10. b | 13. e | 16. m | 19. f | 22. y |
| 2. h | 5. n | 8. r | 11. p | 14. d | 17. v | 20. a | 23. z |
| 3. j | 6. s | 9. u | 12. o | 15. g | 18. l | 21. x | 24. w |

**29th Week / 1st Day:** 1. adherent 2. lithe 3. pathetic 4. obese 5. bliss 6. d 7. b 8. a 9. e 10. c

**29th Week / 2nd Day:** 1. apathy 2. exhort 3. inebriated 4. fracas 5. adversary 6. d 7. c 8. e 9. b 10. a

**29th Week / 3rd Day:** 1. gusto 2. banal 3. platitude 4. indolent 5. garrulous 6. c 7. a 8. d 9. e 10. b

**29th Week / 4th Day:** 1. dilettante 2. atypical 3. nondescript 4. wane 5. pique 6. b 7. c 8. d 9. e 10. a

**29th Week / 5th Day:** REVIEW

| | | | | | | | |
|---|---|---|---|---|---|---|---|
| 1. t | 4. r | 7. p | 10. u | 13. k | 16. l | 19. o | 22. w |
| 2. b | 5. f | 8. a | 11. n | 14. c | 17. d | 20. v | 23. y |
| 3. j | 6. m | 9. s | 12. e | 15. h | 18. g | 21. z | 24. x |

---

**30th Week / 1st Day:** 1. gaudy 2. encumbrance 3. extinct 4. idyllic 5. galvanize 6. e 7. c 8. d 9. a 10. b

**30th Week / 2nd Day:** 1. condescend 2. malign 3. jocose 4. candor 5. mortify 6. c 7. d 8. e 9. a 10. b

**30th Week / 3rd Day:** 1. zenith 2. omnipotent 3. precedent 4. fledgling 5. peremptory 6. e 7. a 8. b 9. c 10. d

**30th Week / 4th Day:** 1. wheedle 2. charlatan 3. rustic 4. decorum 5. jubilant 6. a 7. e 8. b 9. c 10. d

**30th Week / 5th Day:** REVIEW

| | | | | | | | |
|---|---|---|---|---|---|---|---|
| 1. f | 4. l | 7. c | 10. e | 13. t | 16. r | 19. p | 22. w |
| 2. u | 5. j | 8. a | 11. k | 14. b | 17. v | 20. h | 23. z |
| 3. o | 6. n | 9. s | 12. d | 15. m | 18. g | 21. x | 24. y |

---

**31st Week / 1st Day:** 1. fervid 2. heresy 3. prudent 4. ostensible 5. spurious 6. c 7. d 8. e 9. a 10. b

**31st Week / 2nd Day:** 1. propagate 2. milieu 3. anomaly 4. innocuous 5. surfeit 6. d 7. c 8. e 9. a 10. b

**31st Week / 3rd Day:** 1. concomitent 2. strident 3. lassitude 4. deleterious 5. efficacy 6. e 7. c 8. d 9. b 10. a

**31st Week / 4th Day:** 1. incumbent 2. ferment 3. dissent 4. attenuated 5. arbiter 6. c 7. d 8. b 9. e 10. a

**31st Week / 5th Day:** REVIEW

| | | | | | | | |
|---|---|---|---|---|---|---|---|
| 1. c | 4. b | 7. k | 10. h | 13. u | 16. g | 19. f | 22. y |
| 2. n | 5. o | 8. a | 11. j | 14. l | 17. d | 20. p | 23. w |
| 3. s | 6. e | 9. r | 12. t | 15. v | 18. m | 21. z | 24. x |

---

**32nd Week / 1st Day:** 1. expedite 2. celerity 3. profound 4. alleviate 5. prodigious 6. d 7. c 8. e 9. a 10. b

**32nd Week / 2nd Day:** 1. bizarre 2. paltry 3. usurp 4. condone 5. trivial 6. c 7. a 8. b 9. d 10. e

**32nd Week / 3rd Day:** 1. venerable 2. ambiguous 3. succinct 4. menial 5. extraneous 6. b 7. c 8. d 9. a 10. e

**32nd Week / 4th Day:** 1. salubrious 2. archaic 3. facetious 4. rabid 5. emulate 6. b 7. c 8. d 9. e 10. a

**32nd Week / 5th Day:** REVIEW

| | | | | | | | |
|---|---|---|---|---|---|---|---|
| 1. r | 4. h | 7. t | 10. j | 13. l | 16. e | 19. d | 22. y |
| 2. o | 5. g | 8. p | 11. f | 14. c | 17. b | 20. s | 23. x |
| 3. a | 6. m | 9. k | 12. u | 15. n | 18. v | 21. z | 24. w |

*33rd Week / 1st Day:* 1. complacent  2. debilitate  3. occult  4. somber  5. impetuous  6. c  7. e  8. d  9. b  10. a

*33rd Week / 2nd Day:* 1. foment  2. slovenly  3. quarry  4. discreet  5. glean  6. a  7. e  8. b  9. c  10. d

*33rd Week / 3rd Day:* 1. penitent  2. evanescent  3. reproach  4. tantamount  5. abjure  6. c  7. b  8. d  9. e  10. a

*33rd Week / 4th Day:* 1. connoisseur  2. allay  3. propensity  4. wary  5. deter  6. c  7. e  8. d  9. a  10. b

*33rd Week / 5th Day:* REVIEW

| | | | | | | |
|---|---|---|---|---|---|---|
| 1. d | 4. u | 7. s | 10. t | 13. c | 16. p | 19. k | 22. z |
| 2. v | 5. e | 8. r | 11. o | 14. h | 17. b | 20. m | 23. y |
| 3. f | 6. g | 9. a | 12. n | 15. l | 18. j | 21. x | 24. w |

---

*34th Week / 1st Day:* 1. cumbersome  2. interrogate  3. vigil  4. divulge  5. site  6. e  7. c  8. a  9. b  10. d

*34th Week / 2nd Day:* 1. unmitigated  2. commodious  3. antiquated  4. fluctuate  5. disheveled  6. b  7. d  8. a  9. e  10. c

*34th Week / 3rd Day:* 1. tenacious  2. calumny  3. grimace  4. asinine  5. façade  6. d  7. c  8. b  9. e  10. a

*34th Week / 4th Day:* 1. au courant  2. pittance  3. unkempt  4. noisome  5. fastidious  6. c  7. e  8. d  9. b  10. a

*34th Week / 5th Day:* REVIEW

| | | | | | | |
|---|---|---|---|---|---|---|
| 1. r | 4. b | 7. h | 10. t | 13. o | 16. e | 19. p | 22. x |
| 2. s | 5. v | 8. f | 11. g | 14. m | 17. a | 20. n | 23. w |
| 3. l | 6. u | 9. j | 12. k | 15. c | 18. d | 21. z | 24. y |

---

*35th Week / 1st Day:* 1. lampoon  2. whimsical  3. parable  4. sanctimonious  5. countenance  6. d  7. a  8. e  9. c  10. b

*35th Week / 2nd Day:* 1. nonentity  2. effrontery  3. equanimity  4. flabbergasted  5. debacle  6. a  7. c  8. e  9. b  10. d

*35th Week / 3rd Day:* 1. mien  2. refute  3. hirsute  4. vivacious  5. gaunt  6. b  7. a  8. d  9. c  10. e

*35th Week / 4th Day:* 1. stupor  2. cliché  3. wince  4. whet  5. pensive  6. a  7. b  8. e  9. d  10. c

*35th Week / 5th Day:* REVIEW

| | | | | | | |
|---|---|---|---|---|---|---|
| 1. u | 4. p | 7. s | 10. n | 13. t | 16. v | 19. c | 22. x |
| 2. r | 5. h | 8. e | 11. b | 14. f | 17. m | 20. g | 23. z |
| 3. j | 6. a | 9. d | 12. l | 15. k | 18. o | 21. y | 24. w |

---

*36th Week / 1st Day:* 1. degrade  2. venial  3. genre  4. unsavory  5. candid  6. c  7. e  8. b  9. a  10. d

*36th Week / 2nd Day:* 1. grotesque  2. compassion  3. epitome  4. repugnant  5. dexterity  6. b  7. e  8. a  9. d  10. c

*36th Week / 3rd Day:* 1. acme  2. depict  3. naive  4. copious  5. vehemently  6. c  7. d  8. b  9. e  10. a

*36th Week / 4th Day:* 1. ingratiate  2. covet  3. penury  4. perfidious  5. ignominious  6. a  7. b  8. e  9. d  10. c

*36th Week / 5th Day:* REVIEW

| | | | | | | |
|---|---|---|---|---|---|---|
| 1. c | 4. l | 7. n | 10. j | 13. t | 16. e | 19. s | 22. z |
| 2. a | 5. d | 8. r | 11. g | 14. f | 17. k | 20. u | 23. y |
| 3. b | 6. h | 9. o | 12. v | 15. m | 18. p | 21. x | 24. w |

# ANSWERS

*37th Week / 1st Day:* 1. servile  2. sojourn  3. confront  4. volition  5. antipathy 6. d  7. c  8. e  9. b  10. a

*37th Week / 2nd Day:* 1. tenable  2. austere  3. superfluous  4. felicitous  5. halcyon 6. b  7. d  8. c  9. a  10. e

*37th Week / 3rd Day:* 1. iconoclast  2. therapy  3. motivate  4. rationalize 5. nascent  6. c  7. b  8. e  9. a  10. d

*37th Week / 4th Day:* 1. phobia  2. erudite  3. vertigo  4. conducive  5. germane  6. a  7. c  8. e  9. b  10. d

*37th Week / 5th Day:* REVIEW

| | | | | | | | |
|---|---|---|---|---|---|---|---|
| 1. e | 4. k | 7. h | 10. c | 13. u | 16. s | 19. r | 22. y |
| 2. f | 5. m | 8. j | 11. p | 14. o | 17. a | 20. b | 23. w |
| 3. d | 6. n | 9. g | 12. v | 15. t | 18. l | 21. z | 24. x |

*38th Week / 1st Day:* 1. glib  2. trend  3. legerdemain  4. malleable  5. homogenous  6. c  7. d  8. a  9. b  10. e

*38th Week / 2nd Day:* 1. fatal  2. passé  3. facets  4. procrastinate  5. stagnant 6. b  7. c  8. e  9. a  10. d

*38th Week / 3rd Day:* 1. capitulate  2. stigmatize  3. audacity  4. foist 5. tantalize  6. d  7. b  8. a  9. c  10. e

*38th Week / 4th Day:* 1. chicanery  2. docile  3. tacit  4. reticent  5. retort 6. c  7. d  8. a  9. e  10. b

*38th Week / 5th Day:* REVIEW

| | | | | | | | |
|---|---|---|---|---|---|---|---|
| 1. f | 4. t | 7. b | 10. u | 13. k | 16. p | 19. v | 22. w |
| 2. l | 5. e | 8. d | 11. j | 14. a | 17. o | 20. r | 23. y |
| 3. m | 6. c | 9. h | 12. s | 15. g | 18. n | 21. x | 24. z |

*39th Week / 1st Day:* 1. saga  2. imperturbable  3. belated  4. decrepit  5. vacillates  6. b  7. d  8. c  9. e  10. a

*39th Week / 2nd Day:* 1. opprobrium  2. Machiavellian  3. unconscionable 4. pandemonium  5. staunch  6. b  7. a  8. d  9. c 10. e

*39th Week / 3rd Day:* 1. vindicate  2. flay  3. demeanor  4. heinous  5. delineation  6. e  7. d  8. c  9. b  10. a

*39th Week / 4th Day:* 1. infraction  2. callous  3. vituperation  4. redress 5. turpitude  6. b  7. d  8. a  9. c  10. e

*39th Week / 5th Day:* REVIEW

| | | | | | | | |
|---|---|---|---|---|---|---|---|
| 1. n | 4. a | 7. h | 10. l | 13. t | 16. p | 19. u | 22. w |
| 2. o | 5. k | 8. f | 11. v | 14. m | 17. s | 20. e | 23. z |
| 3. r | 6. j | 9. d | 12. g | 15. b | 18. c | 21. x | 24. y |

*40th Week / 1st Day:* 1. clique  2. rhetoric  3. facile  4. extol  5. mentor  6. b 7. e  8. d  9. a  10. c

*40th Week / 2nd Day:* 1. vilify  2. cant  3. magnanimous  4. umbrage  5. elucidate  6. a  7. c  8. e  9. d  10. b

*40th Week / 3rd Day:* 1. proximity  2. lassitude  3. vapid  4. unwieldy  5. vitiate  6. c  7. a  8. d  9. e  10. b

*40th Week / 4th Day:* 1. fatuous  2. repertoire  3. imperceptible  4. contort 5. augment  6. b  7. c  8. d  9. e  10. a

*40th Week / 5th Day:* REVIEW

| | | | | | | | |
|---|---|---|---|---|---|---|---|
| 1. b | 4. a | 7. u | 10. s | 13. c | 16. v | 19. h | 22. w |
| 2. n | 5. g | 8. t | 11. m | 14. k | 17. j | 20. d | 23. x |
| 3. o | 6. e | 9. p | 12. l | 15. f | 18. r | 21. z | 24. y |

*41st Week / 1st Day:* 1. succulent 2. intrinsic 3. curry 4. satiety 5. pall 6. c 7. e 8. d 9. a 10. b

*41st Week / 2nd Day:* 1. sanction 2. insidious 3. allude 4. potpourri 5. denotes 6. d 7. c 8. e 9. b 10. a

*41st Week / 3rd Day:* 1. spate 2. advent 3. propriety 4. proffer 5. impious 6. a 7. c 8. d 9. b 10. e

*41st Week / 4th Day:* 1. nutritive 2. raucous 3. shibboleth 4. bogus 5. substantiate 6. a 7. c 8. e 9. d 10. b

*41st Week / 5th Day:* REVIEW

| | | | |
|---|---|---|---|
| 1. c | 4. k | 7. r | 10. p | 13. f | 16. b | 19. n | 22. w |
| 2. a | 5. j | 8. t | 11. h | 14. v | 17. e | 20. g | 23. y |
| 3. m | 6. l | 9. d | 12. u | 15. s | 18. o | 21. z | 24. x |

---

*42nd Week / 1st Day:* 1. negligible 2. quandary 3. expedient 4. callous 5. blasé 6. c 7. b 8. d 9. e 10. a

*42nd Week / 2nd Day:* 1. diversity 2. ennui 3. comely 4. artifice 5. frenetic 6. b 7. c 8. a 9. d 10. e

*42nd Week / 3rd Day:* 1. artless 2. expurgate 3. qualm 4. gratuity 5. begrudge 6. e 7. a 8. b 9. c 10. d

*42nd Week / 4th Day:* 1. delve 2. replenish 3. manifest 4. capricious 5. requisite 6. b 7. e 8. c 9. a 10. d

*42nd Week / 5th Day:* REVIEW

| | | | |
|---|---|---|---|
| 1. d | 4. f | 7. c | 10. l | 13. s | 16. k | 19. n | 22. x |
| 2. v | 5. r | 8. h | 11. e | 14. u | 17. b | 20. t | 23. w |
| 3. j | 6. g | 9. o | 12. a | 15. m | 18. p | 21. z | 24. y |

---

*43rd Week / 1st Day:* 1. ameliorate 3. roster 3. maim 4. atrophy 5. stunted 6. c 7. a 8. b 9. e 10. d

*43rd Week / 2nd Day:* 1. unctuous 2. cynic 3. benevolent 4. subservient 5. iniquity 6. b 7. c 8. d 9. a 10. e

*43rd Week / 3rd Day:* 1. largess 2. mercenary 3. criterion 4. mollify 5. repent 6. a 7. b 8. e 9. d 10. c

*43rd Week / 4th Day:* 1. vestige 2. pariah 3. aloof 4. guise 5. pragmatic 6. b 7. c 8. e 9. d 10. a

*43rd Week / 5th Day:* REVIEW

| | | | |
|---|---|---|---|
| 1. r | 4. m | 7. b | 10. p | 13. j | 16. c | 19. u | 22. y |
| 2. v | 5. e | 8. o | 11. s | 14. a | 17. h | 20. k | 23. x |
| 3. k | 6. d | 9. t | 12. n | 15. f | 18. g | 21. z | 24. w |

---

*44th Week / 1st Day:* 1. futility 2. technology 3. nullify 4. carnage 5. deluge 6. c 7. b 8. e 9. a 10. d

*44th Week / 2nd Day:* 1. canard 2. defamatory 3. plaintiff 4. libel 5. deprecate 6. c 7. d 8. b 9. e 10. a

*44th Week / 3rd Day:* 1. excoriate 2. frail 3. potent 4. reputed 5. devout 6. a 7. c 8. e 9. d 10. b

*44th Week / 4th Day:* 1. impromptu 2. malevolent 3. profuse 4. diminutive 5. dulcet 6. b 7. e 8. d 9. c 10. a

*44th Week / 5th Day:* REVIEW

| | | | |
|---|---|---|---|
| 1. l | 4. a | 7. m | 10. p | 13. v | 16. r | 19. t | 22. w |
| 2. g | 5. b | 8. e | 11. h | 14. o | 17. c | 20. s | 23. x |
| 3. k | 6. d | 9. j | 12. u | 15. n | 18. f | 21. y | 24. z |

# ANSWERS

**45th Week / 1st Day:** 1. raimant  2. rail  3. corpulent  4. wistful  5. brigand
6. c  7. a  8. d  9. e  10. b

**45th Week / 2nd Day:** 1. rift  2. raconteur  3. sullen  4. emissary  5. ruminate
6. c  7 a  8. d  9. e  10. b

**45th Week / 3rd Day:** 1. livid  2. taut  3. martinet  4. yen  5. bagatelle  6. b
7. c  8. a  9. e  10. d

**45th Week / 4th Day:** 1. decapitate  2. penchant  3. termagant  4. appalled
5. callow  6. a  7. e  8. c  9. b  10. d

**45th Week / 5th Day:** REVIEW

| | | | | | | |
|---|---|---|---|---|---|---|
| 1. b | 4. p | 7. f | 10. m | 13. h | 16. g | 19. l | 22. x |
| 2. d | 5. r | 8. c | 11. o | 14. n | 17. j | 20. v | 23. w |
| 3. e | 6. a | 9. k | 12. u | 15. s | 18. t | 21. z | 24. y |

---

**46th Week / 1st Day:** 1. burgeoned  2. ascertain  3. disseminate  4. dormant
5. potentate  6. b  7. c  8. d  9. e  10. a

**46th Week / 2nd Day:** 1. internecine  2. derived  3. nepotism  4. prerogative
5. dearth  6. d  7. c  8. e  9. a  10. b

**46th Week / 3rd Day:** 1. tyro  2. obloquy  3. sophistry  4. factitious  5. encomiums  6. b  7. c  8. d  9. a  10. e

**46th Week / 4th Day:** 1. charisma  2. genocide  3. prevarication  4. hyperbole
5. munificent  6. e  7. d  8. c  9. a  10. b

**46th Week / 5th Day:** REVIEW

| | | | | | | |
|---|---|---|---|---|---|---|
| 1. v | 4. a | 7. m | 10. o | 13. t | 16. f | 19. p | 22. w |
| 2. n | 5. s | 8. k | 11. u | 14. b | 17. h | 20. c | 23. x |
| 3. l | 6. g | 9. d | 12. r | 15. j | 18. e | 21. y | 24. z |

# Final Review Test

Below are 150 of the words which you have been studying, each followed by four possible definitions. Write the letter of the correct answer in the appropriate space. To attain a mark of 60%, you would have to get 90 correct answers; 105 correct answers are worth a mark of 70%, 120 for 80%, 135 for 90%. After you have completed the test, check your answers on page 254.

_____ 1. implore
 (a) reject
 (b) beg for assistance
 (c) summon
 (d) scold

_____ 2. voracious
 (a) greedy
 (b) vicious
 (c) dull
 (d) careless

_____ 3. badger
 (a) to pester
 (b) to cheat
 (c) remind
 (d) to insult

_____ 4. laconic
 (a) tense
 (b) bashful
 (c) troublesome
 (d) brief in expression

_____ 5. plethora
 (a) overabundance
 (b) helpless fit
 (c) a weakness
 (d) angry reaction

_____ 6. cajole
 (a) force
 (b) demand
 (c) coax
 (d) promise

_____ 7. inadvertent
 (a) unappetizing
 (b) unintentional
 (c) unaware
 (d) unknown

_____ 8. mundane
 (a) forgetful
 (b) friendly
 (c) doubtful
 (d) worldly

_____ 9. jostle
 (a) joke with
 (b) interrupt
 (c) to push
 (d) leap quickly

_____ 10. brash
 (a) impudent
 (b) stubborn
 (c) angry
 (d) upset

_____ 11. sordid
 (a) varied
 (b) guilty
 (c) unable to speak
 (d) dirty

_____ 12. solace
 (a) pity
 (b) comfort
 (c) forgetfulness
 (d) great happiness

_____ 13. acrimonious
 (a) bitter
 (b) brilliant
 (c) tender
 (d) out of tune

_____ 14. egregious
 (a) important
 (b) infected
 (c) remarkably bad
 (d) swollen

_____ 15. paucity
 (a) overweight
 (b) deafness
 (c) shortage
 (d) doubt

_____ 16. eschew
 (a) keep away from
 (b) sneeze repeatedly
 (c) invite
 (d) deny

_____ 17. voluble
 (a) priceless
 (b) talkative
 (c) sinful
 (d) whining

_____ 18. perfunctory
 (a) careless
 (b) hopeful
 (c) without end
 (d) evil

_____ 19. chagrin
 (a) loneliness
 (b) dismay
 (c) opportunity
 (d) suspicion

_____ 20. exacerbate
 (a) present arguments
 (b) plead with
 (c) question closely
 (d) irritate

# FINAL REVIEW TEST

_____21. **indigent**   (a) unreasonable
                        (b) watchful
                        (c) angry
                        (d) poor

_____22. **stymie**     (a) hinder
                        (b) invent
                        (c) confiscate
                        (d) cancel

_____23. **fretful**    (a) lacking ambition
                        (b) dark
                        (c) worrisome
                        (d) mischievous

_____24. **harbinger**  (a) smooth-talker
                        (b) leader
                        (c) forerunner
                        (d) bit of advice

_____25. **sanctuary**  (a) cemetery
                        (b) agreement
                        (c) place of protection
                        (d) approval

_____26. **astute**     (a) keen
                        (b) reliable
                        (c) cheap
                        (d) able

_____27. **blatant**    (a) boastful
                        (b) disagreeably loud
                        (c) blossoming
                        (d) rigid

_____28. **nefarious**  (a) hungry
                        (b) watchful
                        (c) footsore
                        (d) villainous

_____29. **virulent**   (a) harmful
                        (b) sloppy
                        (c) sickly
                        (d) revolutionary

_____30. **histri-**    (a) unreasonable acts
        **onics**       (b) nervousness
                        (c) display of emotions
                        (d) studies of the past

_____31. **salient**    (a) traveling
                        (b) resentful
                        (c) sober
                        (d) outstanding

_____32. **wan**        (a) pale
                        (b) sleepy
                        (c) jealous
                        (d) unlucky

_____33. **corrobo-**   (a) represent
        **rate**        (b) confirm
                        (c) search
                        (d) produce

_____34. **lurid**      (a) outraged
                        (b) sensational
                        (c) capable
                        (d) guilty

_____35. **sanguine**   (a) hopeful
                        (b) objectionable
                        (c) rugged
                        (d) hard to discover

_____36. **sporadic**   (a) occasional
                        (b) special
                        (c) to the point
                        (d) blotchy

_____37. **anathema**   (a) treatment
                        (b) violence
                        (c) apparatus
                        (d) a curse

_____38. **fortuitous** (a) lucky
                        (b) significant
                        (c) accidental
                        (d) huge

_____39. **prestigious** (a) creaking
                        (b) well-known
                        (c) horrible
                        (d) casual

_____40. **timorous**   (a) courageous
                        (b) ambitious
                        (c) fearful
                        (d) tense

_____41. **eventuate**  (a) to result finally
                        (b) pay your respects
                        (c) borrow
                        (d) interrupt

_____42. **inchoate**   (a) vague
                        (b) in an early stage
                        (c) uneasy
                        (d) ingenious

_____43. **propi-**     (a) suspicious
        **tious**       (b) hasty
                        (c) frank
                        (d) favorable

_____44. **viable**     (a) workable
                        (b) sensitive
                        (c) tasty
                        (d) quiet

_____45. incisive
(a) acute
(b) sluggish
(c) massive
(d) jittery

_____46. inveigh
(a) compose
(b) react to
(c) attack verbally
(d) penetrate

_____47. sinecure
(a) urgent message
(b) silly response
(c) big responsibility
(d) soft job

_____48. nettle
(a) mix
(b) suggest
(c) irritate
(d) suspend

_____49. abrogate
(a) publish
(b) portray
(c) permit
(d) cancel

_____50. extrinsic
(a) loaded
(b) containing wisdom
(c) coming from outside
(d) uncertain

_____51. asperity
(a) artful handling
(b) bitterness of temper
(c) foolishness
(d) concern

_____52. altruistic
(a) unselfish
(b) troublesome
(c) dangerous
(d) dignified

_____53. sedentary
(a) hypnotic
(b) largely inactive
(c) scornful
(d) musical

_____54. progeny
(a) vigor
(b) descendants
(c) minority opinion
(d) disease

_____55. cupidity
(a) affection
(b) fate
(c) greed
(d) harmony

_____56. impec-cable
(a) faultless
(b) bold
(c) open to criticism
(d) slow to respond

_____57. perpe-trate
(a) plant
(b) consume in haste
(c) slice
(d) commit

_____58. assiduous
(a) sly
(b) thrifty
(c) busy
(d) educated

_____59. abortive
(a) failing
(b) outside the law
(c) drowsy
(d) unprepared

_____60. tortuous
(a) spiteful
(b) inflicting pain
(c) frank
(d) winding

_____61. peregrina-tion
(a) form of address
(b) travel
(c) insistence
(d) hospitality

_____62. myriad
(a) geometric figure
(b) voter's choice
(c) countless number
(d) minority decision

_____63. fiat
(a) police squad
(b) official order
(c) carriage
(d) council

_____64. menda-cious
(a) lying
(b) abusive
(c) healing
(d) merciful

_____65. profligate
(a) soothing
(b) obvious
(c) distinct
(d) wasteful

_____66. disparate
(a) different
(b) critical
(c) religious
(d) uneven

_____67. lugubri-ous
(a) well-oiled
(b) warlike
(c) very sad
(d) beyond dispute

_____68. puissant
(a) ordinary
(b) studious
(c) powerful
(d) dictatorial

# FINAL REVIEW TEST

_____69. desultory
- (a) disconnected
- (b) incomplete
- (c) polished
- (d) dry

_____70. fulsome
- (a) gratified
- (b) superior
- (c) sensitive
- (d) excessive

_____71. chimerical
- (a) accurate
- (b) imaginary
- (c) regional
- (d) rigid

_____72. recondite
- (a) observant
- (b) sincere
- (c) secret
- (d) willing to bargain

_____73. gamut
- (a) range
- (b) sleeve
- (c) intestine
- (d) bridge

_____74. irascible
- (a) conceited
- (b) patriotic
- (c) bumbling
- (d) irritable

_____75. perspica-cious
- (a) vicious
- (b) shrewd
- (c) sweaty
- (d) light on one's feet

_____76. taint
- (a) weaken
- (b) widen
- (c) contaminate
- (d) cause

_____77. aegis
- (a) fear
- (b) hope
- (c) kinship
- (d) protection

_____78. evince
- (a) prove
- (b) throw away
- (c) exhibit
- (d) wonder

_____79. termagent
- (a) shrew
- (b) insect
- (c) ruler
- (d) coward

_____80. mien
- (a) appearance
- (b) hostile
- (c) cheerful
- (d) important

_____81. elucidate
- (a) hide
- (b) make clear
- (c) paint
- (d) sharpen

_____82. germane
- (a) sickly
- (b) foreign
- (c) charming
- (d) appropriate

_____83. mollify
- (a) turn against
- (b) appease
- (c) hope for
- (d) shorten

_____84. indolent
- (a) lazy
- (b) badly behaved
- (c) owing money
- (d) timely

_____85. impromp-tu
- (a) dangerous
- (b) not understood
- (c) wisely planned
- (d) spur of the moment

_____86. umbrage
- (a) dark color
- (b) offense
- (c) waste
- (d) generosity

_____87. artifice
- (a) trickery
- (b) historic finding
- (c) newness
- (d) gradual change

_____88. vacillate
- (a) follow closely
- (b) fluctuate
- (c) aggravate
- (d) dominate

_____89. vestige
- (a) trace
- (b) cloak
- (c) entrance
- (d) hope

_____90. adamant
- (a) ambitious
- (b) timely
- (c) wasteful
- (d) inflexible

_____91. nepotism
- (a) without religion
- (b) favoritism
- (c) patriotism
- (d) deception

_____92. reticent
- (a) reserved
- (b) in pain
- (c) cooperative
- (d) without example

_____93. tyro
(a) ruler
(b) beginner
(c) fire-setter
(d) warmer

_____94. staunch
(a) evil smelling
(b) tight fitting
(c) whiten
(d) strong

_____95. equanim-
ity
(a) sharing
(b) self-control
(c) hostility
(d) lively

_____96. taut
(a) tense
(b) make fun of
(c) pale
(d) gradual

_____97. mortify
(a) calm down
(b) embarrass
(c) strengthen
(d) pretend

_____98. vapid
(a) wet
(b) quick
(c) remarkable
(d) foolish

_____99. covet
(a) disguise
(b) wish for
(c) bury
(d) change

_____100. condone
(a) repeat
(b) punish
(c) forbid
(d) pardon

_____101. fatuous
(a) heavy
(b) interesting
(c) silly
(d) important

_____102. imbibe
(a) drink
(b) enter
(c) clear away
(d) change

_____103. ennui
(a) fashionable
(b) boredom
(c) together
(d) hopeless

_____104. salu-
brious
(a) sad
(b) dangerous
(c) painful
(d) healthful

_____105. carnage
(a) slaughter
(b) carrying away
(c) marriage
(d) anger

_____106. aloof
(a) painful
(b) reserved
(c) interested
(d) dishonest

_____107. vertigo
(a) dizziness
(b) color blindness
(c) ambition
(d) extreme height

_____108. foment
(a) become alcoholic
(b) investigate
(c) stir up
(d) calm down

_____109. inveter-
ate
(a) anxious
(b) unknown
(c) questionable
(d) habitual

_____110. refute
(a) fame
(b) waste
(c) disobey
(d) disprove

_____111. celerity
(a) stardom
(b) speed
(c) clearness
(d) sourness

_____112. heinous
(a) interference
(b) talkative
(c) evilly wicked
(d) powerful

_____113. quandary
(a) dilemma
(b) quiet place
(c) hopeful sign
(d) crowd

_____114. efficacy
(a) cheapness
(b) ease
(c) mystery
(d) effectiveness

_____115. austere
(a) wild
(b) feverish
(c) unadorned
(d) wishful

_____116. mori-
bund
(a) marvelous
(b) ambitious
(c) gradual
(d) dying

# FINAL REVIEW TEST

_____117. noisome    (a) unwholesome
   (b) challenging
   (c) loud
   (d) newly arrived

_____118. spate    (a) rush
   (b) excess
   (c) insult
   (d) shortage

_____119. nadir    (a) climax
   (b) secret place
   (c) lowest point
   (d) happiest moment

_____120. halcyon    (a) peaceful
   (b) ancient
   (c) innermost
   (d) careful

_____121. pragmatic    (a) repeating
   (b) fat
   (c) practical
   (d) imaginative

_____122. atrophy    (a) prize
   (b) begin again
   (c) change direction
   (d) waste away

_____123. discreet    (a) patient
   (b) colorful
   (c) cautious
   (d) generous

_____124. callow    (a) cowardly
   (b) unfeeling
   (c) inexperienced
   (d) private

_____125. ruminate    (a) reflect upon
   (b) move away
   (c) reclassify
   (d) start anew

_____126. congenial    (a) clever
   (b) agreeable
   (c) masterful
   (d) selective

_____127. decorum    (a) behavior
   (b) attractiveness
   (c) liveliness
   (d) meeting place

_____128. banal    (a) not allowed
   (b) nearly finished
   (c) trivial
   (d) highly respected

_____129. encomium    (a) highest prize
   (b) secret plan
   (c) new idea
   (d) high praise

_____130. avarice    (a) clear path
   (b) wealth
   (c) greed
   (d) positive statement

_____131. malign    (a) slander
   (b) exterminate
   (c) join with
   (d) dismiss

_____132. venial    (a) hopeless
   (b) unseen
   (c) pardonable
   (d) deadly

_____133. dulcet    (a) hard to hear
   (b) sweet to the ear
   (c) soft to the touch
   (d) easy to see

_____134. entreaty    (a) plea
   (b) agreement
   (c) capture
   (d) sudden end

_____135. pensive    (a) limited
   (b) thoughtful
   (c) aged
   (d) retired

_____136. bizarre    (a) busy
   (b) in a hurry
   (c) timely
   (d) fantastic

_____137. requisite    (a) forgotten thought
   (b) requirement
   (c) added problem
   (d) lovely object

_____138. livid    (a) disappointed
   (b) enraged
   (c) bored
   (d) pale

_____139. pique    (a) resentment
   (b) condition
   (c) hidden from light
   (d) wishful thinking

_____140. galvanize    (a) prepare to eat
   (b) arouse to activity
   (c) store away
   (d) experiment

_____141. extol
- (a) explain
- (b) apologize for
- (c) praise highly
- (d) describe honestly

_____142. allude
- (a) avoid
- (b) cover up
- (c) yearn for
- (d) suggest

_____143. slovenly
- (a) slowly
- (b) wisely
- (c) dangerously
- (d) carelessly

_____144. preroga-tive
- (a) ask again
- (b) exclusive right
- (c) divided power
- (d) first born

_____145. raiment
- (a) clothing
- (b) arrest
- (c) left over
- (d) bright color

_____146. abhor
- (a) yearn for
- (b) hate
- (c) distrust
- (d) join together

_____147. jocose
- (a) dizzy
- (b) merry
- (c) sticky
- (d) talkative

_____148. mentor
- (a) coach
- (b) enemy
- (c) stranger
- (d) writer

_____149. hirsute
- (a) overly dressed
- (b) out-of-date
- (c) hairy
- (d) bald

_____150. exco-riate
- (a) complete
- (b) win easily
- (c) criticize severely
- (d) clean thoroughly

## Answers to Final Review Test

| | | | | |
|---|---|---|---|---|
| 1. b | 31. d | 61. b | 91. b | 121. c |
| 2. a | 32. a | 62. c | 92. a | 122. d |
| 3. a | 33. b | 63. b | 93. b | 123. c |
| 4. d | 34. b | 64. a | 94. d | 124. c |
| 5. a | 35. a | 65. d | 95. b | 125. a |
| 6. c | 36. a | 66. a | 96. a | 126. b |
| 7. b | 37. d | 67. c | 97. b | 127. a |
| 8. d | 38. c | 68. c | 98. d | 128. c |
| 9. c | 39. b | 69. a | 99. b | 129. d |
| 10. a | 40. c | 70. d | 100. d | 130. c |
| 11. d | 41. a | 71. b | 101. c | 131. a |
| 12. b | 42. b | 72. c | 102. a | 132. c |
| 13. a | 43. d | 73. a | 103. b | 133. b |
| 14. c | 44. a | 74. d | 104. d | 134. a |
| 15. c | 45. a | 75. b | 105. a | 135. b |
| 16. a | 46. c | 76. c | 106. b | 136. d |
| 17. b | 47. d | 77. d | 107. a | 137. b |
| 18. a | 48. c | 78. c | 108. c | 138. d |
| 19. b | 49. d | 79. a | 109. d | 139. a |
| 20. d | 50. c | 80. a | 110. d | 140. b |
| 21. d | 51. b | 81. b | 111. b | 141. c |
| 22. a | 52. a | 82. d | 112. c | 142. d |
| 23. c | 53. b | 83. b | 113. a | 143. d |
| 24. c | 54. b | 84. d | 114. d | 144. b |
| 25. c | 55. c | 85. d | 115. c | 145. a |
| 26. a | 56. a | 86. b | 116. d | 146. b |
| 27. b | 57. d | 87. a | 117. a | 147. b |
| 28. d | 58. c | 88. b | 118. a | 148. a |
| 29. a | 59. a | 89. a | 119. c | 149. c |
| 30. c | 60. d | 90. d | 120. a | 150. c |

# Index

*The number indicates the first page on which the new word appears.*

250